THE
LONGEST
RESCUE

THE LONGEST RESCUE

THE LIFE AND LEGACY
OF VIETNAM POW
WILLIAM A. ROBINSON

GLENN ROBINS

Foreword by Colonel Bud Day

UNIVERSITY PRESS OF KENTUCKY

Scholarly publisher for the Commonwealth,
serving Bellarmine University, Berea College, Centre College of Kentucky,
Eastern Kentucky University, The Filson Historical Society, Georgetown
College, Kentucky Historical Society, Kentucky State University, Morehead
State University, Murray State University, Northern Kentucky University,
Transylvania University, University of Kentucky, University of Louisville,
and Western Kentucky University.
All rights reserved.

Editorial and Sales Offices: The University Press of Kentucky
663 South Limestone Street, Lexington, Kentucky 40508-4008
www.kentuckypress.com

Maps by Dick Gilbreath, University of Kentucky Cartography Lab

The Library of Congress has cataloged the hardcover edition as follows:

Robins, Glenn.
   The longest rescue : the life and legacy of Vietnam POW William A. Robinson
/ Glenn Robins ; foreword by Colonel Bud Day.
      pages cm
   Includes bibliographical references and index.
   ISBN 978-0-8131-4323-1 (hardcover : alk. paper) —
   ISBN 978-0-8131-4325-5 (epub) — ISBN 978-0-8131-4324-8 (pdf)
   1. Robinson, William A., 1943- 2. Vietnam War, 1961-1975—Prisoners and
prisons, North Vietnamese. 3. Prisoners of war—United States—Biography. 4.
Prisoners of war—Vietnam—Biography. 5. Vietnam War, 1961-1975—Aerial
operations, American. 6. United States. Air Force. Air Rescue Service—
Biography. 7. Airmen—United States—Biography. 8. United States. Air
Force—Non-commissioned officers—Biography. 9. Robinson, William A.,
1943- —Travels—Vietnam. 10. Vietnam War, 1961-1975—Veterans—Biography.
I. Robins, Glenn. II. Title. III. Title: Life and legacy of Vietnam POW William A.
Robinson.
   DS559.4.R57 2013
   959.704′37092—dc23
   [B]   2013018945

ISBN 978-0-8131-6621-6 (pbk. : alk. paper)

This book is printed on acid-free paper meeting the requirements of the American
National Standard for Permanence in Paper for Printed Library Materials.

Manufactured in the United States of America.

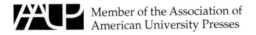 Member of the Association of
American University Presses

Contents

Illustrations follow page 158

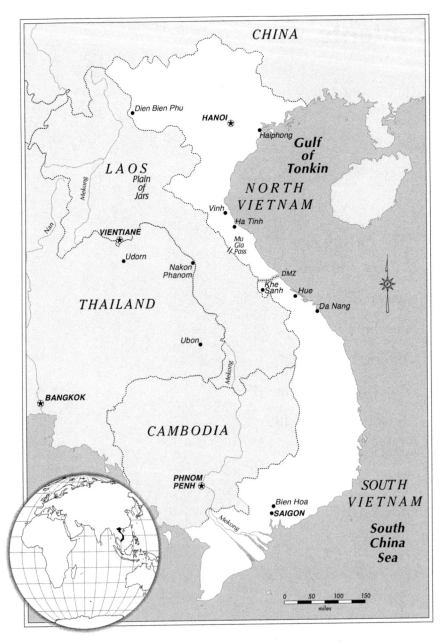

Vietnam

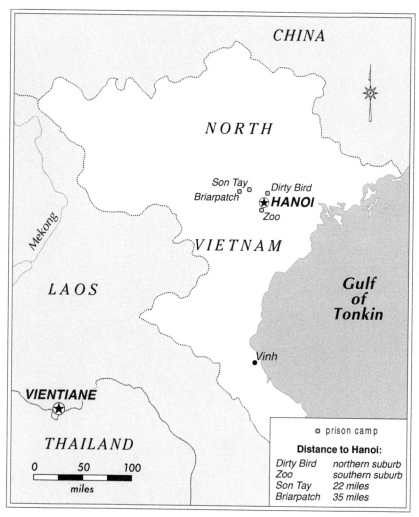

Prisoner-of-War Camp Locations

Foreword

This is a very big book about a very big man, with a big mind, and a huge, unshakable stoicism and innate common sense. These were exactly the qualities he called on to resist the brutal and inhumane conditions that he faced as a prisoner of war. As a reader, you will become a better person for having read this spectacular story and following Billy's example. I was shot down over North Vietnam on 26 August 1967. I was shootdown number 138 of those Americans who actually made it into a prison camp. More than that number had already been shot down and murdered by the North Vietnamese. Little did I expect that I would be held a POW for five years and seven months. Billy Robinson, one of the earliest POWs, had already been in captivity for more than two very hard years before my shootdown.

In Hanoi I was held briefly at the Hanoi Hilton, in the old French jail, and then the communists moved me to the Plantation (a few miles southwest of downtown Hanoi), where my multiple broken bones and gunshot wounds began to heal. In December 1967 Lieutenant Commander John S. McCain became my roommate. That was a great break for me. John was all broken up and wounded, but he absolutely refused to die, although at first I expected he would. He was filthy, emaciated, and in a massive cast from his hip to his shoulder, and he stank like a rotten egg. That was of no consequence. I enjoyed more than four months of John McCain's company, until on 30 April 1968, I was abruptly ordered to roll up my blanket and be ready to move. I was on my way to a camp called the Zoo. The political officer at the Plantation advised that I was "going to a very hard camp, where [I] would have a chance to think about [my] bad conduct in the Plantation Camp." As I would soon learn, the Zoo was a torture camp.

Upon arriving at the Zoo on 1 May, we were immediately put into "kneeling torture," a remarkably painful punishment that consisted of kneeling bare-legged on rough concrete, while keeping one's body erect and holding one's arms straight up as if reaching for the stars. This torture was unrelenting, and after a short time I had holes in the skin over my knees and could see the bones in my leg. I wasn't the only one—the damage to my roommate's knees was severe, too. After a few days of this treatment, the brutality eased off, and we began to peek out through a crack in the door, generated by a little push from us and the poor construction work of the enemy. My roommate, Lieutenant Commander Arv Chauncey (shot down 31 May 1967), was lying on the concrete floor and describing to me what could be seen. I replaced him on the floor, pushed the door a little more, and was startled to see a huge POW about thirty feet away from our cell leaving the building next door to us. He was approximately six foot two inches tall and weighed about 210 pounds. He had a very young and unwrinkled face. He was with three other POWs and a young guard who was not much taller than the length of his rifle. I first assumed that he must be Army or Navy, as he was too large to fit in most cockpits or aircraft of that time. He dwarfed the tiny guard. It was an incongruous sight.

Just as I was whispering about what I saw through the crack, our adjoining neighbor Major Jim Kasler (shot down 8 August 1966) tapped through the wall that there were POWs in the yard. I was later moved alone across the camp to the Stable, and I subsequently only caught a glimpse of this huge man. Later roommates described the existence of three enlisted air rescuemen, of whom Billy Robinson was one. Just before I left the Zoo to go to more punishment at New Guy Village, we got a message through the wall that Billy's roommates were putting him and the other enlisted men through an officer training program. I personally endorsed the idea as a very good use of their time and hoped something of value would result from it. The idea of the training was to make them commissioned officers after the senior officer approved the idea, which he did. I did not see Billy again until after our release, when we were invited to the White House for a reception hosted by President Nixon, although we had no time for anything but a hello. The demands on our time were extremely high, but we were all exhilarated by our freedom.

A short time after our release, I received a call from General John Flynn, who had been the senior officer among the POWs in North

Vietnam. John had spent his entire time in Hanoi essentially in the same cell with one other senior officer and had been totally out of touch with the comings and goings of the other POWs. John and I and Colonel Dave Winn had been moved together in the Plantation just before our release. I gave John and Dave a summary of the seven years of our collective history, much of which had been related to me by the communications officer from the Zoo, Lieutenant Commander Jack Fellowes. (For POW aficionados, the book *P.O.W.: A Definitive History of the American Prisoner-of-War Experience in Vietnam, 1964–1973*, written by John G. Hubbell and published by Reader's Digest in 1976, is one of the two best encyclopedias of the POW story.) John trusted me, and since we were about to get released, he needed to be briefed. He had no idea how many camps there were or where they were located; all he had was his own day-to-day existence, which for some five years and six months was essentially lived out in solitary confinement or extreme isolation.

I had been the senior ranking officer of the Zoo (the largest camp in the system), Chicken Coop, New Guy Village, Skid Row, and Room Four, and I had held other leadership positions as a POW. John wanted to know what I knew about the commissioning of Billy Robinson, Neil Black, and Art Cormier. I gave him a sketchy summary of what I knew and told him that I believed it to be a sterling idea and a very fine use of otherwise wasted prison time; it was also compatible with NCOs' having been commissioned to officer status in previous wars. He thanked me, but he gave me no hint that there was resistance in U.S. Air Force Headquarters to this ad hoc route to an Air Force commission. Apparently, the Air Force's resistance died, as the next time I saw Billy was at Eglin Air Force Base, in my unit, the 33rd Fighter Wing, where we were flying F-4E fighters and he was wearing the bars of an officer; he was the senior flight-line officer in charge of maintenance. The flight-line crews loved him, and I instantly noticed an improvement in the flyability of our combat-fatigued birds. At this time there was a huge cutback in funding; many aircraft repair parts were deemed too expensive and were therefore unobtainable. One hot summer day as I was driving the flight line to make sure that some water and rest were available to flight-line people, I was able to watch Billy's interactions with the maintenance personnel. It was clear that he was a highly respected hero. Even though he held the Air Force Cross, he was humble and effective and humane. The decision to train him as an officer while held as a POW proved to be sound and was consistent with combat-field promotions of previous wars.

My next contact with Billy was confounding. As I turned into my office parking spot at Eglin, I spied a group of men and women running on an improvised oval. The sun was bright in the east, the outdoor temperature was approaching 80 degrees (the day's high was forecast to be 94 or 95 degrees), and the humidity was about 80 percent. It was a typical hot, muggy day on the Gulf Coast of Florida. I instantly recognized Billy Robinson slogging around this track. I realized that he had been put in an Air Force weight control program, derisively labeled Fat Boy. I was the vice wing commander, which meant that I was second in command. I confronted the wing commander, who handed me a copy of the Fat Boy program literature. The thrust of the program was to ensure that no Air Force member was overweight, according to some arbitrary tables that spelled out the height and weight criteria for NCOs and officers. The idea had merit, but it failed to take age into account. As both men and women move into their thirties, forties, and fifties, the dimensions of their waists increase and the uniforms they purchased after commissioning or flight school become tighter. This natural progression was labeled Fat Boy by the regulation writers, and *no* exceptions were permitted. (The policy was clearly a bureaucratic blunder that was promptly junked when the commanding general was pushed into retirement.) I left my office and talked to the flight surgeon, a colonel in charge of medical issues. He responded that several colonels had approached him about exceptions, and that Billy would get no slack. I did not see Billy for some time after this episode. Following my retirement, I opened a law office in Fort Walton Beach and had a thriving military practice. One day out of the blue, I got a phone call from Billy, describing some problems with the pay that the Air Force had been sending to his parents. In short, his accumulated pay from more than seven and a half years in captivity was not properly accounted for. He took this possible catastrophe with the same stoic calm that had characterized his POW years. Eventually, we fixed this dilemma.

Billy's post-retirement years were transformed by a deluge of demands for him to tell his story to the public. These demands only multiplied as he commenced speaking, and countless military and patriotic groups have now heard his tale. Civilian life has not produced a fat boy program, and Billy is out speaking to the public in the same generous body that he had when he was shot down in 1965. He exudes calm, equanimity, and common sense. He is politically astute and in charge of his life. This book is a great addition to those already published about Vietnam POWs. It fills in the gap of much of the story of the enlisted POWs, which has heretofore been neglected. It also deals with Briarpatch prison camp in the most complete fashion of any book I have read. The same is true of the National Prisoner of War Museum at the Andersonville National Historic Site. What is most important is to *read* this authentic story of unshakable loyalty to the United States and discover the best of all things in the best of men.

Colonel Bud Day
Medal of Honor Recipient

Introduction

"We sometimes fondly say that we classify ourselves as one of the longest rescues in history." William Andrew (Bill) Robinson, a bear-like man, grinned and gently shook with laughter as he finished recounting the outline of his capture story during an interview at the National Prisoner of War Museum in Andersonville, Georgia. Robinson was not "rescued" in the literal military sense of the word—quite the contrary. He spent 2,703 days as a prisoner of the North Vietnamese. His use of the phrase refers to the incident that resulted in his capture. On 20 September 1965 Robinson and his fellow crewmembers of an Air Force Search and Rescue team, call sign Dutchy 41, departed Nakhon Phanom Royal Thai Air Force Base, Thailand, on a mission to recover an Air Force pilot, Captain Willis E. Forby, whose F-105D Thunderchief had been shot down in Ha Tinh Province in North Vietnam, near the Laotian border. The Robinson interview took place some thirty years after he, two crewmembers, and Forby returned to the United States following their seven and a half years as prisoners of war (POWs). Perhaps the passage of time had softened the memories of that fateful September day in 1965, or maybe the laughter masked the pain of an omnipresent ordeal. Still, the ability to laugh or see humor in the details of an agonizing period in his life speaks volumes to Robinson's tremendous personal courage, honor, and love of life. In some ways, "the longest rescue" also signifies a type of emotional rescue from, or triumph over, the heartache of a difficult childhood and the long road to fulfillment following his release from captivity. Finally, the phrase extends to the high regard with which many Americans now view former prisoners of war, which has not always been the case, an about-face that stems to a degree from the public perception and memory of Vietnam-era POWs.[1]

Americans have been held as prisoners or captives since the frontier wars of the colonial era, but they have not always been viewed, or remembered, in heroic or patriotic terms. One recent study of American prisoners during the Revolutionary War has been aptly titled *Forgotten Patriots*, and its author, Edwin G. Burrows, explains

1

how "rank historicide," animated by a desire for commercial development and "Anglo-American reconciliation," cast the Revolutionary War prisoners from "the bonds of memory."[2] In many respects, it was the plight of captured Americans during the Civil War that first shaped the nation's public memory of prisoners of war, largely as a consequence of the tragic outcome at Camp Sumter in Andersonville, Georgia, where nearly 13,000 U.S. soldiers died. In the postwar years, former Union prisoners of war were typically viewed as victims of southern atrocities, but they experienced great difficulty in obtaining pensions from the federal government for medical conditions and physical disabilities related to their time in prison.[3] On four separate occasions the U.S. Congress failed to pass federal pension legislation for former prisoners as a distinct group, although some former prisoners obtained them by virtue of special-order private pension awards granted by individual congressmen or as regular veterans.[4] By contrast, former Union prisoners of war could count on politicians to use them for political purposes, most noticeably as a component of a Republican political strategy known as "waving the bloody shirt," but they did not always enjoy a place of honor and respect alongside the hallowed warriors who saved the republic.[5] In fact, northern military and civilian leaders questioned the patriotism and the individual character of captured Union soldiers who subsequently agreed to take an oath of parole from their Confederate captors. These were men who returned to friendly lines and pledged not to bear arms against their captors until they were formally exchanged for an enemy captive. Suspicions arose as early as September 1862, when the number of paroled prisoners increased at an alarming rate. Responding to the perceived crisis, Secretary of War Edwin M. Stanton declared, "There is reason to fear that many voluntarily surrender for the sake of getting home."[6]

America's Civil War generation was not the only one to struggle with reconciling the notions of martial honor and surrender. As the foremost scholar of the American prisoner-of-war experience, Robert C. Doyle, has explained, "The American vision of success demands victory in war. Capture initially signals defeat and failure; captivity, however, does not. Finding a bridge between failure and success requires some analysis."[7] Interestingly, even those former prisoners who were part of World War II's celebrated "greatest generation" fought the stigma of capture and surrender. Russ Gunvalson, a POW captured at the Battle of the Bulge, recalled hearing at an American Legion meeting "that being captured was not a very honorable thing to do." Thus, he remained silent about his time as a POW. "Even my wife says that I didn't say anything," explained Gunvalson. "I never, I didn't say anything to anybody. My diary [of my POW time] lay dormant for thirty-seven years."[8] If the general public expressed interest in the POWs' stories, it was not always willing to believe the most horrific accounts of mistreatment or POW resolve, which would certainly not be the case for Vietnam POWs. A former World War II POW, Irving Silverlieb, remembers that when he shared his captivity experiences, some people responded, "Oh, bullshit! Nobody would do [that] . . . that's impossible. Nobody does that to nobody." Silverlieb, who had an appendectomy without anesthesia, also had his ability to endure the hardships of captivity questioned; disbelievers quipped, "Nobody could take that kind of shit . . . you're making it all up."[9] Though these instances may have been rare and extreme, popular notions of the World War II prisoner-of-war experience, gleaned primarily from movies and television shows and constructed before widespread U.S. involvement in the Vietnam War, tended to portray a benign captivity experience. Taking as their starting points the films *Stalag 17* (1953) and *The Great Escape* (1963) and the television series *Hogan's Heroes* (1965–71), Americans imbibed these lionhearted accounts of captivity and saw American POWs as wildly successful escape artists or well-fed resisters actively engaged in espionage and sabotage against a comically inept Nazi enemy. These depictions lacked war realism, avoided the pain and suffering of imprisonment, and completely ignored the postrelease consequences of the ordeal of captivity. The cultural critic Elliott Gruner believes that these images "of Allied POWs of World War II made Americans happy" at a time when "no one wanted to remember much about the Korean War, at least for entertainment."[10]

No group of American prisoners of war has been more neglected or more maligned than those U.S. soldiers held captive during the Korean War. The number of American POWs, under the supervision first of the North Koreans and later of the Chinese, exceeded 7,000. Of that number, 2,700, or roughly 40 percent, died in captivity, the highest percentage of POW deaths in any American war.[11] The high death rate, along with the decision of twenty-one Americans to refuse repatriation during the final prisoner-exchange program, known as Operation Big Switch, generated concern regarding the performance of all American POWs during the Korean War. Critics charged that the POWs had been brainwashed during indoctrination sessions, had betrayed their country, and were a threat to national security. They also alleged that a disturbing number of POWs had been cooperative during indoctrination sessions and had expended little effort in attempting to escape, and they explained the high death rate as a function of personal weakness. In searching for causal factors, critics pointed to "momism," a condition precipitated by emasculating mothers who coddled their sons and prevented them from developing the "traditional American values of patriotism" and masculine toughness.[12] This psychosociological profile dominated Richard Condon's novel *The Manchurian Candidate,* as well as the Hollywood film of the same title. The main character in these works, a fictitious former Korean War POW, Sergeant Raymond Shaw, has been brainwashed by his captors and possibly has had an incestuous relationship with his mother. Upon his return home, Shaw, still under the manipulative powers of communist agents, plots the assassination of the president of the United States and the overthrow of the American government. The bizarre plotline actually reflected the view held by some Americans regarding the Korean War POWs. During a return trip to the United States aboard a troop transport ship following the end of the war, an American intelligence officer asked a recently released POW, "You ever have sex with your mother?"[13] As outrageous and far-fetched as these ideas may seem in the twenty-first century, the Cold War hysteria, generated in large part by Senator Joseph McCarthy, tarnished the legacy of American POWs of the Korean War, and this myth of failure once more attached itself to the legacy of the American POW. The Department of Defense, concerned about the performance of American POWs during the Korean War, appointed an eleven-man commission that ultimately produced the military Code of Conduct. More than just a prohibition against revealing anything more than the Big Four—name, rank, serial number, and date of birth—the Code of Conduct outlines the ethical guidelines for POW behavior. Therefore, as American service personnel set off for Vietnam, a rigid and specific set of expectations had been established in the event of their capture. At the same time, *The Manchurian Candidate* and *Hogan's Heroes* perpetuated historical fictions about the POW captivity experience.

American prisoners of the Vietnam War emerged, for a variety of reasons, as the heroes of what many deemed a lost war, and their iconic status became a cultural appropriation that redefined the image of American POWs of past wars. The transfiguration was illustrated when the U.S. Congress authorized and President Ronald Reagan signed into law on 8 November 1985 the creation of the Prisoner of War Medal, which could be awarded to anyone held as a prisoner of war after 5 April 1917, the day before America's entrance into World War I. The POW medal represented an important milestone in the history of the POW image, as former prisoners received praise and recognition for their unique military service. Over time, many Americans came to view the POWs of World War II and Korea through the same patriotic lenses that they viewed Vietnam POWs, and they applied this new understanding to subsequent generations of American captives. Take as but one example the outpouring of concern and interest in the plight of Army Chief Warrant Officer Michael Durant, a helicopter pilot who was shot down and held as a prisoner for eleven days by a Somali clan during Operation Gothic Serpent in October 1993. Durant became the first individual to appear simultaneously on the covers of *Time*, *Newsweek*, and *U.S. News & World Report*, even trumping the announcement of Michael Jordan's first retirement from professional basketball. Durant's story became part of American popular culture after the success of *Black Hawk Down*, both a book and a Hollywood film, and later through a best-selling memoir, *In the Company of Heroes*.[14] A similar outburst was manifested after the capture and recovery of Army Private First Class Jessica Lynch during the commencement of Operation Iraqi Freedom in 2003. Since the "forgotten patriots" of the Revolutionary War, the American POW image has undergone a complete about-face, from neglected and unappreciated Americans to celebrated paragons of courage, self-sacrifice, and honor. And the Vietnam POWs were a critical link in that transformation.

By some official U.S. government estimates there were slightly fewer than eight hundred American prisoners of war during the Vietnam War, 1961–73. Generally speaking, the existing literature on the Vietnam POW experience has been written by and about the officer-aviators who were held in various prison camps of North Vietnam.[15] These accounts seem to follow a uniform pattern, and certain themes or events tend to dominate the accounts. The literary theorist Maureen Ryan advances this argument in *The Other Side of Grief: The Home Front and the Aftermath in American Narratives of the Vietnam War.* According to Ryan, "Throughout the Hanoi memoirs . . . the trajectory of the official story is consistent: shoot down; biographical backstory; early torture and the privations of imprisonment; eventual reconciliation to a long, Spartan incarceration; commentary on individual POWs, daily conditions, and the author's particular vulnerabilities and coping strategies. And almost without exception, the recital of the slow unfolding of the grim years is underscored by a recurrent declaration of the author's faith in God."[16] Ryan's assessment of published biographies and memoirs has merit. But certainly the American prisoner-of-war experience in Vietnam did not fit into a neatly defined master narrative or conform to an "official history." Indeed, the American POW experience in Vietnam was a mosaic of stories, stories as complex as the war itself, and stories of success, disappointment, and even failure, as exemplified in the life and legacy of Bill Robinson.

Born in the cotton-mill town of Roanoke Rapids, North Carolina, in 1943, Robinson encountered hardship and heartache at an early age. His father, William, served in the U.S. Army during and immediately following World War II. He was seldom around to care for Bill or his two sisters. Sadly, William completely abandoned his parental responsibilities before his son reached the age of eight. Bill's mother struggled to provide for her three children, and they depended on Bill's maternal grandparents for support. When Bill was fifteen, his mother died suddenly after a brief fight with ovarian cancer. He lived with his grandparents for the remainder of his high school years and, after graduating, joined the Air Force to serve his country and to break free from the suffocating grip of the cotton factories. He chose aircraft maintenance as a military career path and became a helicopter crew chief. As an enlisted man in the Cold War Air Force, he completed several uneventful assignments in the United States and South Korea before shipping out to Thailand in early 1965, when the air war intensified in Vietnam with the start of Operation Rolling Thunder. As a member of the Air Force's nascent air rescue operations in Southeast Asia, Robinson participated on several missions before his capture, including one in which he and seven others earned the Silver Star.

Among the first three dozen captives in North Vietnam, Robinson witnessed the initial development of the North Vietnamese prison network. He spent time at the Hanoi Hilton, but as the number of prisoners increased and the prison system expanded, Robinson was moved to Briarpatch, described by some as the most primitive of the northern camps because of its lack of electricity and running water as well as the prevalence of malnutrition among the prisoners. Later he was held at a camp called the Zoo, where he spent most of his seven and a half years of captivity and endured the full range of North Vietnam's torture program. He also survived, without the benefit of general anesthesia, an emergency appendectomy at the four-year mark of his captivity. The officers held in the cells and camps with Robinson recognized his exemplary conduct and took the unusual step of awarding him and two other enlisted men battlefield promotions to the rank of second lieutenant. The three men completed an officer training program, taught by their fellow POWs, while imprisoned in North Vietnam.

Throughout Robinson's captivity, his family lived through a nightmare of their own. They received letters from Bill on an intermittent basis, which offered very little information about how he was treated by his captors or the conditions of his cells or prison camps. Several photos of Robinson appeared during his imprisonment in major media outlets, at sporadic intervals, beginning with a dramatic depiction of his capture and a disturbing snapshot published in *Life* magazine. These glimpses provided some assurance that Robinson was still alive, but the family continued to worry about his well-being. During their private ordeal the Robinsons worked publicly to promote POW and MIA (missing in action) awareness in the state of North Carolina and the southeastern United States.

After their release from North Vietnam in 1973, Robinson and his fellow crewmember Arthur Neil Black became the first two enlisted men to receive the Air Force Cross, a combat award that ranks second only to the Medal of Honor. In 1986 the service permanently established Robinson's place in the storied history of its enlisted corps by inducting him into the Enlisted Heritage Hall. Still, his homecoming did not follow an idyllic or storybook script. He had disappointments in his military life as well as his personal life. Tension and unrealized dreams shadowed his first marriage. Old wounds and new injuries once again dominated Robinson's relationship with his father. These conflicts led to a twenty-year-long estrangement between Robinson and much of his nuclear family. Robinson remarried in 1994, following his first wife's death. His second marriage marked a new beginning, personally and with respect to his POW legacy. He repaired the rift with his family, with the assistance of his new wife, and he became more involved in former prisoner-of-war organizations such as American Ex-Prisoners of War and NAM-POWs. In May 1995 Robinson and his second wife traveled to Vietnam and met with some of his former captors. The visit formed the basis for a documentary produced by the Japan Broadcasting Corporation. Since the mid-1990s Robinson has become a much-in-demand speaker, but rather than charge huge speaking fees, he tends to appear most often before school groups and enlisted personnel and at informal veterans' reunions. Robinson's story offers a unique opportunity to examine the POW experience in North Vietnam from the perspective of an enlisted man. During the Vietnam War no enlisted man, in either the North or the South, was held longer than Bill Robinson. His very compelling personal story also serves as a vehicle for studying the legacy of the Vietnam POW. Thus, *The Longest Rescue* is not simply another book about capture, torture, and release. Instead, it chronicles the journey of a man who has fought some rather painful and difficult battles, both personally and in behalf of his country, and in the process it provides a corrective to some of the myths and stereotypes of the American Vietnam-era prisoners of war.

1

Unfortunate Sons

Late in the evening of 4 August 1964, President Lyndon Johnson appeared on television to inform the world of U.S. retaliatory strikes against North Vietnam in response to the Gulf of Tonkin incidents involving the U.S.S. *Maddox* and *C. Turner Joy.* "As I speak to you tonight," the president announced, "air action is now in execution against gunboats and certain supporting facilities in North Vietnam which have been used in these hostile operations." In concluding his brief remarks, the president stated, "Our response for the present will be limited and fitting."[1] Unfortunately for those involved in the mission, Johnson's irresponsible demand to appear on television before the end of the late-night news and "the final deadline for the major East Coast papers" eliminated the element of surprise.[2] When the president addressed the nation, only four of the fifty-nine planes making up Operation Pierce Arrow were actually airborne, and those four were 350 miles from their targets. Among those yet to take off was Lieutenant (j.g.) Everett Alvarez Jr., a navy pilot. In a bizarre twist of fate, Alvarez had been part of the response to the alleged attacks on the *Maddox* and *C. Turner Joy* the previous night. He had dropped illumination flares for a fellow navy pilot, Commander James Stockdale, as they attempted to identify the two American ships and any would-be attackers.[3]

Called into action again, Alvarez was part of a squadron of A-4C Skyhawks "assigned to hit the naval base at Hon Gai harbor, about twenty-five miles northeast of Haiphong and only fifty miles south of the Chinese" border. Because of an eleven-hour time difference between Washington, D.C., and Hanoi, the bulk of the strike force launched during the afternoon hours of 5 August. At 2:30 P.M. local time, Alvarez was the first launch off of the U.S.S. *Constellation.* He reached his target seventy-five minutes later, only to discover that the "briefers had guessed" wrong and the torpedo boats were on the opposite side of the harbor. He made a second pass, and as he headed out over the southern edge of the town, he received fire on the port side of his windshield. Forced to eject, Alvarez splashed into the choppy waters of the Gulf of Tonkin. He successfully extracted himself from his parachute but discovered that he was coated with a black dye; the vial of shark repellent in his survival vest had broken. As militiamen approached in sampans, Alvarez's thoughts shifted to his wife of seven months, Tangee, and his beloved mother, Chloe. He then realized that he had forgotten to remove his wedding ring; pilots had been warned that captors could use information about family members to exploit prisoners during interrogations. Alvarez worked quickly to slip off the ring, and as the symbol of love floated to the bottom of the gulf, the young pilot made a promise to his bride: "Don't worry, sweetheart . . . someday I'll get you another one." The vow was not necessary. Tangee divorced her prisoner husband nearly two years before his release from North Vietnam.[4]

Everett Alvarez was the first American serviceman captured in North Vietnam, and his more than eight and a half years in captivity would earn him the sobriquet the Old Man of the North. His chronological counterpart in the South was Army Captain Floyd "Jim" Thompson, whose nine years in captivity marked him as the Old Man of the South, and more grimly, the longest-held serviceman in American military history.[5] Among those to follow Alvarez and Thompson in captivity were some men who were born to wave the flag, including an admiral's legacy, and they would be asked to sacrifice a great deal for their country. Years of torture, torment, frustration, and lack of freedom meant that there would be no fortunate sons in North Vietnam. One of those unfortunate sons was Bill Robinson.

Life in a Cotton-Mill Town

The small cotton-mill town of Roanoke Rapids, North Carolina, was home to the Robinson clan. Eugene William (Gene) Robinson, Bill's grandfather, planted roots there in 1920, when, at the age of sixteen, he moved from southeastern Virginia to the tight-knit community in northeastern North Carolina. Gene Robinson was not alone. Between 1910 and 1920 the population of Roanoke Rapids more than doubled, from 1,670 to 3,369, as southerners throughout the region left the life of sharecropping and subsistence farming and moved to the cities in pursuit of the New South dream.[6] The boosters of the New South hoped, as most articulately expressed by Henry Grady, editor of the *Atlanta Constitution*, to build a "new economic and social order based on industry and scientific agriculture." For Roanoke Rapids, and much of the region, the promise of a New South seemed to rest on textile manufacturing.[7] In reality, "Roanoke Rapids did not exist before its mills," suggests the journalist and historian Mimi Conway. "From its beginnings, the history of the town has been the history of the mills, a history of power struggles." By 1910 several family-owned mills had been built in Roanoke Rapids, including the Rosemary Manufacturing Company, which "produced one third of all the damask tablecloths in the nation."[8]

Although Gene Robinson had traveled only ten miles from southeastern Virginia to Roanoke Rapids, he in actuality had entered a new world of economic opportunity and a class system based on noblesse oblige. The paternalistic ethos of the family-owned mills manifested itself in a variety of forms: affordable and comfortable housing, community gardens maintained at company expense, canning facilities constructed by the company, as well as recreation centers, a hospital, and a library. Mill work did not offer an easy living, but by the sweat of his brow, Robinson forged a successful life. He married Geneva Cox in 1922 and they soon started a family. For Geneva, who had been raised in an orphanage, the only family that she ever truly knew was the one she raised with her husband. Their first child, William Jackson Robinson, the father of Bill Robinson, was born in November 1922. Their second son, Harold, was born in 1924, and their only daughter, Hazel, was born in 1928. By almost any cultural or economic measure, the family of Gene and Geneva Robinson was a typical cotton-mill family. They worked hard, went to church, and raised their family.[9]

When all of the family-owned mills in Roanoke Rapids sold out in 1928 to the Simmons Company, a mattress manufacturer, the prevailing attitude of paternalism did not change. In 1956, however,

when the J. P. Stevens Company, one of the largest and most aggressively anti-union textile firms doing business in the South, purchased the mills, it wasted little time in dismantling the vestiges of
the former social contract between the workers and the mill owners.
It sold the company-owned homes and recreation center and withdrew its support from the hospital. As Mimi Conway explains, "With
the old system gone, many families . . . were left to shuttle between
the memories of the old paternalistic way of life and the jarring reality of the new, corporate mode."[10] Not only did the era of noblesse
oblige end in Roanoke Rapids with the J. P. Stevens takeover, but the
textile conglomerate introduced a management strategy that had a
devastating effect on the community, including the Robinson family. During his thirty-plus years in the mills, Gene Robinson had
risen from the lowly position of floor worker to that of shift supervi-
sor. But when the Stevens company inserted "college-educated people" into management and supervisory positions, Robinson found
himself "doing at fifty-eight years old what he previously did at
sixteen years old." Despite the demotion and cut in pay, Robinson
was among the fortunate survivors, as J. P. Stevens slashed its pay-
roll by eliminating thousands of jobs. Nevertheless, he decided that
he had had enough of mill life. "Always prepared for a rainy day,"
Robinson used his savings to purchase a little grocery store, where
he spent his remaining days "trying to help himself as well as others." He had survived the Great Depression raising rabbits and veg-
etables and sharing with and feeding those in the neighborhood,
and he would overcome this newest challenge.[11]

By this time Gene and Geneva's children had all married and
started lives of their own. In 1940 their son William met Lillian
Coppedge, and they married on Christmas Day of that year. In a
span of a little more than fifteen months they had two children; the
first child, a daughter named Jacqueline, was born 14 May 1942, and
Bill Robinson was born 28 August 1943. Many members of the Robinson family considered Bill "a miracle baby." He had been a breech
baby, "or what they referred to as a blue baby" in those days, and
family members considered him "lucky to survive just to get here
on earth." During his childhood Bill also survived several brushes
with death. When he was a youngster, the Robinsons often visited

family in nearby Virginia Beach, Virginia, and on one occasion Bill "actually drowned" but was revived by a quick-thinking uncle who performed mouth-to-mouth resuscitation. He then went through a period during which he was "a bleeder." His mother worried that even a minor cut might produce massive hemorrhaging, so she prevented young Bill from walking barefoot and carefully monitored his activities. His closest encounter with death came as a result of complications from a tonsillectomy. Robinson's heart stopped beating during the operation and the doctors informed the family that the boy "was dead and there was nothing that they could do." After he was revived, Robinson remained in the hospital for seventeen days, and the doctor believed that it was a miracle that he survived.[12]

Religion and family defined Bill's formative years. Lillian Robinson raised her children in the Methodist tradition, but other members of the Robinson clan were Baptist, and, ultimately, Bill remembers, "it didn't matter where we went to Sunday School, as long as we went to Sunday School." His mother eventually joined the Union Mission in Roanoke Rapids, an independent nondenominational church that held services four times a week and conducted a number of children's programs. Lillian taught Sunday School and helped organize the annual Easter egg hunt and Christmas parade. She supervised the "Clothes Closet," which accepted donated new and used clothing and distributed items free of charge to needy families. On Saturdays Lillian and another Union Mission member canvassed the neighborhoods and downtown areas for donations. Bill had a close relationship with his older sister, whom everyone called Jackie, and Ginger, the youngest of the family, who was born 24 June 1945. Ginger inherited her mother's temperament, and the two were nearly inseparable, to the point that Ginger followed "like a puppy dog" in her mother's footsteps. Ginger's older siblings regularly picked on her, the baby of the family. At times Jackie played the role of big brother; she was Bill's sparring partner. Their mother had a unique technique for settling disputes between the two. "She wouldn't take it out on us," Bill recalled. "She would give us the switch and would make us take it out on each other. She became the referee, and that took a lot of the fun out of it." The process certainly affected their characters, especially Jackie's: "She was the tough one of the family; she would take on anything and anybody at anytime." Toughness was something the children needed because their father was rarely around to either nurture them or provide for them. In many ways and on numerous occasions, William's actions caused considerable heartache among the Robinson children, especially Bill.[13]

A Son in Search of a Father

William Robinson just had "a wild streak that existed in him," and apparently "married life or the responsibility of a family was not part of his makings." Trouble appeared on the horizon shortly before the end of World War II, when Robinson was drafted into the Army. He completed basic training at Fort Jackson, South Carolina, and was assigned to a military police unit. He never deployed overseas and in fact was released from the Army following the birth of his third child, Ginger. At the time the U.S. Army draft policy conscripted fathers who had two children but exempted those with three; thus, Robinson served about six months before returning home. His stay was brief. He rejoined the Army and accepted a three-year assignment in Panama. He left the Army in 1949 and returned to Roanoke Rapids. His presence confused Ginger, who had no real awareness that he was her father, and with a child's innocence asked her mother if she "was going to sleep with that man." The romance of reunion did not last long, and William began to drift away from Lillian. Although they never legally separated or divorced, William left his family, forcing his wife to raise their children in a single-parent home. He would drop by from time to time, and on those occasions he sometimes seemed intent on reminding everyone why he left. The mere presence of young children seemed to cause him considerable annoyance; he could be heard complaining, "Damn children underneath your feet anywhere you go." If William had simply left without ever returning, he might have actually caused less pain. But he did not. He reappeared on special occasions and on holidays, often attempting to win approval by giving gifts. One Christmas William came back to Roanoke Rapids and brought gifts for his entire family, including his children, his brother and sister, and his parents, but he did not bring his wife anything. He claimed that he had bought her some dishes but he had forgotten to pick them up. Lillian never received the set of dishes.[14]

Lillian Robinson was no stranger to hardship or familial burden. She was one of thirteen children. While Lillian was in high school, her mother suffered a stroke and was paralyzed on one side. Lillian became her mother's caregiver and also raised three of her younger siblings in her parents' house. Her father worked as an overseer at a lumberyard, and, although he died in 1947, his wife, Lillian's mother, retained lifetime rights to the house. Here in the house on Henry Street, Bill lived with his mother, two siblings and invalid grandmother while his father was stationed in Panama and for a short while after his return in 1949. Life here could be hectic. Lillian's sisters had their own versions of marital discord, divorced their husbands, and intermittently dropped their kids off at the house on Henry Street, so that for a time a couple of cousins grew up with Bill and his siblings.[15]

Lillian Robinson then moved her family into a series of old shotgun houses. The rent at the first place was five dollars per week, a second place cost seven dollars per week, or "a dollar a day for a house." Financial uncertainty weighed heavily on the mother of three. She rarely knew where she would find the money to support her family. As a young child, Bill witnessed the mounting strain on his mother. His grandfather came by their house each Wednesday to take his mother grocery shopping, which meant that Tuesday nights were "either a glorious night or a night of tears. It was a good night if mother [had] received something in the mail from dad and she was able to buy our own groceries [the next day] rather than having to depend on granddaddy." But there would be "teardrops all night long" if Lillian did not receive financial assistance from her husband: William's disregard for their welfare left Lillian no choice but to ask her father-in-law "for money to buy groceries to feed her children." Throughout this ordeal of callous neglect, Lillian "scraped by the best she could, working with a friend of hers who owned a little grocery store." Whatever the circumstances, she taught her children to be proud and to accept responsibility at a young age, advising them, "You might not have much, but you can be clean." Even in the face of these difficult times, the children knew they could depend on their mother and "trust her guidance and leadership." Still, young Bill suffered from the emotional strain caused by his father's actions, and little Ginger "sensed that things were not as they should be."[16]

Sometime in 1952 or 1953 William Robinson succumbed to a woman "who promised him the world." They worked and traveled in North Carolina, Tennessee, and South Carolina for Olin Mills Photography. He still returned to Roanoke Rapids periodically, but the visits were rife with deception. To his children he claimed that he too had fallen into "dire straits." He lied. And what "hurt" Bill the "most" was that when his father visited he parked his car three blocks away, telling everyone that he had walked to see them because he had no way to get around; he actually had driven a brand-new automobile, a 1953 Oldsmobile, to town. Years later, Bill learned that the other woman had given his father thirty-five dollars a week—conscience money—to help Lillian and her children. William routinely kept the money for himself, however, forsaking his family and transferring the care of and responsibility for his children to his own father. The contrast in character between Gene Robinson and William was not lost on Bill, who lived by the creed, "If I was half the man my grandfather was then I would be twice the man that my daddy was." Indeed, when Bill was in the fifth grade, his mother and his siblings moved in with Gene and Geneva. Soon Grandmother Coppedge followed them. The new residence certainly pleased Bill: "This was the first time that we had actually had a toilet; up to that point we had an outhouse behind the house, but it was neat to have [a modern bathroom]. We ended up getting a hot water heater and a refrigerator. We thought we had died and gone to heaven. We had a washing machine and life was just getting good."[17]

Life without a Mother

The material improvements certainly made life better for Bill and his sisters, but the late 1950s also brought an unimaginable loss. His Grandmother Coppedge died in 1956. Then, in May 1958, his mother became ill. At first Lillian experienced severe headaches and the doctor prescribed a week of bed rest, which prevented her from collecting donations for the Union Mission. A determined soul, she resumed her fund-raising efforts the following Saturday, but her health was not improving. On Thursday night, 19 June 1958, while sitting at the kitchen table, she began to hemorrhage. Gene had already reported to work, but the children were able to contact him, and he returned home while a neighbor came to help prepare Lillian for the trip to the hospital. She was diagnosed with ovarian cancer. By Sunday Lillian was on her way to the Duke University Medical Center in Durham, North Carolina. Gene had a sister in Durham who agreed to care for Lillian at her home if the treatments made her too sick to return to Roanoke Rapids, which they did.[18]

Ultimately the disease was so advanced that the doctors declared Lillian terminally ill and made the arrangements to—in effect—send her home to die. The hemorrhaging persisted and Lillian was in and out of the local hospital. At times the pain was so great that she was brought to tears, and she remained weak in body and confined to her bed. Her faith in God remained steadfast, however, and she calmly embraced the biblical axiom "His will not my will be done" throughout the crisis. As the family cared for Lillian, her husband stopped by now and then to check on her but made no special efforts to help his dying wife. William's thirty-sixth birthday was on 5 November 1958. He telephoned Ginger to let her know that he was coming home to visit and he wanted his mother to cook him a pot of navy beans to celebrate the occasion. When Ginger relayed the information to her grandmother, her mother overheard the conversation and she began to weep uncontrollably. After Lillian gained her composure, family members asked why she had broken down, and she told them that she was upset because she was too sick to bake her husband a birthday cake. The day after William's birthday, Lillian returned to the hospital. On 7 November 1958, after a nearly five-month battle with cancer, Lillian slipped into a coma and passed away around three o'clock in the afternoon.[19]

Even in these tragic circumstances, William refused to take on the responsibility of raising his son. Shortly before her mother's illness, Jackie, Bill's older sister, married, and his younger sister, Ginger, "married at a very young age." This left Bill alone to be raised by his grandparents. Through all the disappointment, the betrayal, the abandonment, and the grievous loss of his mother, Bill not only survived but developed into a resilient young man. He would draw on this personal fortitude in subsequent dealings with his father as well as in the challenges he would face in North Vietnam. In general, school proved difficult for him because he suffered from a mild form of dyslexia, which went undiagnosed in his youth. During his grade school and junior high years, he performed well in math, "average in science, and had a little bit of a problem in English." Because of his struggles, Robinson in essence received a probationary pass from the eighth grade to the ninth grade. At the end of the first six-week grading period, however, he had made satisfactory progress and remained in the ninth grade. Sports provided a major incentive. He participated in football and served as the manager of the school's basketball and baseball teams. He also participated on the track team, mainly for conditioning purposes and to improve his agility for football. Robinson played football all four years of high school, mostly the center position on offense, and filled in at long-snapper on special teams. He lettered in football, but was not quite good enough to earn a starting position.[20]

As a result of Robinson's extensive involvement in athletics, he developed a close relationship with one of his coaches. Coach Hoyle was Robinson's history teacher and Sunday School teacher as well as his coach. After Robinson's mother died in 1958, Coach Hoyle played a very active role in Robinson's life, helping him find a job in a clothing store and giving him financial advice. Robinson described Coach Hoyle as "the type of person who was close to everyone." The school integration struggle, which began at Central High School in Little Rock, Arkansas, in 1957 and moved at a glacial pace throughout the South, had not reached Roanoke Rapids during Robinson's school days. This is not surprising, given that only 10 percent of schools in the Upper South and a scant 1 percent of public schools in the Deep South integrated in the decade following the 1954 *Brown vs. Board of Education* decision. If a racial problem existed in Roanoke Rapids, Robinson was unaware, or, he admitted, he turned a blind eye to the issue. Of course, he encountered separate "water fountains and bathrooms and all these other things," but never made the connection to the larger concern of social injustice.

Like some southern families, the Robinsons felt more comfortable dealing with blacks as individuals than as a racial group. For example, Gene Robinson had "dear friends" who were African American, including "one lady who came to his house once a week" and helped his wife clean and organize the house. When she came, "she always sat at the table" with the Robinson family during meals. It took moving away from Roanoke Rapids for Bill to realize a racial problem existed in the South and the nation.[21]

Joining the Cold War Air Force

When Bill Robinson graduated from high school in 1961, he applied to the nearby Newport News Shipyard and Dry Dock Company's apprentice program in welding. The southeastern Virginia shipyard, one of the largest on the East Coast, employed tens of thousands and offered the region's young men a chance to learn valuable mechanical skills. The Newport News Shipyard, because it received numerous military contracts, also offered young men an alternative, a type of deferment, to military service. In limbo as he waited for official notification of his acceptance to the shipyard program, Robinson began to discuss with family, friends, and recruiters the prospects of joining the military. His grandfather's experience with J. P. Stevens had so hardened Robinson that he firmly rejected the cotton mills as an employment option. Perhaps in an effort to keep her grandson close by, Geneva asked him if he considered himself "too good to work in the cotton mills." The respectful grandchild replied, "Absolutely not. I appreciate the people who work in the cotton mills . . . but there are other options." He vowed to stay in the service the rest of his life rather than return home to work in the cotton mills. In reviewing the military services, he examined the Marine Corps and Navy before "finally settling on the Air Force." At the age of seventeen, Robinson needed formal parental approval to join the military, "but the thought of somebody else deciding" his future did not appeal to him, and so he waited until he turned eighteen to join the Air Force, when he was able to make his own decisions.[22]

Once Robinson made the commitment, during the summer of

1961, to join the Air Force, he hoped that he could start basic training in September. Robinson suspected, however, that his recruiter
"had filled his quota for September and October," because "the only
available date was November." Robinson therefore opted for November, but with a family philosophy based on the notion that "if
you didn't work, you shouldn't get hungry," the recent high school
graduate "had to find something to do." Still having a misplaced
faith in his father, Bill turned to William for help. His father had
married the other woman after his mother's death, and in addition
to the photography job had started working construction. Sadly,
the outcome seemed predetermined from the start. The night that
Bill graduated from high school he left his grandparents' home
and went to live with his father and stepmother. The move and attempted reunion precipitated another "downhill run" for Bill: "Less
than twenty-four hours after graduating high school I'm driving a
dump truck and getting cussed out on the side of the road because I
couldn't keep up. I had never driven a dump truck in my life, but I
was my dad's son, so I could do anything that he could do, that's the
way he looked at it." The experiment continued until Bill wrecked
one of his father's dump trucks, which prompted a rare moment of
agreement between the son and the father: "He thought I should get
into another line of work, and I did too." The failed attempt at reconciliation did not deter the resolute Bill, and he managed to turn
disappointment into what may have been the best training he ever
received. After parting with his father, Robinson teamed up with
a master carpenter. They built a house from the foundation to the
roof. Earning fifty cents an hour, Robinson dug the footing, put up
drywall, and hung the roof trusses. He also spent some time working in a tobacco market, performing manual labor in the warehouse
and driving a delivery truck to and from the market. Finally, Robinson went to work and "turned wrenches for a month" at the garage
of a friend of his father's while he waited to join the Air Force.[23]

Robinson's Air Force career began in near-comical fashion. The
week before Thanksgiving 1961, he reported for his physical, which
he failed. The news devastated Robinson, and he had to take the
bus back home and inform his family that the Air Force had rejected
him. Apparently, anxiety and "the excitement of the whole world

changing" had caused some unsatisfactory readings during a check of his vital signs. Robinson remained at home for a week, relaxing and composing himself, and he returned for a second physical the day before Thanksgiving. He passed the second physical and "by pure accident ended up" at Lackland Air Force Base in San Antonio, Texas, on Thanksgiving morning. The failed physical had delayed Robinson's presumed arrival by one week and probably added to a confusing incident upon his eventual arrival. During roll call the first sergeant omitted his name, and when the young trainee pointed out the omission, the first sergeant replied, "Well, you're not supposed to be here." Two weeks later the Air Force finally corrected the mistake. Basic training consisted of two phases when an airman received an assignment to a technical school, which was the case for Robinson; the introductory phase took place at Lackland and lasted five weeks, and the technical training took an additional three weeks. On his written examinations Robinson scored well in both mechanics and electronics, but because of his affinity for "turning wrenches" he chose to be a mechanic. He completed his technical training in a helicopter group at nearby Sheppard Air Force Base in Wichita Falls, Texas, on all three active-duty helicopters, the H-19, H-21, and H-43. Aside from the unusual beginning, Robinson's basic training entailed no additional surprises, excepting a notification that he had been accepted to the Newport News Shipyard's apprentice program. He drew Altus Air Force Base, in Altus, Oklahoma, as his first post–basic training assignment.[24]

When Robinson called home to inform his family of his impending graduation from basic training, he learned that his father intended to continue the charade of parenthood. The latest game of deception had begun as Robinson left for basic training and centered on an unfulfilled pledge from his childhood. Before his mother's death, his father had purchased a 1938 Ford, and as Bill recalls, his father, "standing over my mother's grave," promised him the car. The occasion of the promise had obvious sentimental meaning for Bill, and as he prepared to enter the Air Force, a vehicle became something of a practical necessity for him. The car, however, needed to be repaired and restored, but William never seemed to have the time or inclination to complete the project. As his son prepared to leave for Lackland, William had told him that he had discovered another 1938 Ford that he intended to purchase. The plan now was to use the first car for parts and to restore the second car, and when Bill came home after basic training, he could take the car with him to his next assignment. As the time for graduation approached, Bill phoned home with details of his upcoming travel plans, at which time his stepmother informed him that his father had sold the first car on the very day that he had left North Carolina for Texas. This angered and "upset" Robinson to the degree that he canceled his plans to go home after graduation and instead went directly to Altus, Oklahoma, where a friend from his hometown resided. The same friend eventually convinced Robinson to return to Roanoke Rapids a year later.[25]

When Robinson entered the Air Force in November 1961, U.S. military involvement in Vietnam barely registered, if at all, on the collective consciousness of the American public. In his region of the South, where evangelical denominations such as the Southern Baptist and Methodist significantly influenced public perceptions, Robinson sensed more concern over the election of a Yankee Catholic president than the expansion of war in Southeast Asia. For Robinson himself, the prospect of having to go to Vietnam "was not even in [his] thought process. . . . It was not even on the radar."[26] Yet only a month after Robinson started basic training, Army Specialist George Fryett became the first American captured by the Viet Cong. Fryett was a clerk in the Saigon office of the chief of staff at Military Assistance Command, Vietnam. On the day after Christmas 1961, in search of some relaxation, Fryett decided to visit a local swimming pool. While he was riding a bicycle to his destination, two Vietnamese cyclists ambushed him with hand grenades. He suffered shrapnel wounds during the explosion, and his attackers quickly subdued him. For the next six months, Fryett endured what has been described as "harsh but not brutal [treatment]. The Viet Cong beat him when he was uncooperative, fed him little, and several times forced him to dig his own grave." He escaped once but was immediately recaptured. The Viet Cong interrogated him, but they appeared to follow no routine or system for information gathering. Abruptly, the Viet Cong released Fryett in late June 1962.[27]

If Robinson had no awareness of Vietnam when he entered the Air Force, he certainly never contemplated being a prisoner of war. In fact, his assignments at Altus Air Force Base and later at Osan Air Force Base in South Korea typified some of the Air Force's more routine duty assignments during the early stages of the Cold War. Although assigned to a B-52 bomber wing, Robinson's helicopter group at Altus basically provided missile support for Atlas missiles, a first generation intercontinental ballistic missile (ICBM), which occupied a prominent place in the nation's nuclear deterrence program in the late 1950s and early 1960s. Their primary responsibility was to fly spare parts and personnel to twelve Atlas missile sites in Oklahoma and Texas, a task Robinson considered at "the bottom of the totem pole," both in terms of importance and in presenting a mental or physical challenge. Put simply, the Air Force used ground transportation to send nonemergency parts to missile sites, and it used helicopters to move technical personnel and emergency parts to reduce the downtime for Atlas sites. Occasionally, Robinson's cargo generated a little excitement, such as the time he made a short flight to Clinton-Sherman Air Force Base, Oklahoma, and signed for a box that was "no bigger than the size of a suitcase." The paperwork indicated that the part cost $334,000. Upon his return to Altus, someone tried to grab the part off of the helicopter, and Robinson responded by "essentially standing on the box and held out the paper and made them sign it" before releasing the expensive freight.[28] In September 1963 Robinson left Altus for Osan, South Korea. His unit ostensibly supported military negotiations between the two Koreas at the Joint Security Area at Panmunjom by ferrying high-ranking military officials to and from the talks. Among the various tasks performed by Robinson's unit at Osan, one of the most common was taking a particular general and his wife "up to Seoul for grocery shopping." To be precise, "every once in a while we took the general," Robinson clarified, "but we took his wife more times than him." The frequency of these missions led to a discussion among the airmen about creating a unit patch featuring a "bag of groceries." Robinson's first two years in the Air Force ended with very little drama, and none appeared likely at his next assignment, Grand Forks Air Force Base in North Dakota, at least not on a professional level.[29]

An Enlisted Man's Heritage

On a personal level, though, Robinson felt the pain of rejection again; but this time his father had not created the anguish. In December 1964, after leaving Korea, he stopped in North Carolina before reporting to Grand Rapids. Since high school, he had dated, off and on, a girl named Jane who had been a year behind him in school. Their roller-coaster courtship produced moments when they sometimes "would have a real cozy relationship and sometimes it was a bit of a debacle." Yet they corresponded while Robinson was in South Korea and she was in college. In one letter Robinson mentioned his upcoming move to North Dakota, and she raised the possibility of transferring from her school to another school in the Grand Forks area. Her suggestion, aided by the 12,000-mile separation, filled Robinson's head with visions of "beautiful things." Convinced that he was in love, Robinson scraped up enough money to buy an engagement ring. When they reunited, he proposed. Jane accepted. By all indications, things were wonderful; then, three days later, the bride-to-be returned the ring, saying that "it was too small." Robinson offered to have the ring resized but she countered that the ring was not the style or cut that she wanted. Her quibbles about the ring, in reality, masked a more serious issue. Her father had been an officer during World War II, and in college she and her friends had dated only "officers or officers-to-be." She informed Robinson that "she couldn't stand the thought of being married to an enlisted man." Robinson could not envision a more "devastating" attitude, and the comment "hurt" him deeply. He rejected the notion "that an officer could serve his country better than an enlisted man." He viewed the military as an assemblage of men not separated by rank, but rather a brotherhood bound together based on a common pledge "to serve their country."[30]

Needless to say, this incident ended their relationship, and Robinson abruptly departed for North Dakota. Not long after arriving at Grand Forks, Robinson met Beverly, a local nursing student. They "became good friends and things looked very promising . . . and headed in the right direction." But a meddling father and an upcoming transfer cast a cloud of uncertainty over the young couple's future. Beverly's father offered to buy her a new Plymouth Satellite if she would end her relationship with Robinson. The offer certainly tempted her, but the Air Force may have played a larger role in keeping the two apart. In January 1965 Robinson learned that his unit was being disbanded and he would be leaving North Dakota for a temporary duty assignment. Still, he could hope. On 23 April 1965 Robinson left Grand Forks "as an individual with a toolbox." Like most American servicemen sent to Southeast Asia during the Vietnam War, Robinson flew on a military charter flight from Travis Air Force Base, just outside San Francisco. He jokes that it cost "the government more to fly the toolbox than to fly me." His return to Travis Air Base, nearly eight years later, would be much more memorable. On 25 April he arrived in Bangkok, Thailand, and made his way to Nakhon Phanom Royal Thai Air Base, in northeastern Thailand, a mere seven miles from the Laotian border.[31]

That Others May Live

The origins of the United States Air Force (USAF) helicopter air rescue operations can be dated to the close of World War II, when U.S. Army Air Forces used Sikorsky R-6 helicopters to rescue a few dozen downed airmen in the China-Burma-India Theater. Statistically speaking, the number of rescues was minimal. According to the Air Force historian Forrest L. Marion, however, "The limited accomplishments of helicopters heralded the birth of a new technology with immense potential for military applications, notably, medical evacuation and aircrew rescue." From these humble origins rose the Air Rescue Service, established in 1946. The first commander of the Air Rescue Service was Colonel Richard T. Kight. He held the command from 1946 to 1952, and he also penned "The Code of the Air Rescueman": "It is my duty as a Pararescueman to save life and to aid the injured. I will be prepared at all times to perform my assigned duties quickly and efficiently, placing these duties before personal desires and comforts. These things I do, 'That Others May

Live.'" The opportunity for the USAF to realize the "immense potential" of helicopter air rescue occurred in 1950 with the outbreak of war in Korea, and the opportunity was led by the 3rd Air Rescue Squadron (ARS). It has been estimated that the combined U.S. military services used helicopters to evacuate or rescue approximately 25,000 personnel during the Korean War. Of that number, the 3rd ARS evacuated more than 7,000 soldiers and rescued nearly 1,000 U.S. and United Nations personnel from behind enemy lines. One of the more heralded missions happened on 23 December 1950 after a T-6 Mosquito aircraft observed "the letters PW spelled in the snow with pieces of straw," and the crew determined that American soldiers were in the area. Members of Detachment F, 3rd ARS, launched a rescue mission eight miles behind enemy lines. The rescue operation took twelve sorties to complete and recovered eleven American and twenty-four South Korean POWs.[32]

During the Korean War the primary helicopter used by the USAF was the Sikorsky S-51, which the Air Force designated the H-5. Although well-suited for "mountainous terrain . . . , the H-5 had several significant operational limitations." Flying the H-5 under instrument conditions was dangerous; therefore, night rescues or rescues during inclement weather were rare. The H-5 lacked armor and armament, which made the helicopter dependent on "fighter cover or friendly ground fire for protection during the most vulnerable phase of a rescue or recovery—the pickup." Normally, pilots were issued .45-caliber automatic pistols and medics carried carbines, but the helicopters remained unarmed for several reasons. Originally, the H-5 had been designed for commercial purposes, and in its air rescue role it flew at payload capacity. The helicopter also lacked cabin space for a machine gun. Despite these aircraft limitations and liabilities, the pilots and crews of the H-5s performed admirably during the Korean War, accounting for 73 percent of the nearly one thousand U.S. and U.N. personnel rescued by the 3rd ARS. These accomplishments were impressive given the fact that "at the outset of the war, the concept of using helicopters to rescue pilots from behind enemy lines was largely untested, and the USAF lacked a doctrine and experience for such a mission, World War II notwithstanding." The performance of the

Air Rescue Service has led some Air Force historians to conclude that the adoption of helicopter air rescue as an established component of the USAF was a very real possibility following the Korean War. The changing nature of the Cold War and the election of a new U.S. president, however, presented the Air Force with a different set of priorities.[33]

In assessing American foreign policy in the aftermath of the Korean War, the administration of President Dwight Eisenhower decided on a new strategy for fighting the Cold War. Looking to avoid limited proxy wars, such as the conflict in Korea, the New Look approach emphasized the option of using nuclear weapons. The Eisenhower administration hoped that the threat of "massive retaliation" would deter Soviet aggression and allow the United States to reduce spending on conventional forces while it invested more in technological superiority. Within this new posture, the Air Force would play an important role as strategic airpower, most identifiable in the form of long-range jet bombers, emerged as a crucial means for delivering nuclear weapons.[34] To be sure, the USAF received the largest share of New Look defense budgets, and "the emphasis remained on SAC [Strategic Air Command] and not preparations for another Korea." The attention placed on strategic nuclear bombing gave rise to the claim, especially within the USAF, that airpower represented the predominate component of America's military capabilities.[35] The doctrinal and budgetary emphasis on strategic nuclear bombing led to the neglect of other types of air operations, including air rescue. Between 1954 and 1961 Air Rescue Service personnel dropped from 7,900 to 1,600, and "headquarters USAF deleted the wartime mission statement from the National Search and Rescue Plan [and] in its place . . . inserted a clause making combat search and rescue an extension of the USAF's peacetime mission."[36] As a result of the Eisenhower administration's New Look strategy, and the Air Force's desire to be the centerpiece of that policy, Dennis Drew, an expert on airpower and USAF doctrine, has concluded that during the decade of the 1950s the Air Force's basic doctrine "seemed to assume that the struggles in Southeast Asia did not exist and, for the most part, that the Korean War had not happened."[37]

By early 1961, when President John Kennedy assumed office, American-backed governments in Laos and South Vietnam faced renewed challenges from insurgencies within their respective borders, and North Vietnamese incursions along the Ho Chi Minh Trail threatened both governments. The Kennedy administration sponsored "a range of assistance programs" to bolster South Vietnam's President Ngo Dinh Diem and the Army of the Republic of Vietnam (ARVN). In Laos, the Central Intelligence Agency (CIA) expanded its role in what some would call a shadow war. Following the deaths of Diem and Kennedy in late 1963, the Pathet Lao (Laotian communists), the North Vietnamese, and the Viet Cong seized the initiative. The pace of American escalation continued under President Lyndon Johnson, who in February 1965 authorized Operation Rolling Thunder. Lasting three years and nine months, Rolling Thunder became the longest bombing campaign in American military history.[38] Despite the evolution and corresponding intensification of the air war in Southeast Asia, the respected Air Force historian Earl H. Tilford Jr. characterized the early 1960s as the "dark ages" for air search and rescue.[39] Likewise, the U.S. Navy prepared poorly for search-and-rescue operations. Indeed, Lieutenant (j.g.) Everett Alvarez recounted in his memoir that "nothing at all was said about search and rescue" during his intelligence briefing for Operation Pierce Arrow, the retaliatory strikes for the Gulf of Tonkin incidents and the mission that he was flying when shot down and captured.[40]

In the case of the Air Force, Tilford argues that in the early 1960s "the rescue mission in Southeast Asia suffered from inadequate forces, nonexistent doctrine, and ill-suited aircraft." To address personnel shortages, the Air Force in mid-1964 transferred a number of rescue units from stateside detachments to Southeast Asia under a temporary duty status. A year later a major "organization change restructured Air Service units in Southeast Asia" and led to the activation of the 38th ARS, headquartered at Tan Son Nhut, South Vietnam. The detachments of the 38th ARS included Detachment 1, Nakhon Phanom Royal Thai Air Force Base (RTAFB); Detachment 2, Takhli RTAFB; Detachment 3, Ubon RTAFB; Detachment 4, Korat RTAFB; Detachment 5, Udorn RTAFB; Detachment 6, Bien Hoa Air

Base, South Vietnam; and Detachment 7, Da Nang Air Base, South Vietnam. On 15 September 1965 the Air Force added Detachment 9, Pleiku Air Base, South Vietnam; and Detachment 10, Binh Thuy Air Base, South Vietnam.[41]

During the developmental years of air rescue in Southeast Asia, two models of the Kaman HH-43 helicopter, nicknamed the Huskie, served as the primary recovery vehicles for the USAF. The HH-43s dominated the ARS inventory at the end of 1965, representing 64 percent of assigned rescue helicopters. Their forerunner, the HH-43B, was originally conceived to perform Local Base Rescue (LBR) missions, whereby "a small, high performance helicopter . . . could respond quickly, perform hoist rescue, carry firefighting and rescue personnel, and serve as an aerial ambulance." The HH-43s provided exceptional firefighting capabilities that included counterrotating rotors designed to generate "huge volumes of low velocity air with a longitudinal forward thrust, which opened a 'cool' corridor" for firefighters. Some HH-43s included a Fire Suppression Kit (FSK) that could be attached to and detached from the helicopter's external cargo hook. The FSK, nicknamed Sputnik, was a spherical pressurized tank containing a mixture of water and foam fluid and a dispensing hose some 150 feet long. An LBR mission's objective was aircrew recovery in a nonhostile environment, and rescue personnel focused on fire suppression "rather than attempt to extinguish the entire blaze." The mission objective in Southeast Asia would be substantially different from those in peacetime, and the HH-43B proved to be poorly suited for the task of recovering pilots behind enemy lines. The HH-43B had a limited fuel capacity, 198 gallons, which at cruise speed produced a range of only 212 miles, and it lacked protective armor to deflect small arms fire. Although M-60 machine guns could have been mounted in the HH-43B, they rarely were: as a practical matter, minimal cabin space precluded the placement of a gunner. Additionally, the Air Rescue Service was uncomfortable with the idea of an armed rescue gunship. The obvious limitations necessitated combat modifications, and Kaman produced the HH-43F. The F-model was equipped with a greater fuel capacity, 350 gallons, which at cruise speed extended the helicopter's range to 500 miles, titanium armor plating covered portions of the cabin and engine areas, and its engine generated more horsepower (1,150 versus 750) than the B-model. But for the same reasons that the B-model went unarmed, so did the HH-43F.[42]

As the USAF's air rescue mission unfolded in Southeast Asia, doctrine and tactics evolved in accordance with the HH-43's capabilities. Typically, the crew of an HH-43 consisted of a pilot, copilot, crew chief, and pararescueman, or PJ. Once an airman had been downed, his actual location had to be verified (audibly or visually) and an assessment of enemy forces in the area had to be made before a rescue mission commenced. Optimally, two helicopters conducted the rescue, escorted by propeller-driven aircraft such as the A-1 Skyraider or jet fighters such as the F-4 Phantom, or both. To coordinate the rescue efforts, an airborne command, usually flying in an HU-16 Albatross, accompanied the mission, gathering and relaying information. The HH-43B's limited flight range often required a leapfrogging approach to the rescue site, stopping at "Lima Sites" (slang for landing sites) along the route for refueling. Upon reaching the downed pilot, the crew chief, who manned the hoist, worked with the PJ, who sometimes descended from the helicopter to provide medical aid or otherwise assist the downed pilot. On the HH-43B, the hoist apparatus was a one-hundred-foot-long wire cable with a simple harness, which had limited effectiveness in the jungle-canopied terrain of Southeast Asia. Accordingly, the HH-43F came equipped with a jungle penetrator, a spring-loaded device "that parted jungle foliage as it was lowered to the survivor who, after strapping himself to the penetrator, released a set of spring-loaded arms at the other end to protect himself as he was hauled up through the branches of trees." By the end of 1965 the USAF had begun to address personnel shortages, to develop doctrine and tactics, and to modify existing or introduce new aircraft in its search-and-rescue operations. From 1 January to 30 June 1965 the Air Rescue Service recorded twenty-nine "combat saves," and it recorded an additional ninety-three rescues from 1 July 1965 to 1 January 1966. Earl Tilford described "the summer of 1965 . . . [as] a watershed period for search and rescue in Southeast Asia," and he concluded that by 1966 "combat search and rescue was indispensable to tactical air operations."[43]

NKP

Clearly, when Bill Robinson arrived at Nakhon Phanom RTAB in late April 1965, the USAF was in a transitional phase in its air rescue operations. The air base at Nakhon Phanom, known as NKP, was nothing more than an outpost with a pierced-steel-planking (PSP) runway, which was "basically just a little bit better than a grass strip." The Navy's Seabees had originally constructed the runway and ramp for Thailand as part of a South East Asia Treaty Organization (SEATO) agreement. Although primitive, NKP had a contingency of about forty Americans who served as cooks, Air Force police, and refueling technicians. The base included an officers' club and an NCO club, both of which were converted hooches, and an unofficial PX run by an entrepreneurial radar operator. Most of the servicemen assigned to Detachment 1 of the 38th ARS at NKP had experience with LBR; however, at NKP they would be conducting Aircrew Combat Recovery (ACR) missions, something completely new to most of the crew. Moreover, as Detachment 1's commander, Air Force Captain Joe E. Ballinger, explained, "We were the only group in the military who were granted in regulations the option to prosecute a mission on 'Calculated Risk,' [which] meant that in the fields we could make the decision to risk our lives and our machines, if we thought we could get away with it and save a life." For rescue operations at NKP, the crews flew the HH-43B, which Robinson realized did not "really have the range we needed . . . but, again, coming out of peacetime going into wartime, you didn't always have the equipment that you needed." The crew chiefs and mechanics at NKP modified the HH-43Bs for combat operations. They added a piece of quarter-inch steel to the floor beneath the pilot's and co-pilot's seats, and the crew chief and PJ used their World War II–era flight vests, "the old shingle type," "to sit on to protect our butts" because the vests were useless in flights. Robinson's HH-43B was essentially unarmed: "We carried an M-16 and a P38 [pistol]. . . . We had a Smith & Wesson combat special and that was the extent of our firepower." The crews that preceded Robinson at NKP had developed a system for in-flight refueling to increase the HH-43B's flight range. Ordinarily, the range of the HH-43 was approximately seventy-five miles to the site, thirty minutes onsite, seventy-five miles back to base; this left a remainder of twenty minutes of reserve fuel. By carrying extra fuel in fifty-five-gallon barrels in the cabin area and using quick-disconnect hoses for refueling, crews could extend the range to 105 miles out and back, while maintaining the same time onsite and amount of reserve fuel. Flight-planning duty officers often marked maps with circles that equaled the "range of one barrel of extra fuel, two barrels, and three barrels." Once the fuel was consumed, the crews would "kick the barrel out of the back" of the helicopter and continue with the flight. Robinson and the rest of Detachment 1 practiced this in-flight refueling system. Aside from air rescue, Detachment 1 flew a number of "cats and dogs" missions, including support for a radar site, explosive ordnance disposal (EOD) missions, and medical support missions.[44]

Robinson met most of his crewmembers for the first time in Bangkok. As he recalls, "They put us up at the same hotel in Thailand and we realized we were all going to end up at the same place." The deploying unit to Nakhon Phanom was from Kirtland Air Force Base in Albuquerque, New Mexico, and individuals such as Bill Robinson were assigned as support for that group. The same was the case for Robinson's pilot, Captain Thomas J. Curtis. Born on 24 August 1932 as the youngest of nine children, Curtis was raised in Houston, Texas, and spent two years at the University of Houston before enlisting in the Air Force in October 1952. He received his commission and wings on 18 December 1954. "Through the luck of the draw," Curtis found himself assigned to an air rescue unit, and, despite squadron closures and base closures, subsequent reassignments kept Curtis in air rescue or flying rotary-wing aircraft for much of his pre-Vietnam Air Force career. From September 1962 to April 1965 Captain Curtis served as commander, Detachment 9, Central Air Rescue Center, England AFB, Louisiana. He volunteered for the temporary duty assignment that took him to NKP. Robinson's copilot, 1st Lieutenant Duane W. Martin, born 2 January 1940, hailed from Denver, Colorado. He received his commission at Lackland AFB on 5 February 1963 and completed helicopter pilot training at Webb AFB, in Big Spring, Texas. He served in Detachment 9, Western Air Rescue Center, Portland, Oregon, his first and only assignment before arriving in Thailand in spring 1965. The final crewmember, Airman Third Class Arthur Neil Black, was born 12 December 1944 in Bethlehem, Pennsylvania. He enlisted in the Air Force in January 1963 and trained as a pararescueman. He served with the 79th Air Rescue Squadron at Andersen AFB, Guam, from October 1963 to May 1965, and briefly with an air rescue squadron in California, before his assignment to Southeast Asia. Black was the only crewmember that Robinson did not meet in Bangkok.[45]

The piecemeal fashion in which the Air Force built up its air rescue personnel force, a resignation, and the quirks of flight schedules fated these four men—Robinson, Curtis, Martin, and Black—to be crewmembers on 20 September 1965. Before arriving at Nakhon Phanom, the four men had not trained together and they possessed different personalities and levels of experience. Lieutenant Martin was something of an unknown quantity, as he had limited experience in the Air Force and as a pilot. Martin had been rushed in as a replacement for a pilot who had reached a burnout point and had lost a bit of his nerve. This pilot felt he could no longer do his job and wanted to return to the states to resign his commission. Martin had been sent in his stead. Black was a bit of "wild hair." He personified the gung-ho, snake eater, Superman attitude of the Vietnam-era PJ, a trace of which still exists among their clan today. The nineteen-year-old was "full of vinegar and tiger piss" and ready to tackle any challenge. During after-duty hours he required some adult supervision, but as part of a rescue team, Neil Black knew his job and could be counted on to perform at a high level. Curtis exuded a kind of quiet yet powerful confidence, a confidence reinforced by his massive forearms, which seemed better suited to a lumberjack than a helicopter pilot, as well as his nearly thirteen years of experience in the Air Force. He was "very comfortable" with his crew chief, Bill Robinson, as the two shared similar backgrounds, and there was a strong degree of trust between the two men.[46]

Despite their respective pedigrees, each of the four men had received specialized preparation for his duties, and it did not take long to jell as a team. The key was learning the most efficient techniques and doctrines for the unique air rescue mission in Southeast Asia. The setup at NKP had "two birds on standby every day" and three aircrews, meaning pilot and copilot "rotated between high and low bird." The crew chief and PJ also followed a rotating schedule. During a typical rescue mission both helicopters flew to the rescue site, where the low bird executed the pickup and the high bird orbited the site in support of the low bird. Depending on the number and availability of A1-E Skyraider fighter escorts, the possibility existed that some A1-Es, nicknamed Sandy, flew as "Sandy Low" and some as "Sandy High." On these missions, each member of the HH-43B helicopter had a specific task to fulfill. In Robinson's experience, the low-bird pilot served as a type of mission leader, ensuring that all crewmembers worked together as a team. The co-pilot assisted the pilot with the navigation of the helicopter and the planning for the flight. The crew chief operated the hoist and "basically hung on the side of" the helicopter while directing the pilot for the pickup. The PJ, if necessary, would rappel to the ground and render first aid or assistance. As USAF air rescue doctrine evolved, Robinson underwent some degree of frustration with the so-called rules of engagement: "There were so many rules of engagement at that particular time; they wouldn't even let us get airborne until the pilot was identified on the ground. Well, the same time we're [U.S. aircraft] trying to identify him, the enemy is looking for him. So we were already put behind the power curve: flying at 10,000 feet, we could only fly sixty miles per hour." These procedures placed rescue crews in difficult circumstances, especially if the travel time to the target area was two to three hours. Robinson believed that the inadequate equipment issues brought about ill-conceived rescue procedures. Subsequently, the USAF made procedural changes in airborne rescue and in-flight refueling that allowed rescue teams to arrive within moments of a pilot's being downed. This learning curve occurred too late to benefit Robinson.[47]

Robinson flew on two rescue missions before 20 September 1965. On both occasions the operations included "two birds, a high and a low," and both times Robinson flew in the high bird. From the support position, Robinson's helicopter assisted the low bird "in setting up a search grid to locate the downed pilots," and then hovered over the rescue site as the low bird descended and retrieved the pilots before flying back to the base together. The two missions averaged about three and a half to four hours each, from start to finish, and one took place northeast of Nakhon Phanom, in the narrow strip of southern North Vietnam, the other approximately ninety miles southwest of Hanoi. Both times Robinson and his crewmembers encountered enemy fire at about 3,700 feet and avoided serious damage by simply climbing to a higher altitude.[48]

20 September 1965

The aviation historian Chris Hobson called 20 September 1965 "a bad day for U.S. airmen." The ill winds of fate resulted in more than 13,800 days of captivity, one pilot being killed in action, and four pilots surviving shootdowns or crashes. On that morning the misfortune began during an armed reconnaissance mission flown by USAF Captain Edgar Lee Hawkins. Flying an F-105D Thunderchief, Captain Hawkins attacked a bridge thirty miles southwest of Sop Cop, not far from the Laotian border. His aircraft received ground fire, his plane crashed, and Hawkins did not survive. An apparent mechanical failure contributed to the plight of USAF Captain Phillip Eldon Smith. During a Combat Air Patrol mission over the Gulf of Tonkin, Captain Smith lost his navigation system in his F-104C Starfighter, and as he tracked eastward he encountered two Chinese Navy Shenyang J-6s (MiG-19s). His plane was shot down and he became a prisoner of the Chinese, "the only USAF pilot known to have been held by the Chinese" during the Vietnam War. Smith remained in captivity until 15 March 1973. Compounding the loss of Smith was the fact that two F-104Cs collided while returning from a failed attempt to locate him. Both F-104C pilots survived the crash. Among those eleven airmen killed, captured, shot down, or crashed on that eventful September day, only Lieutenant (j.g.) John R. Harris served in the Navy. Launched from the U.S.S. *Independence*, Harris's A-4E Skyhawk was part of a major strike on a railway bridge at Cao Hung, a vital supply route between China and Hanoi. After sustaining significant ground fire, Harris ejected from his plane and was picked up in "the first overland rescue by a U.S. Navy helicopter in North Vietnam and the first anywhere in the Southeast Asian theater by a ship-based Navy helicopter." Lieutenant Harris also became "the first American pilot to be shot down to the east of Hanoi, an area that had been largely out of bounds up to this point."[49]

The remaining airmen connected to this life-altering September day included USAF Captain Willis E. Forby, Bill Robinson, and his crewmembers, Thomas Curtis, Duane Martin, and Neil Black. Flying an F-105D Thunderchief as part of an armed reconnaissance mission, Captain Forby attacked a railway bridge near Ha Tinh, some thirty-five miles south of Vinh. Anti-aircraft fire hit and heavily damaged Forby's plane, causing an on-board fire and forcing him to eject. Forby's wingman witnessed the shootdown and radioed for help.[50] Air Force rescue teams from the 38th ARS at Nakhon Phanom responded to the call. On that day Robinson, Curtis, Martin, and Black drew the low-bird assignment and flew their HH-43B, call sign Dutchy 41, to the rescue site. Experience had proved that helicopters flying at low altitudes during rescue missions risked exposure to enemy fire, and that was the case that day. Flying at 3,700 feet, Dutchy 41 drew small arms fire, and Captain Curtis climbed to 10,000 feet. But flying at a higher altitude consumed more fuel and increased the time required to reach the rescue site. In addition, Forby had ejected near his target area, which gave enemy forces time to envelop the area.[51]

Once Dutchy 41 reached the rescue site, sometime around three-thirty in the afternoon, crewmembers set up a grid and began their search. Escort aircraft had accompanied Dutchy 41 into the area where previous visual contact with Forby had been made, but the jungle cover required that they determine a more exact location before a pickup could be completed. The crew looked for "anything out of the ordinary, a crash site, anything that would give you some identifying marks." In most instances, a downed pilot carried, at minimum, a flare pen, and sometimes a handheld radio. Dutchy 41 did not have radio contact with Forby, but the fighter escorts orbiting the area received a good beacon from the downed aircraft, and Forby was able to fire a pistol flare, allowing the rescue team to pinpoint his location. Still, a hoist extraction in an area with thick brush and rugged terrain would not be completed easily. At this point, as the helicopter hovered over the downed pilot, Captain Curtis could not "see straight down," and so as crew chief, Robinson had to become his pilot's eyes and "hold him in a position to be able to drop" the hoist to Forby. Forby's position on a hillside required Curtis to maneuver the helicopter below the treetops in such a way that Robinson could "swing the cable up to" Forby, because Dutchy 41 "did not have enough cable to go straight down to him." The HH-43B was equipped with a hundred-foot cable hoist, of which the last ten feet were painted red. Robinson distinctly remembers: "I had red cable in my hands so I know we were in excess of ninety feet above him. We swung the cable to him and [at] the same time we're taking small arms fire." Then the situation got even worse.[52]

One of the A1-E Skyraider fighter escort planes took a hit in its rocket pod and caught on fire. The last radio transmission that Robinson heard was "not authorized to dispose of your ordnance in the local area." Consequently, both A1-Es withdrew from the operation. Now the crew of Dutchy 41 had a decision to make, its difficulty compounded by the fact that they were low on fuel, so low that they were at "bingo fuel": on the basis of the planning briefs, they had just enough fuel to get home. With no fighter escort and being low on fuel, Dutchy 41 decided to continue the mission. No matter the risks, they would not leave an American pilot behind. Suddenly "all hell broke loose." The ground fire intensified, and the crew could see holes appearing in the helicopter. Airman Black returned fire out of the back of the helicopter and Lieutenant Martin out the side. Meanwhile, Robinson had managed to swing the cable and harness over to Forby and had temporarily brought him off the ground. Curtis even detected the additional weight. But the helicopter had been heavily damaged. To prevent a catastrophic crash, Robinson hit the fuel control, causing a momentary stall before the HH-43B dropped out of the sky. As the helicopter fell, the rotor blades began to chop the jungle bamboo, which disintegrated from the friction. Dutchy 41 fell approximately ninety feet to the jungle floor. Curtis had an M-16 propped next to his seat, and the force of the crash broke the stock of his weapon. All the helicopter's antennae were on the underside of the aircraft, so all the radios became useless. Fortunately, the jungle floor provided a certain amount of cushion. If they had hit solid ground, there might have been no survivors.[53]

Of the five downed airmen, only Robinson had received no survival training. His entire career with the USAF Air Rescue Service had been an on-the-job training apprenticeship. Understandably, all the men had difficulty getting out of the helicopter, given the violent and abrupt nature of the crash. Although he didn't know it at the time, Robinson, the first to exit the helicopter, had suffered two hairline fractures in his back and had "crushed both knees." Yet the proximity of enemy forces sent the airmen scurrying for cover. Additionally, the men had thirty minutes to get away from the crashed helicopter, because, under standing operating procedure, the Air Force would send in a team to blow it up to prevent the enemy from recovering anything of value from it. The initial confusion had caused a brief separation, but the men soon "met up at a little creek bed," and Forby informed everyone that "the place was infested with Vietnamese." At that moment, Martin and Forby took off, as the high bird from the original rescue mission flew over the three remaining airmen.[54]

The group of three attempted to make radio contact, but when they pulled out the lone radio, its antennae fell off. Curtis fired his flare pistol, and the flare "went right up through the rotor blades [of the high bird], but they did not see it"; they were directly over the men and too close to see the flare but too far to see the men hidden by the jungle cover. The high bird began receiving heavy ground fire and was forced to leave the area. Curtis's "plan had always been to get away from the crash [site], wait until dark, and to get back into a SAFE area," a reference to the military's acronym for Superior Area for Evasion. Curtis conceded that in a war zone a SAFE area is something of a misnomer. The helicopter pilot had completed survival school in 1955, but he had never fired the M-16 "except dry fire." He was confident, though, that he "could make it talk" if the situation warranted. Once he learned his weapon had been damaged in the crash, he drifted back to a decision he had made long before. If faced with a hopeless situation, Curtis was not going to engage in a shootout armed "with an aircrew .38-caliber pistol." Curtis, Robinson, and Black "had a quick conversation" and concluded that they needed some place to hide, and they hoped to sneak past the enemy forces at night. As they headed west, toward Thailand, they discovered what amounted to a "hole in the wall," and they felt pretty confident that they were well concealed. From this cave the three men every once in a while observed a presumed Vietnamese search party. As time passed, the group increased in number and drew closer and closer to their hideout. Suddenly, what seemed like "a hundred of them" appeared at the entrance to the cave armed with pitchforks and other assorted weapons. Although each American had a .38-caliber pistol, armed resistance would have been suicidal. They could "live to fight another day." The elapsed time from shootdown to capture was approximately one and a half hours.[55]

The captors first separated their prisoners and began independent transfers of the American airmen. Forby had returned to his original hiding place and he too had been captured. The fate of Lieutenant Martin was unknown. Next, the captors bound the prisoners with vines and prepared to transport them through a ravine. They tied their arms just above the elbows, and again just below the elbows, and then finally just above the wrists. The captors used a second vine to lasso the prisoners' necks. Robinson compared the application of the second vine to being "leashed like a dog," especially when he was pulled out of the ravine to the top of a hill by his captors. There Robinson noticed a number of aircraft flying overhead. The captors had confiscated Robinson's .38, and he had the unsettling experience of "looking down the barrel" of his own weapon as an excitable North Vietnamese held the weapon with a "trembling hand." An inadvertent discharge of the weapon could have easily ended Robinson's life. He certainly realized the gravity of the situation: "Your whole life passes through your mind, especially all of the good things that have gone on in your life. You just kind of wonder, how did I get myself into this situation and what am I going to do to get out of it? I guess the main thing was to try to maintain a cool head. . . . I don't think any of us were thinking about captivity." In such moments the mind sometimes conjures unusual thoughts, and Robinson appeared somewhat relieved when he remembered that he had loaded only five bullets in his pistol.[56]

After the intense initial encounter, "things settled down" and Robinson's captors took him to a nearby village. Because of the American air activity around the crash site and the open spaces that afforded no concealment, Robinson and his captors traveled in spurts, starting and stopping to avoid unnecessary exposure. The trip lasted several hours but covered not more than two or three miles. The village they were taken to was quite small, and nothing about the place suggested anything about Robinson's future. There he received something to drink, probably water. Possibly in shock or overstimulated by the heat, emotion, and trauma of recent events, Robinson began "heaving [his] guts out." Follow-up attempts by his captors to provide food and drink caused similar reactions, as his body rejected the sustenance. To this day Robinson does not know whether he was captured first by Laotians, maybe even members of the Pathet Lao, who quickly turned him over to the North Vietnamese militia, or captured by North Vietnamese militia and turned over to the regular army. What is certain is that on 20 September 1965 Airman First Class Bill Robinson began a seven-and-a-half-year-long journey, one that would take him down his own separate path to hell.[57]

2

Separate Paths to Hell

After only one night in the first village, Robinson's North Vietnamese captors moved him to a second location, a village that was a little bit larger than the first. He never developed a clear visual of the place because he arrived after dark, and his handlers kept him preoccupied by using him in a series of well-orchestrated propaganda displays over the next three days. Robinson was the star attraction in what many prisoners referred to as pep rallies. Typically, guards paraded prisoners out in front of a crowd, suggesting to the locals that the captured American pilots had been responsible for the bombing and ensuing death and destruction in their villages. In Robinson's case, the fact that he was not a pilot and had not been on a bombing run was immaterial to his captors. His uniform and his large physical stature suited him for the role. When he was presented to the villagers, they were reserved initially, mainly curious, but they were easily excited by a few instigators. Once they had been incited, they started "shaking their fists and rifles" at the American airman. He worried that the pep rally might turn from mere taunting to something more sinister, especially when the North Vietnamese threatened him with a public execution. While American planes circled overhead, his captors lined him up next to a freshly dug grave and placed him in front of a firing squad. As it turned out, the North Vietnamese performance was only a ruse, but it certainly unsettled Robinson and added to an already tense situation. In addition to the so-called pep rallies, the North Vietnamese used American POWs as part of more sophisticated propaganda programs.[1]

On the second or third day of his captivity, Robinson found himself in the middle of a fairly elaborate production. Somewhere between twenty-five and fifty guards, some obscured by the shadows and others standing in the open, formed a secure ring around the prisoner. Without any warning or explanation, Robinson's captors forced him to simply walk along a narrow path, and he soon realized that a photographer stood poised to take his picture. Robinson walked erect, with his head up, and he could see the person walking beside him, a teenage girl wearing a uniform and pith helmet and carrying a rifle. The directors of this unfolding drama were not satisfied with Robinson's performance, and someone—not the girl next to him—began to beat him in the back of the head with a rifle butt. Robinson was sure the girl "never touched" him. After repeated blows to the head, Robinson got the message that the Vietnamese were sending and he lowered his head. At that moment the photographer snapped the image of a young girl appearing to capture and detain an American soldier. Obviously, the entire scene had been carefully planned; Robinson had not dropped his head as a gesture of humility or an admission of defeat. In some small way, at least for Robinson, the incident had a silver lining. He had been briefed that, in the event of capture, "if you see a camera, look straight into it." The reasoning was that if the captors ever released the photo, "they would have to account for you at the end of the war." Such optimism may have provided some consolation to a captured American serviceman, but the North Vietnamese were more concerned with the propaganda value of the photos than they were about whether they had created evidence of Robinson's captivity. It would be some time before Robinson learned the full extent of this propaganda exhibition.[2]

Throughout the three-day period at the second village, Robinson's captors used a number of tactics to confuse and disorient the prisoners, largely in an effort to discourage escapes before transferring the POWs to the North Vietnamese regular army. While at the second location, Robinson, Curtis, Black, and Forby were confined in different huts, and they had no direct contact with each other. When conducting the pep rallies, the captors took each prisoner out separately, although the village was small enough that Robinson could hear the shouts of the angry crowds from his hut when another prisoner was on display. The isolation heightened his anxiety, as did the language barrier. None of Robinson's captors spoke English.

They understood a few words, such as "food," "sleep," "water," but more often than not he communicated with his captors through hand signals. At night the captors removed Robinson and the other prisoners from their holding areas, and they marched for a good part of the night. To prevent communication or visual contact, the prisoners were kept apart from one another. Obviously, the captors hoped to convince the prisoners that they had changed locations, but in reality they had just walked around in circles. Moreover, the four- or five-hour hikes had the supplemental effect of wearing the prisoners out, so that they slept most of the day. On the third day the prisoners "could sense the difference in what was going on . . . they [their captors] got real serious now." This seemed to indicate, not through spoken word but through demeanor, that their transfer from the militia to the regular army was imminent.[3]

The Road to Hanoi

Despite the gravity of the situation, the actual transfer was a fairly low-key affair accompanied by no ceremony or "formal changing of the guard." Robinson remembered that this new group of captors simply arrived "in better-looking uniforms" and were equipped with more modern weaponry than were those who had held him for four days. But they did not demonstrate a greater degree of organization than the militia, whom Robinson judged sufficiently competent at their task. Once the North Vietnamese assumed control of the prisoners, they guided Robinson and his fellow POWs on a weeklong journey of some two hundred miles to Hanoi, a journey fraught with danger, abuse, and uncertainty for the Americans. Always leery of a possible escape attempt, the North Vietnamese removed one shoe from each prisoner but allowed them to keep the other. The captors believed that when the Americans' tender, unprotected feet were exposed to the coarse terrain, the prisoners would be discouraged from attempting an escape or would be more easily apprehended in the event that they temporarily broke free. The trip to Hanoi was not a simple drive, or even march, along a major thoroughfare, but one that required the prisoners to alternate their travel by truck, car, and boat. Sometimes Robinson, Curtis, Black, and Forby traveled in the same vehicle. On such occasions the vehicle was usually a truck and the prisoners were all in the back and instructed not to speak or communicate in any way. Often a guard rode in the back of the truck for security purposes.[4]

The presence of a lightly armed North Vietnamese guard in the back of a relatively small transport vehicle did not serve as a deterrent to U.S. planes on interdiction missions or armed reconnaissance missions. Once the truck transporting Robinson became a target of U.S. planes. When the attack began, the North Vietnamese "bailed out of the back of the truck," leaving Robinson bound and exposed in the truck bed. Fortunately for him, the pilots missed their target each of the three times that they strafed the truck, expending their ammunition without hitting anything. Still, literally and figuratively, Robinson had dodged a bullet. He realized these first few days were "just the introduction." He pondered, "What's next?" He "never thought or never allowed the thought to enter [his] mind that [he] wasn't going to make it, [but] deep down" he considered the possibility he might not reach his twenty-third birthday. He took some solace in the notion that if the North Vietnamese intended to kill him, then the deed would have already happened. They would not have expended so much time and manpower to conduct a simple execution. His greater fear as he moved northward to Hanoi stemmed from concerns about exposure to friendly fire and the illogical hazards of war. Traveling by car, even at night, did not eliminate the danger, in part because the North Vietnamese typically turned off their headlights and taillights when driving at night to avoid detection by American aircraft. During one segment of the trip to Hanoi, Robinson found himself paired in a car with Captain Forby. The shield of darkness was compromised when an Air Force C-130 gunship flew over the caravan and dropped illumination flares. The car's driver "pulled into a little hiding place" amid some underbrush to wait until it was safe to proceed, when suddenly another car traveling at "a great rate of speed" plowed into the back of the parked car. Luckily, Robinson and Forby sustained no serious injuries. The most difficult traveling conditions occurred when the North Vietnamese moved the prisoners by boat. The boats were small vessels that carried only one prisoner apiece.

They blindfolded each prisoner, bound his hands and feet together, and forced him to lie in the bottom of the boat. Robinson felt a sense of relief whenever he exited one of these boats.[5]

The One-Armed Bandit

The North Vietnamese held a mere three dozen captives in late September 1965, but since the capture of Everett Alvarez in August 1964, some patterns in the treatment of prisoners had begun to emerge. Americans captured in the southern provinces of North Vietnam, for example, were typically routed through the town of Vinh, in Nghe An Province. Some 160 miles south of Hanoi and near Kim Lien, the birthplace of Ho Chi Minh, Vinh functioned as a type of processing center for migrating POWs. At Vinh, Robinson met a dastardly individual known as the One-Armed Bandit. This wounded veteran of the First Indochina War spoke fairly decent English, although he boasted that his French was more refined. Rather than conduct intensive interrogations, the One-Armed Bandit, who gave the impression that he was a native of Vinh who had returned home to serve as a type of political commissar, devoted most of his time to talking about himself, including telling the tale of how he had lost his arm fighting the French. He lectured the Americans on how the French colonialists had exploited the Vietnamese people first, and he accused the United States of the same imperialist ambitions in Southeast Asia. The One-Armed Bandit never mentioned torture in his interactions with the American POWs, but, while at Vinh, they experienced handcuffs and leg irons for the first time. These simple devices produced intense pain. The adjustable-ratchet cuffs could be so forcefully tightened around the wrist that they cut to the bone. Sometimes the cuffs were placed on the forearms and the prisoner's arms were pulled behind him, which caused a progression of sensations, starting with an acute burning feeling and ending with numbness. The application of leg irons produced similar results, but occasionally the North Vietnamese improvised. Because the leg irons, which were designed to confine the much smaller Asian limbs, would not fit Robinson's larger limbs, they tied ropes around his feet, tied his elbows together behind his back, and tied his wrists together. He spent the next three days bound in this manner, just lying on the floor. Periodically the North Vietnamese untied him long enough for a drink of water and a little food, and once a day Robinson received a bathroom break. Because he was so dehydrated, the one bathroom break sufficed. A pigpen served as the prisoner's latrine.[6]

After less than a week, the strains of captivity started to take a toll on Robinson and the other three POWs. Still attired in a short-sleeve shirt, Robinson had a number of cuts and scratches on his arms from the crash and the forced marches through the jungle. Therefore, the various restraints and bindings caused "the blood to just ooze out of" his arm, and his hands swelled to what appeared to him to be twice their normal size. At this point Robinson's captors concentrated on obtaining name, rank, and serial number, and on intimidating the prisoners. The One-Armed Bandit, whom Robinson described as a "vicious individual," berated the American POWs, calling them "war criminals" and castigating them for their "grave crimes" against the Vietnamese people. He asked for no pertinent military information while questioning them, but the One-Armed Bandit warned Robinson, "A time will come when you will tell us everything." The threat really did not register with Robinson. He convinced himself that he "was running an obstacle course," and if he made it to Hanoi, then he might be released. He did not allow himself to consider a long-term captivity. In retrospect, Robinson viewed the One-Armed Bandit as part of the North Vietnamese' "introduction to the prison system," a type of "softening-up program" to let the POWs know who was in charge.[7]

A Code to Keep

After a ten-day odyssey, Robinson reached, on 1 October, the North Vietnamese capital of Hanoi and entered the Hoa Lo prison complex. Completed in 1898, the Hoa Lo prison, known by the Vietnamese as the Oven, was one of four colonial central prisons administered by the French; in contrast to the smaller provincial prisons, it housed a number of high-profile Vietnamese political prisoners. Poor rations, inadequate medical care, and overcrowding added to the prisoners' misery, but as the historian Peter Zinoman has concluded, "The brutality and squalor of the prison system itself ultimately killed . . . most of the prisoners who died in captivity." In 1934, 168 prisoners died at Hoa Lo, approximately 12 percent of its total population.[8] Under French authority, maximum capacity at the Hanoi Central Prison approached 1,500, but when the North Vietnamese converted Hoa Lo to a detention center for American POWs, it could scarcely accommodate fifty captives. Still, the prison complex covered an entire "trapezoidal block in the center of the city," and a fifteen- to twenty-foot-high wall, trimmed with barbed wire, surrounded the compound. An imposing feature of the prison's architecture was its single entrance that "was divided by a series of heavy iron gates that sealed shut one after another." The Americans dubbed this historic prison the Hanoi Hilton, which actually consisted of three primary sections, "New Guy Village," "Heartbreak Hotel," and "Little Vegas"; the North Vietnamese added a fourth section in late 1970.[9]

As part of his in-processing, the North Vietnamese stripped Robinson of everything, leaving him to stand in his "birthday suit." They issued him "a pair of shorts, a long shirt, and long pants . . . a toothbrush, toothpaste, a bar of soap and a towel, and a blanket and a mat." Standing with his "meager belongings," Robinson for the first time admitted to himself that "this was not temporary." Despite the well-publicized capture of the Navy airman Everett Alvarez, who had been in captivity for more than a year at the time of Robinson's capture, and the addition of twenty-seven more Americans to the North Vietnamese prison population from August 1964 to 19 September 1965, Bill Robinson had no awareness of how American POWs were being treated by the Vietnamese or how the French had fared as prisoners during the First Indochina War. In many respects, no degree of historical acumen would have ever prepared Robinson for what he was about to experience. The North Vietnamese assigned Robinson to New Guy Village, where he received a dire greeting from a fellow POW. As he sat in his cell, he heard a voice echoing down the corridor: "This is Robinson Risner, senior ranking officer. Be prepared to die for your country." Having just reached the age of twenty-two, Robinson admitted: "This is not what I planned for my life." Feeling overwhelmed, he then did the only thing he could think of, "some tall praying."[10]

Virtually every early captive in the North has asserted that two keys to survival and resistance were the establishment of communication techniques and a chain of command. No one played a greater role in the area of communication than Air Force Captain Carlyle (Smitty) Harris. The sixth pilot captured in the north, on 4 April 1965, Harris arrived at the Hanoi Hilton the next day. As Harris recalled during a television interview a few years after the release of the POWs, "From the very beginning the North Vietnamese tried to prevent us from communicating with each other. They went to almost insane efforts to keep us from even seeing another American by putting up blinds, and when we went out to pick up our food or dump our [waste] bucket, there was no way we could see another American." Joking that the Morse code was not an option because "the only tools we had were our knuckles and a bare wall, and it's really tough to send a dash with the knuckle," Harris explained the introduction of the tap code that he had picked up during survival training at Stead Air Force Base in Nevada.[11]

A prisoner could tap out or spell on the prison walls a message based on the arrangement of a five-character-by-five-character matrix of the alphabet. The letter C also functioned as a K. The letters were arranged as follows:

A	B	C	D	E
F	G	H	I	J
L	M	N	O	P
Q	R	S	T	U
V	W	X	Y	Z

The first tap or taps signified the location of the letter in the horizontal rows and the second signified the location in the vertical rows. For example, 2-3, 1-1, 4-2, 4-2, 2-4, 4-3 spelled H-A-R-R-I-S. The tap code could be transmitted by coughs, shuffling feet, or whisking brooms. Prisoners used the tap code to compile a list of names of all known captives, to offer encouragement to one another, to announce policies, or simply to pass the time. The military's propensity to use acronyms and abbreviations facilitated communications. Most important, the tap code was used to inform prisoners about interrogation techniques and convey strategies for coping with torture. In addition to the tap code, POWs used a form of sign language to communicate, they used cigarette ash, bamboo slivers, and toilet tissue as pen and paper, and they scratched messages on the bottoms of plates and cups. They even discovered that they "could talk directly through a brick-and-mortar wall eighteen or more inches thick" by pressing a tin cup up against the wall. They covered their heads with blankets to muffle their conversations and to avoid detection by the guards. In a fortuitous twist of fate, the Vietnamese policy of shuffling prisoners "from cell to cell and camp to camp," in an effort to disrupt group solidarity, actually spread vital information and communication techniques throughout the prison grapevine.[12]

As these various forms of communication were being developed, a chain of command was quickly being formulated, and four men stand out for their decisive leadership. They were, in order of capture, Air Force Major Lawrence Guarino, Navy Commanders Jeremiah Denton and James Stockdale, and Air Force Lieutenant Colonel Robinson (Robbie) Risner. Following the dictates of the military Code of Conduct, the four men worked through the process of establishing who was the senior ranking officer (SRO) and "decided to base seniority on rank at the time of shootdown." Between 1965 and 1970 the SRO and his executive assistants interpreted the Code of Conduct and set the policies for resistance and responding to torture.[13]

The Code of Conduct

I. I am an American fighting man. I serve in the forces which guard my country and our way of life. I am prepared to give my life in their defense.

II. I will never surrender of my own free will. If in command, I will never surrender my men while they still have the means to resist.

III. If I am captured I will continue to resist by all means available. I will make every effort to escape and aid others to escape. I will accept neither parole nor special favors from the enemy.

IV. If I become a prisoner of war, I will keep faith with my fellow prisoners. I will give no information or take part in any action which might be harmful to my comrades. If I am senior, I will take command. If not, I will obey the lawful orders of those appointed over me, and will back them up in every way.

V. When questioned, should I become a prisoner of war, I am bound to give only name, rank, service number, and date of birth. I will evade answering further questions to the utmost of my ability. I will make no oral or written statements disloyal to my country and its allies or harmful to their cause.

VI. I will never forget that I am an American, fighting for freedom, responsible for my actions, and dedicated to the principles which made my country free. I will trust in my God and in the United States of America.

If interpreted literally, the six articles would have set unrealistic expectations for American service personnel held in enemy hands. Thus, the SRO and his executive assistants formulated the standards for resistance and interpreted the Code of Conduct for all POWs. One of the first decisions made by the senior officers concerned the acceptable responses to interrogation. To a man, former prisoners of war have conceded that everyone had a breaking point. Moreover, any interrogator, given enough time and with no restrictions on interrogation methods, could extract a statement from a POW. Except for vital military information, senior officers instructed their fellow prisoners to resist to a point short of permanent bodily harm before making a statement.

After a few more days at the New Guy Village, Robinson was moved to a part of the Hilton complex known as Heartbreak Hotel. A self-contained unit, Heartbreak had interrogation and torture rooms, a courtyard, six cells, and a community shower. The five-by-six-foot cells came furnished with concrete-slab beds on each side of the room, and each was equipped with its own set of leg irons. At that time all the POWs in Heartbreak were in solitary confinement, but the prisoners could easily remove the panels above the cell doors and then stand on their beds and look directly into the cells on the opposite side of the hall. Robinson discovered that the small coterie of Americans, who had all been captured between 24 August and 27 September 1965, included Captain George Hall, Major Ray Merritt, and Captain Willis Forby from the Air Force and, from the Navy, Lieutenant Commander Robert Doremus and Commander Bill Franke, who served as the group's senior ranking officer. Interrogations at Heartbreak were "very infrequent" for Franke's group and did not entail physical violence or torture. George Hall recalled, "It seemed like it was just a square-filling exercise for them, that they were supposed to talk to each one of us [every] so often. . . . I was a captain . . . and possibly was of little interest to them, and so they didn't bother me very much." Robinson received pretty much the same treatment; there was some verbal haranguing and the occasional rifle butt or "punch to the back" as a way to intimidate the young enlisted man.[14]

Commander Franke accepted the responsibility of initiating communication with each new arrival and briefing him on procedures and passing along pertinent information. Everyone was aware of the risks—leg irons or handcuffs—if the guards caught them communicating. Nevertheless, they persisted. Franke also took it on himself to lift the spirits of his men, frequently resorting to humor to charge his troops. Each morning he addressed one of the guards, derisively called Dipstick by the prisoners, with this salutation: "Good morning, Dipstick. It looks like a beautiful day for a bombing." For Robinson, even on gloomy, rainy days, Franke had the ability to spark their day and boost morale. Much of the conversation between the prisoners revolved around an anticipated move to a prisoner-of-war camp that would more closely resemble the prison compounds of World War II and Korea, where American POWs typically interacted with one another in large groups on a regular basis. The prisoners, of course, were just speculating, perhaps hoping, because none of them in Heartbreak had been to this "other" camp.[15]

Beyond the Hilton

Generally speaking, by September 1965, once a prisoner completed "registration and initial interrogations" at Hoa Lo, he was
transferred to another prison, although the North Vietnamese periodically returned POWs to Hoa Lo "for special punishment or an
intensive extortion or indoctrination sessions." The North Vietnamese operated a total of fifteen camps over the course of the war. Most
of the camps were in Hanoi or just outside the city; however, there
were several camps well beyond the capital's boundaries. Once the
Hanoi Hilton reached maximum capacity, the North Vietnamese
opened two overflow camps, the Zoo (Cu Loc) and Briarpatch (Xom
Ap Lo). Robinson spent time at both of these camps during the early
stages of his captivity, and both differed considerably from the more
famous Hilton. The Zoo, located a few miles southwest of the Hoa
Lo complex, originally served as a French movie studio or possibly
an art colony. When the first prisoners arrived, they noticed faded
posters and "old film cans and damaged [film] reels" littering the
grounds. The presence of farm animals at the compound contributed to its designation as the Zoo, and several smaller buildings
were given such names as Pigsty and the Barn.[16]

In late October 1965 Robinson and Commander Franke were
transferred to what Robinson sarcastically referred to as "the freshly
completed Zoo." They went on the same day, in the same vehicle,
and were placed in cells beside one another. When Robinson entered
the twelve-by-twelve-foot cell, he noticed two bunks, or "wooden
bed boards on stilts," which he deemed an "encouraging" sign. He
did not, however, receive a roommate right away. Because the North
Vietnamese continued to expand the Zoo, construction was ongoing and prisoners were constantly being shuffled around. Over the
course of the next few months, Everett Alvarez moved into the other
cell beside Robinson; his pilot, Tom Curtis, moved into one of the
cells behind him, as did Willis Forby. Navy Lieutenant Commander
Robert Shumaker and Smitty Harris were paired together as roommates on the other side of Commander Franke. The Shumaker-Harris
pairing was the first that Robinson recalled in the Zoo. Although
Robinson remained in isolation until early December 1965, he did

not suffer absolute solitary confinement, as he was not cut off from all contact with his fellow Americans. When the guards were not in the immediate area, the prisoners could stand by the windows in their cell doors and talk relatively freely. They also had the option of communicating by the tap code. After two months in confinement, Robinson began to mark time in unusual ways. On 22 November he tapped a message to Curtis indicating that he expected to go home that day. A surprised Curtis asked for an explanation, and Robinson responded, "My enlistment is up." Without missing a beat, Curtis rejoined, "You need to get Commander Franke to issue the oath of enlistment so they won't cut your check off."[17]

Notwithstanding these moments of camaraderie, the months of isolation had a dark side. In many respects, the worst part of isolation, from Robinson's perspective, was the fear of dying in anonymity, as an unknown soldier, as an MIA (missing in action), with no one to preserve his memory. As they all experienced this fear to some degree, the prisoners shared with one another their hopes, dreams, and weaknesses in a deeply personal way. These dying declarations became sacred communications, and Robinson admits that the overwhelming majority of POWs will take these confidential confessions "to their graves." For a man so candidly open about his personal life and captivity experience, Robinson remains stoically silent about the content of these exchanges. He insists that the purpose was to ensure that if a prisoner died in captivity, a surviving POW could go to a family member, "and without a shadow of a doubt" confirm to the family that he knew the identity of their loved one and knew his ultimate fate because he carried such intimate knowledge of the deceased.[18]

In early December 1965, without any advance notice, Robinson received his first roommate, Air Force Captain Kile "Red" Berg. An F-105 Thunderchief pilot, Berg, of the 563rd Tactical Fighter Squadron, led one of the first attacks against a defended surface-to-air missile (SAM) site in the Hanoi area. On 27 July 1965 Berg registered a hit on his assigned target, but his plane took anti-aircraft fire, which forced him to eject. Berg had flown approximately twenty missions in Laos and twenty-seven in North Vietnam before being shot down. During his captivity, Red Berg earned a reputation for having "a keen imagination and sense of humor." Berg created quite a comical buzz when he taught an unsuspecting North Vietnamese guard, who wanted to learn some basic English, to say, "I'm queer," when making the rounds of the cellblock. Everett Alvarez recalled that Berg taught him to use his rubber Ho Chi Minh sandals to cover the sharp edges of his *bo* (his personal latrine bucket) when he squatted, to avoid cutting his buttocks on the ragged metal rim. Berg and Robinson got along well. Although they both possessed the ability to use humor as a coping mechanism, certain actions by the North Vietnamese instantly provoked their ire.[19]

One particular incident "really pissed off" the two airmen. All things considered, Berg and Robinson were reasonably healthy young men, ages twenty-six and twenty-two, respectively. In a nearby cell were Marine Warrant Officer John William Frederick and Air Force Captain John Joseph Pitchford. Frederick, a WWII and Korean War veteran, was the back seater in an F-4B Phantom II piloted by Major J. Howard Dunn when his plane was shot down on 7 December 1965 during a high-altitude fighter escort mission. Dunn evaded capture for six days, but Frederick was recovered by the North Vietnamese on the day of his shootdown. Frederick and Dunn were the second and third Marines captured by the North Vietnamese; Captain Harlan Chapman, captured on 5 November 1965, was the first. Pitchford, who entered the Air Force in 1952 after graduating from Louisiana State University with a degree in forestry and an ROTC commission, volunteered for the Wild Weasel program in the fall of 1965. After three weeks of stateside training, Pitchford deployed to Korat RTAFB to participate in Operation Iron Hand, whose purpose was "to suppress and/or destroy enemy surface-to-air missile sites." In the early stages of Iron Hand, the nicknames Wild Weasel and Weasel identified the aircrafts' weapon systems and the pilots' ability to ferret out targets. During typical Iron Hand missions, an F-100 would identify the SAM site by exposing itself to enemy radar systems, and an F-105D would conduct the actual strike. On 20 December 1965, while he was flying his third mission, Pitchford's F-100 Super Saber encountered anti-aircraft fire, and he was forced to eject. He was the first Weasel pilot shot down in the Vietnam War. Both Frederick and Pitchford suffered serious injuries during their shootdowns. Frederick "had burned his hands severely, and rather than wrap them individually so that they would heal properly," the North Vietnamese wrapped the hands together, thereby impeding the healing process and leaving the Marine somewhat incapacitated. Pitchford had "about two inches shot out of his upper right arm." Robinson thought this "was cruelty to the utmost—they had one hand between the two of them and right next to them . . . were two healthy individuals." Robinson deemed the situation "worse than any torture, knowing there were guys right next to you that really needed help and you couldn't do anything about it." Robinson and Berg had many discussions over the callous disregard the North Vietnamese had for the wounded Americans.[20]

While cellmates, both Berg and Robinson received letters from and wrote letters to their loved ones. Berg had married in October 1960 and had two small boys, Kim and Kelly. The two men discussed the challenge of raising children, and Robinson, who hoped to one day have children of his own, listened intently as Berg explained his parenting philosophy. Berg once recounted a story in which he reprimanded his kids for jumping on the family couch. The offense seemed somewhat innocuous, given that the couch was inexpensive. Yet Berg explained that one day their family would be able to afford more expensive home furnishings, and children needed to be taught at an early age to treat all their possessions with care and appreciation. The simple lesson of responsibility resonated with Robinson, and he stored it in his memory for future reference, perhaps in a relationship with Beverly. Not long into his captivity, Robinson received a letter from Beverly and a picture of her in a white nursing uniform. To Robinson "she looked like a little angel," and the image nearly brought tears of joy to his eyes. He beamed with pride over Beverly's recent graduation from nursing school and regretted that he had not been able to attend her ceremony. Beverly's news that she had started a hope chest boosted Robinson's spirits; though he cautioned himself about unrealistic expectations regarding his release, he clung to the prospects of a brighter future. "Let's just hope and pray that it will be soon," he told Beverly in a letter, "but [we] can't forget that it could be a long stay. But as long as I know you are waiting for me then life isn't as bad." As the months and years of captivity pressed down on the prisoners, each man developed a personal survival strategy. Sometimes the conditions were so punitive and the mistreatment so inhumane that the POWs could not see forward and lived only in the moment. As they resurrected themselves, some contemplated the possibility that some of their loved ones had already abandoned them—or would do so eventually.[21]

Because Robinson's cell was adjacent to the lone shower at the Zoo compound, he became part of a "communications hub" as prisoners relayed information to him and his roommate each time they were allowed to bathe, typically on a weekly or biweekly basis. The shower stall at the Zoo was a converted cell and had windows with louvers; this allowed a prisoner to enter the shower area, turn on the water, and then position himself so that he could be easily heard by Robinson and his roommate. Often Robinson received word of the identity of the POWs held in the various buildings at the Zoo. To avoid detection, a "bang on the wall with your elbow" signaled that all communication should cease. On one occasion Navy Lieutenant (j.g.) Rodney Knutson missed the signal, perhaps because of the noise of the water, and continued to talk while the POWs persisted in sending the keep-quiet warning. Exasperated by the silence, Knutson hollered, "All right, you chicken fucks, if you are not going to talk to me, I am going back to my damn room."[22]

The brash naval aviator tested the resolve of North Vietnamese interrogators during his first days in captivity by refusing to answer questions beyond name, rank, and serial number. With each refusal, the North Vietnamese expanded their repertoire of punishments. They affixed ankle straps, withheld food and water, used their fists to break his nose and chip several teeth, and beat his back and buttocks with clubs. But the worst treatment occurred on 25 October, after just eight days in captivity, when Knutson experienced the so-called ropes torture. Guards entered his cell, "forced him face down on his bunk, set his ankles into stocks, and bound him tightly with rope at the elbows. The long end of the rope was then pulled up through a hook attached to the ceiling. As a guard hoisted the prisoner, he lifted him off the bunk enough so that he could not relieve any of his weight, producing incredible pain—with shoulders seemingly being torn from their sockets—and horribly constricting breathing." Unable to endure the pain any longer, Knutson agreed to answer questions. Knutson was the first person whom Robinson was aware of who experienced the ropes torture at the Zoo. As the war unfolded, guards and interrogators used a variety of torture techniques, but few were as debilitating as the ropes torture, or what the POWs simply referred to as "the ropes," and they applied it to 95 percent of Americans held in North Vietnam, including Bill Robinson.[23]

Hell in Laos

For much of their captivity, the paths of Forby, Curtis, Black, and Robinson intertwined, whether in the same cell, cellblock, or prison camp in North Vietnam. The fate of Lieutenant Duane Martin unfolded in neighboring Laos and intersected that of a young naval aviator, Lieutenant (j.g.) Dieter Dengler. As a child in Germany during World War II, Dengler had experienced the savagery of war. First, he lost his father, a German soldier, when the Russians reclaimed Kiev in the Ukraine in late 1943. The Allied bombing of his small Black Forest village of Wildberg, in southwestern Germany, forced Dengler to flee with his mother and two brothers to nearby Calw, where he lived with his grandparents. Once Germany fell, Calw became part of the French occupation zone, and Moroccan Goumiers, still serving their colonial masters, enacted their atrocities in the small town. Dengler overcame these early hardships and succeeded in making a decent life for himself in postwar Germany; but he plotted, with the encouragement of an American relative, to leave his native land one day and go to America to fulfill his dream of becoming a pilot. On 12 May 1957 Dengler arrived in New York City aboard the ocean liner S.S. *America.* Less than four weeks later he joined the U.S. Air Force. Before he completed basic training, he learned that he had been duped by his recruiter, who had convinced the recent immigrant that any enlisted man in the Air Force could be a pilot. He completed four years in the Air Force before being discharged, having worked in mess halls and motor pools before earning an assignment at the Air Force's new marksmanship school. Frustrated but undeterred, Dengler headed to California in pursuit of a college education. With an associate of arts degree, he would be eligible for the Naval Aviation Cadet program. Despite some detours for fun, girls, and bad grades, the aspiring pilot graduated from the College of San Mateo with a degree in aeronautics in January 1963 and shortly thereafter enlisted in the Navy. He received his naval aviator wings on 14 August 1964.[24]

In February 1965 Dengler joined VA-145, an A-1 Skyraider squadron, based at Alameda Naval Air Station in California. He spent most of the year training before deploying with the carrier U.S.S. *Ranger* on 10 December, bound for the South China Sea. The VA-145, also known as the Swordsmen, in early January 1966 reached Yankee Station, a staging area in international waters used by the U.S. Navy's Seventh Fleet Attack Carrier Force. The Swordsmen soon began flying missions over the southern demilitarized zone (DMZ), which separated North and South Vietnam. On 1 February Dieter Dengler flew his first mission into Laos. The target was "an intersection of Route 27 at a river crossing used by trucks heading south" along the Ho Chi Minh Trail, and "the mission was to crater the highway and river crossing with 500-pound bombs left over from World War II, making the intersection impassible for a while." Flying in a four-plane division, Dengler dropped his two tons of 500-pounders fourth in the single-file bombing run. When he pulled out of his dive a series of violent explosions off the right wingtip knocked out the engine and "threw the aircraft totally out of control." Dengler, however, did not eject. He made a remarkable crash landing, and the plane cartwheeled to a stop near Mu Gia Pass, thirty or so miles from Robinson and Martin's crash site several months earlier. Despite an injured knee and some abrasions, Dengler evaded capture for twenty-four hours before two Laotian mountain tribesmen snared him when he arrived at the crossing of several jungle trails. For seven days the captors marched the naval aviator through an assortment of Laotian villages, proudly displaying their prize along the way. Each night they staked Dengler, spread-eagle, to the ground. He managed a brief escape after a week in captivity but suffered a severe beating as punishment. On 14 February 1966 Dengler arrived at his first Pathet Lao prison camp, Par Kung, approximately eighty-five miles southeast of his crash site. There he met Lieutenant Duane Martin for the first time.[25]

Martin's journey to Par Kung had been nothing short of miraculous. After the initial chaos of the 20 September 1965 shootdown, Martin headed in the opposite direction from his crewmates, hoping to cross all of Laos to reach safety in Thailand. An experienced hiker and outdoorsman, Martin evaded capture for several weeks before succumbing to fatigue and dehydration. A Hmong family discovered him in the jungle and took him to their village, where a young mother breast-fed him for a week "just to keep him alive." (Many members of the Hmong tribe fought against the communist Pathet Lao during the Laotian Civil War.) Subsequently, Pathet Lao soldiers found Martin convalescing in the village and claimed him as their prisoner. The Pathet Lao group departed the village with two girls carrying Martin by litter. They carried him for a week before he gained enough strength to walk on his own. He entered Par Kung prison on 3 December 1965; he was not alone. Nearly nine months earlier, five members of an Air America cargo crew, "an airline secretly owned by the CIA" and a vital component in the Shadow War against the Pathet Lao, had arrived at Par Kung. They had been prisoners of the Pathet Lao since 5 September 1963, when their plane was shot down during a supply drop in Ban Houei Sane Province in southern Laos. Among the Air America crew were three Thai nationals, all civilians: Prasit Promsuwan, Prasit Thanee, and Pisidhi Indradat, formerly a paratrooper in the Royal Thai Army. The group also included a Hong Kong native, To Yick Chiu, known as T.C., and the American Eugene (Gene) DeBruin, an Air Force veteran and Alaska smoke jumper. This eclectic group greeted Dengler upon his arrival and introduced him to the world of tiger cages and jungle prison camps.[26]

The conditions of the prison camps operated by the Pathet Lao in Laos more closely resembled those operated by the Viet Cong in South Vietnam than those maintained by the Vietminh in North Vietnam. Generally speaking, the jungle prison camps of the south were small and typically held no more than six prisoners at a time. The individual prison cells—or, more accurately, cages—varied in size and construction. They were most often made of bamboo and thatch, and their height, width, and depth could be 10 feet by 8 feet by 10 feet. Or they could be so small that a man had room only to sit up, but not enough to stand. Sometimes caves were used as prison cells. When not in their cells, the prisoners had to battle a primitive environment, diseases, and malnutrition. The jungle itself could be a cruel tormentor. The leeches, snakes, fire ants, scorpions, and rats presented daily threats, but the swarms of mosquitoes, which could cover a man's hand or foot in a matter of seconds, exposed the POWs to several strains of malaria. The thick foliage of the massive trees created multiple canopies that concealed the camps from detection and shielded the prisoners from direct sunlight. During the monsoon seasons the POWs therefore languished in damp or muddied conditions. Their diet consisted of not much more than three cups of rice per day—rice that was often rotting or contaminated by animal feces—and supplemented with manioc, an edible root, high in starch content but low in nutritional value. Most of the prisoners developed severe cases of dysentery. Some men defecated fifty to one hundred times a day and were in such a weakened state they were often unable to reach their jungle latrines. The camps became cesspools of human excrement. The unforgiving environment, diseases, and malnutrition contributed to extreme weight loss. It was not uncommon for a 175-pound American to lose 50 to 75 pounds in a brief period. In terms of sheer survival, the POWs in South Vietnam confronted a mortality rate of 20 percent, compared to 5 percent for those held in North Vietnam.[27]

Despite any similarities, the experience of downed American airmen and prisoners of war in Laos differed considerably from that in either North or South Vietnam. The prospects for immediate rescue in Laos after shootdown were higher, at 61 percent, than those in North Vietnam (45 percent) but lower than those in South Vietnam (70 percent). "Among those not rescued, most became MIA statistics," however. A mere "9 out of 300 U.S. personnel listed in 1973 as having been lost in Laos turned up on the capture rolls . . . released by the Communists." The percentage of immediate rescues, along with several early releases and an occasional escape, offered temporary reassurances about surviving Laotian captivity, but the tales of brutality and barbarity "became so widespread, that [by

1968] U.S. pilots commonly elected to avoid going down in Pathet Lao territory even if it meant nursing a crippled aircraft into North Vietnam." The fate of Duane Martin contributed to this harrowing legacy.[28]

When Dengler first observed his fellow POWs, he recoiled in dismay and disbelief. Martin appeared in his Air Force fatigues; his "hair was long and his face was covered with a light-colored beard. He was only in his twenties but he walked bent over, as if someone had just hit him in the guts and knocked the wind out of him." The Air America crew looked far worse, "their clothes—old, worn, stitched haphazardly." Conditions at Par Kung were severe, and the burden of nearly two and a half years in captivity was "etched on their faces, and in their sunken, haunted eyes there was a sadness that could not be hidden by their brief smiles." Indradat, who had previously spent time in six jungle prisons, labeled Par Kung "the cruelest prison." A bamboo fence surrounded Par Kung, which consisted of an area of no more than "twenty-one steps by twenty-one steps." Several huts dotted the prison yard, in addition to two rectangular-shaped cages that the prisoners called coffins. Dengler's cage measured eight feet by fifteen feet. While confined in the cages, the prisoners did not have room to stand and were often locked in foot stocks. Their diet consisted of minuscule portions of rice, rarely supplemented by rat, snake, or tadpole. The jungle canopy blocked the sun and the damp atmosphere helped breed swarms of malaria-carrying mosquitoes. Malaria became a shared affliction that produced recurring episodes of fever, chills, and nausea.[29]

During the week, the men pursued a number of activities to occupy their time. Martin, who had majored in history during his college days and who aspired to teach history at the United States Air Force Academy, talked for "hours and hours" on various historical topics, to the delight of his fellow prisoners. Movie night allowed each prisoner to recall lines and scenes from his favorite films and provide a little thespian release. Dengler specialized in comedies, and one of his favorites was *It's a Mad, Mad, Mad, Mad World*. He regaled his comrades by performing the roles of Spencer Tracy, Milton Berle, Sid Caesar, Buddy Hackett, and Mickey Rooney. Dengler also possessed a cerebral side and crafted a chessboard and taught each man how to play, which resulted in some fierce competition among the prisoners. On Sundays, Martin, a devout Christian Scientist, conducted religious services that sometimes entailed simple recollections of biblical stories but also might involve more philosophical discussions on the nature of God. These diversions and amusements helped the men fight the boredom of captivity and gave them something to think about other than home, although home was never far from their minds. Dengler dreamed of returning home and marrying his fiancée. Martin, already married, simply wanted "to see his wife and girls and have a hamburger."[30]

On 1 May 1966 the small group of prisoners was moved to a prison near the village of Ban Houei Het, a short distance from Par Kung. The compound, concealed by dense jungle foliage and surrounded by a fifteen-foot-high bamboo fence, was approximately forty feet by forty feet and appeared new. There were two identical log-and-bamboo cells, roughly eighteen feet long and six feet wide, with thatched roofs. Dengler, Martin, and DeBruin occupied one cell, and the three Thai and T.C. the other. For some time the prisoners had discussed an escape attempt. In fact, the original group of five had escaped once before for six days in late May and early June 1964. They all agreed that the rainy season, which typically commenced in May, offered the optimal chance for success because the rain provided a reliable source of drinking water and often washed away footprints, which made the escapees more difficult to track. There was widespread disagreement about other details of the escape plan. Dengler wanted to steal weapons from the guards, kill them, gather supplies, and wait in camp to signal a passing plane or move to a nearby river and float down to Thailand or South Vietnam. Everyone else objected to killing the guards. Yet they began to save part of their daily rice ration in anticipation of an escape attempt and mentally recorded the routine of the guards. They observed that at mealtime in the late afternoon the guards gathered in the camp kitchen to eat, leaving their weapons in their huts. The guard towers, which loomed over the compound, were vacant during mealtime as well. But there was still no agreement on whether to kill the guards.[31]

The rainy season did not begin in May, as it had in 1965, and drinking water became so scarce that the prisoners drank from cups polluted with "dirt, algae, and worms." Rations dwindled and prisoners ate the testicles and penis of a deer—the guards consumed the preferred cuts of venison—and a type of tadpole soup, "black and thick as highway tar." The mood of the camp turned tense and desperate. Then one night several guards, including two nicknamed Little Hitler and Crazy Horse, started playing a variation of Russian roulette with the prisoners. They pointed loaded and unloaded rifles at the heads of the prisoners and "with every click of a trigger, the prisoners would jump with fright, causing much merriment among the guards." Afterward, the traumatized prisoners finalized their escape plans and agreed to kill the guards if necessary. Specifically, they would overpower the guards, drag them into the jungle, strangle some, and hold the survivors "for information about the jungle topography or to trade as hostages." Now the captives needed only an opportunity. In mid-June conditions were so bad that ten guards departed on a rice-gathering detail, leaving just seven guards for seven prisoners. Prasit Thanee overheard the remaining guards discussing the probable execution of the prisoners; the guards reasoned that, with no prisoners to watch, they could return to their native villages. On 29 June 1966, feeling that they could no longer afford to wait, the band of hopeful captives launched their escape plot. From the start, their plan went awry.[32]

Briarpatch

In late August 1965 the North Vietnamese opened the Briarpatch, located some thirty-five miles west of Hanoi in a remote, mountainous region near Xom Ap Lo. The camp, which held only ten POWs during its first weeks of operation, closed temporarily in September after U.S. bombers pounded the region in an effort to destroy a North Vietnamese military complex situated just two miles from the prison. Briarpatch reopened in December 1965, during a bitterly cold winter, and housed a dozen prisoners, including Willis Forby. In April 1966 nine more POWs arrived, including Tom Curtis. Bill Robinson followed with six others, including Everett Alvarez, and Neil Black arrived with a group of eleven others in June. Robinson received no advance notice of the move. Just before departing the Zoo, the prisoners underwent a physical, which caused some to speculate that they might soon be going home. They were sadly mistaken. Robinson rode to Briarpatch in a truck carrying pigs, chickens, and other supplies. Perhaps the most primitive of the northern camps, Briarpatch had no electricity or running water, and the "inside walls of the cells were dabbed with cement and painted with muddy water which gave them a cavelike appearance." The POWs constantly battled poor sanitation and meager rations. Rats, mosquitoes, ants, and roaches infested the cells, and a "mosquito net was necessary for survival." In April 1966 the North Vietnamese constructed a bath area for the prisoners, but the Briarpatch officials gave prisoners only "ten minutes to draw water from the well, wash clothes, [and] bathe." Moreover, whereas prisoners were allowed a bath "once or twice a week" at the Zoo, they were fortunate if they bathed once every six weeks at Briarpatch. Although the North Vietnamese attempted to boil drinking water, it was often "murky, very greasy, and tasted of wood smoke." The POWs consumed a diet comprising rice, greasy pumpkin soup, and "occasionally a piece of hairy pork fat," as well as three cigarettes per day. This change in the substance and quality of the diet—at the Zoo prisoners sometimes received a small loaf of French bread with their meal—hastened the spread of diarrhea and dysentery among the prisoners. Robinson reached a level of sickness that he had not experienced in his entire life. Briarpatch was one of the few northern prisons where POWs suffered from malnutrition, and Robinson shared in their misery.[33]

The entire camp, including prison cells, consisted of nine brick huts. For a brief moment Robinson was reunited with Curtis, Forby, and Black, before he was placed in solitary again, where he battled boredom and doubt. He exercised and "counted the holes" in his mosquito net. He imagined repairing cars and thought about automobiles. He feared the loss of basic knowledge and reviewed his high school lessons on geography and North Carolina history. He realized that he did not know much about the Vietnam War or how and why America got involved. He regretted neglecting to speak with his fellow servicemen in South Korea and Oklahoma about their earlier tours in Vietnam and not tapping the reservoir of knowledge possessed by the airmen who had served in World War II or Korea. He questioned some of the decisions that he had made in life, wondering if he had done "the right thing or the wrong thing." But Robinson did not wallow in self-pity. In fact, he made a promise to better himself. "It never dawned on me how long I would be there," Robinson admits, "but I wanted to be prepared when I got out to go on with my life." He would not let captivity defeat him.[34]

The primitive conditions at Briarpatch momentarily placed some of the prisoners at ease, and Robinson assumed that since they "were out in the middle of nowhere," they could not possibly be of any use to the North Vietnamese. He soon learned otherwise. Although the North Vietnamese kept prisoners isolated from one another at Briarpatch, which resulted in limited POW organization and communication, the Americans had fortunately received instructions on resistance strategies while at their earlier places of confinement. From April to July 1966 the North Vietnamese conducted extensive and repeated indoctrination and interrogation sessions, which they considered "educational programs" designed to help the prisoners understand the communists' revolutionary cause. They installed a public address system, powered by a gasoline generator, and broadcast indoctrination lessons on what was characterized as the 4,000-year history of Vietnam and its struggle for independence. The captors placed propaganda materials in the cells, including the *Vietnam Courier*, an English-language communist news weekly. The Americans as a group rebuffed the North Vietnamese proselytizing efforts. Robinson was not persuaded by the communist view of history or its prescription for an egalitarian social order, and, most important, he rejected its strategy of revolutionary violence. He also read a lot about the Russian Revolution and failed to understand "how people were so willing to give up their freedom." In addition to the indoctrination sessions, the North Vietnamese sought detailed biographical and military information from the POWs and presented prisoners with a carefully prepared questionnaire, approximately twenty pages long. The goal was to collect evidence or formulate charges that could be used against Americans during a trial for war crimes.[35]

The precedents for the prosecution of war crimes established at

Nuremberg and Tokyo at the end of World War II lent credence to North Vietnam's intentions, as did the efforts of the noted antiwar activist Bertrand Russell. Since the mid-1950s Russell had been investigating American involvement in Vietnam. In 1966 he published *War Crimes in Vietnam* and later organized the Russell International War Crimes Tribunal, which essentially tried the United States for war crimes in absentia.[36] Although the government of Ho Chi Minh ratified the 1949 Geneva Convention in 1957, Hanoi filed an important "reservation" at the time regarding its view of Article 85, which stipulated that "prisoners of war prosecuted under the laws of the Detaining Power for acts committed prior to capture shall retain, even if convicted, the benefits of the present Convention." The North Vietnamese response to Article 85 was that "the Democratic Republic of Vietnam declares that prisoners of war prosecuted for and convicted of war crimes or crimes against humanity, in accordance with the principles established by the Nuremberg Tribunal, will not enjoy the benefits of the provisions of the present Convention as provided in Article 85." It should be noted that the delegation representing the Soviet Union had submitted a similar objection at the diplomatic convention that drafted the original articles.[37] In addition to frequent broadcasts over Hanoi Radio, various news outlets reported during the summer of 1966 that the North Vietnamese had notified the Egyptian foreign minister as well as Czechoslovakian diplomats of impending trials. Some predicted that the trials would occur on 20 July, which coincided with the signing of the 1954 Geneva Agreements, or 4 August, the anniversary of the Gulf of Tonkin incident.[38]

On 6 July 1966, fifty-two POWs, sixteen from Briarpatch and another thirty-six from the Zoo, participated in what became known as the Hanoi March. Upon arriving in the northern capital, the POWs quickly learned that unless they publicly renounced their role in the American military effort in Vietnam, they would be tried and executed as war criminals. Paired and handcuffed, the POWs formed two long columns; the distance between each pair was roughly ten feet. The guards then instructed the POWs to bow their heads, as a sign of contrition and respect, and march through a throng of Vietnamese people, some of whom had gathered in bleachers or reviewing stands. Uncertain about what to expect, the Americans stood firm and held their heads high. Slowly, but progressively, men, women, and even children filtered into the procession of prisoners. Pandemonium ensued. Indeed, the crowd completely engulfed the two columns of prisoners, and the guards had clearly lost control of the staged event. One POW was clubbed in the head, another in the groin, another kicked in the testicles, and it appeared that several prisoners were on the verge of being beaten to death. In a panicked reaction, the guards tried to shield the prisoners from the enraged mob.[39]

The POWs fought their way through a two-mile-long gauntlet, which lasted for nearly an hour, escaping with their lives when they reached the safety of one of the city's stadiums. Amazingly, international media witnessed and reported on the entire ordeal. As news stories circulated, world opinion, for once, worked against the North Vietnamese. From the floor of the U.S. Senate, the junior senator from New York, Robert F. Kennedy, made these remarks: "I have dissented at many points from this war and its conduct. But I am at one with all Americans in regarding any reprisals against these young men and indirectly against their families, as an intolerable act—contrary to the laws of war, contrary to all past practices in this war, a plunge into barbarism which could serve the interest of no man and no nation."[40] Such condemnation, and a more general global backlash, convinced the North Vietnamese to retreat from their public stance for a war crimes tribunal, but, as Bill Robinson understood it, Hanoi still maintained its right to try American service personnel for war crimes once the war was over. Until then, the North Vietnamese focused on obtaining criminal confessions and antiwar statements so they could exploit prisoners for domestic propaganda purposes.[41]

Although Robinson was not one of the sixteen men from Briarpatch who participated in the Hanoi March, he and everyone else at the camp suffered during the sadistic era of torture that followed in its wake. This marked Robinson's "first major" experience with prolonged torture. Until this point, he "had been brutalized a little bit here and there," but during this latest period, known as "Make Your Choice" or "Choose the Way," there "was no mercy" shown. Under this new approach, the North Vietnamese interrogators forced the POWs to choose between confessing their crimes against the "peace-loving Vietnamese people" on the one hand or condemning the Johnson administration's involvement in Southeast Asia on the other hand. In simple terms, the prisoners had the choice of cooperating or resisting. The North Vietnamese forced those who chose to resist to undergo indoctrination and torture until they produced an acceptable response. When faced with the option to condemn their president and the American war effort, Robinson and his fellow POWs "naturally . . . refused." As the men later joked, they soon found out that "we chose the wrong way." The interrogation sessions were brutal. The North Vietnamese used various torture methods to maximize pain and force compliance. Prisoners were forced to kneel on concrete floors, sometimes with an iron bar between their kneecaps and the floor, for extended periods. The prisoners were unable to remain still, and their bare knees soon became bloodied or swollen from the constant friction with the coarse surfaces. Sleep, food, and water deprivation added to their misery. Strangely, a sense of release washed over the POWs after they completed a round of torture. "Sometimes physical torture was a relief, once you got through it," Robinson attested, because "you were going to be left alone for a while. But if it was going on and you hadn't had your turn in the barrel yet, then you were under [a severe] mental strain—you knew it was going to happen, you just didn't know when." No matter how painful or traumatic the torture session, Robinson "never" contemplated suicide. "If things were to turn [really] bad," he imagined taking two or three Vietnamese with him in a fight to the death, but suicide was not an option. Although some may have considered ending their lives, Robinson always assumed that "one way or another [the POWs] would find a way home." Until that day, they continued to battle their tormentors.[42]

Because of Briarpatch's proximity to U.S. bombing targets, it contained numerous bomb shelters and trenches, which prison officials converted into torture chambers. To Robinson, the trenches seemed "to run for miles" and were perfectly suited to the North Vietnamese' maniacal plans. The guards blindfolded the prisoners, tied their hands behind their backs, and forced them to run blindly and wildly through the trenches to simulate a type of air raid drill. The trenches, designed to protect the shorter Vietnamese, carried natural hazards. "If you were tall and blindfolded going through, every once in a while they would have a damn bridge across" the trench and you would crack your head against the board, Robinson recounted. "That is when you learn to run stooped over with your arms held behind you," barefoot, "in mud up to your knees." Being forced into these positions and to endure these conditions was a miserable existence. Similarly, the North Vietnamese used caves to inflict torment on the POWs for failing to cooperate. Inside such a cave, "you could not sit down because the damn thing was half full of water, and you could not stand up because the caves were only four feet tall." Robinson marveled that his captors were able to affix doors to the caves, which allowed them to leave prisoners in this perverse situation for days. After only "five minutes it seemed like forever. . . . Sitting in a puddle of water, of course, no matter how hot it is, when you're sitting in water on a cold side of the hill it can really sap" your strength. During the Make Your Choice phase, their captors' favorite torture method involved a simple cinderblock. The guards forced the prisoners to sit on a cinderblock, which rose a mere eight inches from the floor, with their hands tied behind their backs, in a darkened room with a single beam of light shining in their faces. "The problem," according to Robinson, was that "no matter whether you weighed a hundred pounds or three hundred pounds, when you get your butt below your knees, it puts all of the weight on your tailbone": it becomes excruciating after a short period. Robinson spent countless days squatting on the cinderblock.[43]

At the end of each round of torture during the Make Your Choice period, the North Vietnamese offered the POWs a chance to reconsider and make another phony confession. One day in early August, Robinson, who had been reunited with Neil Black, tapped a message to SRO Larry Guarino asking if they had "to take torture every time" they went out for a session. Both Guarino and his cellmate, Air Force Major Ronald Byrne, had survived the Hanoi March and had since been subjected to abusive treatment. In fact, Guarino "was too weak to tap an answer" himself, and he instructed Byrne: "Tell them to do their best and try to minimize what they do. Try to bullshit their way out of it." Of course, this approach meant more mistreatment. The utility of the Make Your Choice program was simple. The North Vietnamese wanted to destroy prisoner morale and to demonstrate their control over the POWs, all of them. "As far as I ever knew," Guarino stated, "not a single man of the fifty-six of us escaped torture. Every man got it at least once, and some of us over and over again."[44] Some historians have concluded that "in terms of prolonged misery, no prisoners suffered more than the men confined at Briarpatch."[45] At some point in August 1966, security at the prison tightened over concerns of a possible camp bombing. New preventive measures added to the prisoners' suffering. Anticipating the need to evacuate the prisoners at a moment's notice, the North Vietnamese loosely cuffed the POWs' hands behind their backs each day, from the conclusion of the morning meal at dawn to just before the second meal at dusk. After three weeks, the captors replaced the cuffs with short ropes, and late in September 1966 the North Vietnamese allowed the ropes to "be worn on one arm like a bracelet," a practice that continued until the camp closed. Nearly sixty Americans spent time at Briarpatch. In early February 1967 the camp closed, presumably because of severe water shortages, and the POWs were sent to the Little Vegas complex at the Hanoi Hilton or to the Zoo.[46]

A Family Crisis

President Lyndon Johnson had not prepared the nation for an expanded war in Southeast Asia, and equally derelict was the U.S. military in establishing protocols for casualty notification. In the 2002 film *We Were Soldiers*, a dramatic account of the first large-scale battle between North Vietnamese and American forces in November 1965, viewers get a glimpse of this unpreparedness. The widow of the 7th Cavalry's first member killed in action (KIA), Sergeant Billy R. Elliott, receives the news of her husband's death via telegram, delivered by a Yellow Cab driver. Subsequently, Julia Compton Moore, the wife of Colonel Harold Moore, who commanded the 1st Battalion, 7th Cavalry, confronts a subservient and contrite cab driver who obviously regrets the role that he has been forced to play, and she bravely assumes responsibility for delivering casualty notifications. Hollywood's fictitious rendering of the casualty notification conceals a more disturbing reality. In actuality, the cabbie who notified Sara Elliott that her husband had been killed in action arrived "blind drunk and staggering" and "fell backward off her porch and passed out in her flower bed" after he presented the telegram. Incredibly, the Army "briefly lost her husband's body on its return journey home." The madness continued with subsequent notifications to the family members of the men in the 7th Cavalry.[47] The Air Force did not hire a drunken cabbie to deliver news to the Robinson family; instead, they employed a phantom notifier.

No one in the Robinson family knows precisely when the notice explaining that Bill had been shot down arrived at his parents' home in Robersonville, North Carolina. His father and stepmother lived in a simple house, which they typically entered through the back door. They rarely used the front door unless special guests visited. In fact, they rarely paid attention to the front foyer during their daily routines. One day, upon returning home, the couple noticed a mysterious envelope in the foyer. Presumably, someone, military or civilian, had slid the envelope through the letter slot on the front door. It could have been on the floor for a few hours or even a few days. Inside was word that Bill Robinson's helicopter had crashed in Vietnam and he was missing in action. The letter offered few details, and the insensitive handling of the notification foreshadowed the kind of treatment the families whose loved ones were being held as prisoners of war would receive. His parents, of course, were stunned by the news, and they quickly reached out to family members in nearby Roanoke Rapids.[48]

When Robinson had joined the Air Force in 1961, he, like many young men, especially in the South, was fulfilling a societal obligation and a male rite of passage. Family members, including his sister Ginger, simply believed that "he would serve his period of time and come home." She understood his need to see and explore the world. As children, they had rarely traveled outside their local community, except for the occasional summer vacation in Virginia Beach, Virginia, or when their grandfather took them "on Sunday afternoon . . . to the old airport in Rocky Mount [North Carolina] to sit and watch the planes go in and out" or to Emporia, Virginia, for ice cream cones. Ginger felt that these family excursions compensated for their lack of material possessions and produced a familial bond based on love and interdependence. She believed that Roanoke Rapids "had as much to offer as any place else," and, because of Bill's strong affection for his grandfather, Ginger expectantly awaited her brother's return, which she assumed would be followed by marriage and the raising of a large family. Nothing could have prepared her for the news of her brother's being shot down. Ginger learned that her brother was missing and presumed captured while at her mother-in-law's house. Her father and stepmother, Jessie, informed her of the incident, but it just did not register with her. She could not "realize the seriousness" of the situation and believed that "he would be home in a few days." The day on which the family learned of Bill's misfortune seemed surreal; they had not prepared, they had not even believed that this day was possible. Only after four or five months had passed did Ginger begin to comprehend the gravity of the situation and confront the possibility that her brother might not return home. On that day, "when it finally hit" her, she cried all day. Then there were days when she "could barely function" because of the sadness and grief, but the needs of her husband and two children pulled her along.[49]

Following the initial shock, the family coped with the situation both as a group and as individuals. But the immediate family was somewhat scattered, and Bill's sister Jackie was dealing with a difficult situation of her own when she learned of his being shot down. She had married in 1957, left Roanoke Rapids shortly thereafter, and followed her husband, a member of the Air Force, to England in 1958. She returned to the states in 1962 and saw her brother just before he left for South Korea in 1963. They would not see one another for ten years. In 1965, when William Robinson traveled to Elizabeth City, North Carolina, to tell his daughter of her brother's fate, he found a woman struggling to make ends meet. She had recently separated from her husband and had four children to support. Sometimes the refrigerator and cupboards were bare, and Jackie had to rely on support from her father and stepmother, her grandparents, and her sister and brother-in-law just to get by.[50]

Despite the geographical distance between them (Roanoke Rapids and Elizabeth City were roughly one hundred miles apart), the family "gathered as often as they could" to console one another, and they talked about the situation and prayed about it. Ginger, a deeply religious woman, prayed frequently with her daughter, Pam, who was only five years old when her uncle was captured. Her son, Tim, was only one year old in 1965 and had no ability to fathom the loss or heartache within his immediate and extended family. Relying on their Christian faith, Ginger and her family learned to cope one day at a time. Gene Robinson often sat in a swing on the front porch of his home contemplating the fate of his grandson. Once he revealed to Ginger his thoughts about her mother's death, explaining that in the past he had questioned why "the Lord took" their mother from them at such a young age. Now Gene Robinson accepted Lillian's death as a way to spare her from this ordeal of pain and worry.[51]

As best as she can recall, Ginger dates the arrival of the first letter from her brother to February 1966. The envelope addressed to Bill's father and stepmother appeared to have been postmarked in fourteen different countries and came directly to North Carolina. Family members wondered why this first letter had not been intercepted by the U.S. government or by the Air Force.[52] When Robinson had written the letter on 20 December 1965, the North Vietnamese had not yet developed the abbreviated postcard-style form letter that they would implement in mid-1968. Consequently, Robinson composed a two-page, handwritten letter outlining his first three months in captivity.

Dear Mother & Dad,

It has been a long time since the 20th of September and I'm sure you'll be glad to hear from me.
I'm in hope that this letter finds all doing very well.
As for me, my health is good, I'm getting adequate food and clothing from the Vietnamese people. I'm still at my normal 200 pounds.
I'm happy to say that I was unhurt in the plane crash

and I thank God for that. I know he is with me and will see me thru all of this.

Tell all hello for me and that I send my love to all. Thanks so much for the many prayers that have been said for me while I have been away.

I'll leave it up to you as to what to do about my car. It is ok with me if you sell it and put the money in the bank until I return. You could ask Bev and if she thinks we should keep it, well I'll let you work that out for me. I know you'll do what is best.

I hope my being away has not caused too much of a hardship on you. I know since my being here I have been closer to God in so many ways. I have put all my trust in him, knowing that he is ruler of all.

I am grateful for the treatment I have received from the Vietnamese people.

If all my things were sent home, there should be a jewelry box in it somewhere. If so, send it on to Bev for me. Ok?

I hope that Grandmother & Granddaddy are getting along well. Tell Grandmother I'm sorry that I didn't take time to answer her last letter. Let them know that I am OK and most of all not to worry about me for I'm getting good care from the Vietnamese people and that all is going well for me.

I am just happy that I have been given the chance by the Vietnamese people to write home to let you hear from me and to know that I'm getting along very well.

I'd like to wish you all a very Merry Christmas and a Happy New Year. Most of all not to worry about me for God will be with me all the way.

I'll close for now in hopes that I'll be hearing from you very soon.

Love From Your
Son Billy[53]

Obviously, Robinson could not reveal the terror of his shootdown and capture, the difficult ten-day trek to Hanoi, the savage encounter with the One-Armed Bandit, or the harsh conditions at Briarpatch. This first letter contained one coded message; his "normal" weight was 240 pounds, not 200 pounds. Otherwise, Robinson used the opportunity to encourage his family; even the requests to manage and handle some of his affairs were a way to occupy their time and, in a manner of speaking, keep them connected. Robinson also confessed his devotion to Beverly with talk of a future together. In consoling his loved ones, he no doubt gained strength to battle his current circumstances. From 26 April 1966 to 7 December 1967 Robinson received permission to write ten letters to his parents and Beverly; in most instances he wrote to both on the same day and on the same four-paneled sheet of paper. He asked simple questions about their daily routines and the weather. He inquired about their health. He expressed his hopes of a successful future after his release. He worked from his prison cell to arrange a meeting between Beverly and his parents; they had not previously met. And he constantly mentioned his faith in and reliance on God, and he consistently maintained a positive attitude and tried to reassure them that he was doing well.[54]

More than a year into his captivity, Robinson sent a deeply reflective letter to his father and stepmother. After claiming that he was "fit as a fiddle and doing just great," he explained that the passing of time ebbed and flowed: "Sometimes it feels like ages and other times like only yesterday." He recognized that his faith had become "stronger than ever," and professed, "I know He has been with me and will continue to be with me until the end." He fondly remembered his nieces and nephews. He urged Pam "to study hard in school," and he sent his love to Jackie and her kids. Although it was only late October, Robinson thought ahead to Christmas. He did not expect to be home. And so he asked his stepmother to "send one dozen 'long stem' red roses to Bev" on his behalf as a Christmas present. He also included the following poem.

During this Holy Christmas Season
When families and loved ones are near

I send red roses to you, my love
In hopes they bring you cheer.

Even though there's an ocean to cross
And many mountains to climb
I know each love has a loss
But I pray that ours is nothing but time.

Till then, My Love Forever,
Billy

He concluded his letter with his customary well wishes, prayers, and expectations of receiving and writing future letters. The very last line of the two-page letter read: "Thanks for sending the flowers to Bev for me, I'll repay you when I get home." Bill Robinson never intended for his captivity to be a burden to his family.[55]

Every piece of news about or photo of Bill or any other American POW in Vietnam received solemn attention and reflection and made the family "more aware of the war itself." Additional news, however, did not always provide consolation. For instance, on 7 April 1967 *Life* magazine published a twelve-page photo essay, "North Vietnam under Siege," based on the work of Lee Lockwood. Lockwood, the first American photographer allowed in North Vietnam, had recently finished a four-week stay in the country. The timing of the photo essay no doubt deeply disturbed the Robinson family. Two weeks earlier casualty reports "showed the highest single weekly toll of the war for both sides: 2,675 Communists killed; 211 Americans killed, 1,874 more Americans wounded and seven missing." Each page revealed scenes of bomb devastation and a landscape of rice patties and oxen tended by peasants carrying automatic weapons. One section described Hanoi, a city of some 500,000 Vietnamese and the central place of confinement for most American POWs, as "an anxious city." Its residents expected a more sustained air campaign against the capital city in the coming months. The last two pages of the essay, subtitled "U.S. Prisoners and an Eerie Puppet Show," certainly unnerved both the American public and the Robinson family. The first page of the two-page section included head shots of four American POWs, Bill Robinson, Neil Black, Captain Murphy N. Jones, and Captain Glendon Perkins, and full-frame photos of Lieutenant Colonel Robinson Risner, 1st Lieutenant Joseph Crecca, and Captain Edward L. Hubbard. All the men were members of the Air Force, and the color photos "were taken by a North Vietnamese photographer, using Lockwood's camera and film." Only one black-and-white photo appeared on the entire second page, that of Navy Lieutenant Commander Richard A. Stratton.[56]

Stratton, the first pilot captured by the North Vietnamese in 1967, underwent immediate and prolonged torture. For two weeks he endured beatings, cigarette burns, and the ropes, before making a taped confession. On 6 March the North Vietnamese displayed Stratton, who was being held at the Plantation, a prison in north central Hanoi, during a press conference. Lockwood attended the staged event and recorded the following observations in the *Life* photo essay, in essence transporting the reader to Vietnam.

Stratton appeared, flanked by two soldiers. He wore striped pajamas, socks, and sandals. Except for a red, swollen nose, he appeared healthy. His eyes were empty. He stood stiffly at attention while movie lights were turned on and photographers took pictures. His expression never changed.

This continued for about a minute. Then an officer snapped out a command in Vietnamese. Like a puppet, the prisoner bowed deeply from the waist toward the audience without changing expression. He straightened up, made a quarter-turn left and then bowed again, slowly and deeply. He turned to the right and bowed once more. After four or five bows he stopped. The officer shouted another command and the whole process began again—the prisoner bowing in all directions, his expression blank. After the cycle was completed one more time, the officer gave another command. The whole tableau took only about four minutes. Then the pilot did an about-face and padded silently through the curtain.[57]

The U.S. Defense Department reported that, as of 11 March 1967, the North Vietnamese communists and the Viet Cong held a combined

143 prisoners, Robinson and Stratton among them. In performing the robotic bows, Stratton took a chance that his bizarre behavior would ignite further inquiries into the treatment of U.S. POWs.[58] As if on cue, Averell Harriman, a senior State Department official who headed the Interdepartmental Prisoner of War Committee, accused the North Vietnamese of "using mental or physical torture on American prisoners of war." He compared the incident to "the ugly record of 'brainwashing' during the Korean war," and he worried that the North Vietnamese were using similar tactics. He renewed the call for independent inspections of POW facilities by the International Committee of the Red Cross; he insisted that without "independent verification," North Vietnam's professions of humane treatment could not be accepted.[59]

The picture of Robinson in *Life* jolted his sister Ginger. She could not ignore the enormous change between the brother who left Roanoke Rapids to join the Air Force and the brother who was a prisoner of war. "His eyes were dark and sad," she noticed upon reviewing the photo, and especially troubling to her was that "his face was thin and he had lost so much weight." Had her brother received the same treatment as Lieutenant Commander Stratton? Had he been brainwashed? Was he a puppet? The limitations of the head shot prompted additional uncertainty, as did his prison garb. Robinson, Neil Black, and Robbie Risner all wore off-white pajamas over a dark-colored turtleneck shirt, which differed from the red-and-gray-striped outfits of Stratton and the other four prisoners. Did the different uniforms mean the prisoners were held in different locations under different conditions? The caption under each photo listed the prisoner's name, rank, branch of service, but it classified each man as missing in action, not as a prisoner of war. The North Vietnam government did not release an official list of Americans held in captivity until December 1970, by which time Robinson had been a prisoner of war for more than five years.[60] During a 2006 POW symposium, Robinson and another former prisoner fielded questions on how their families coped during their imprisonment. Each man felt that the families who did not know whether their loved ones were alive or dead endured more hardship than the POWs themselves. Robinson expressed deep and heartfelt regret that his family suffered so much during his captivity. "If I hold anything against the Vietnamese it would be the fact that they put our families through torment that was so unnecessary, unwarranted, and undeserving," Robinson told the audience.[61] By mid-1967 his family's pain had just begun. And yet the young prisoner of war still had to experience several seasons of horror.

The Daily Grind

Upon leaving Briarpatch, Robinson returned to the Zoo compound on 2 February 1967. The camp had changed considerably in terms of its population since his first stay. The number of prisoners held increased from 50 in February 1966 to 120 in January 1967.[62] Robinson and Neil Black had first become roommates at Briarpatch "and were pretty much glued to each other's hip . . . from that point on." Their new cell at the Zoo was in an area known as the Office. Before they were captured, the two airmen had "walked in different circles." In many respects, the different types and lengths of training completed by pararescuemen, such as jungle training, survival school, and medical training, distanced them from the crew chiefs, who completed a fourteen-week course on aviation mechanics and then learned the rest through on-the-job training. As Robinson sensed, PJs "were young and cocky; I was just young." The two men were barely out of their teens when they were shot down, Robinson the elder at age twenty-two and Black only twenty. After they became cellmates at Briarpatch, the two men "exhausted everything about true confessions," and they "discussed everything from politics to religion." Both "basically figured out that neither one knew a lot" about the other's religious traditions—Robinson was Methodist and Black was Jewish—or the philosophical basis for their political inclinations. They soon learned to agree to disagree, but they had "one common bond, and that was to survive and to do what was right and to support their leaders," no matter the costs. When the stakes were high at Briarpatch, they "stood shoulder to shoulder" and gave an honorable effort. It was their good fortune that there was a lull in the torture routine at the Zoo compound for much of 1967. Thus, they concentrated on coping with the daily grind.[63]

Humor was a powerful combatant to the drudgery of captivity for many POWs, especially Bill Robinson and Neil Black. The pair could be creative and silly and occasionally venture into a little off-color comedy, all in an effort to stay sane. Black possessed genuine musical abilities, including "a good ear for music," but without access to instruments, he could not readily take advantage of his talents. So he improvised. Black pulled a piece of string out of his blanket and attached it to pegs mounted in the cell's doorframe. He added some marks to it and plucked out some tunes. If a prisoner "leaned up against the wall," he could "hear an echo throughout the building." One night the two enlisted men tapped out a message indicating that Black was taking requests. Several inquiries were made, but Black could not perform the requests. Finally, in desperation, someone tapped, "Do you know 'Row, Row, Row Your Boat'?" Despite their age and rank, the duo of Robinson and Black belonged to the coterie known as the old guys or old-timers, those men captured during the early stages of the war. Whenever new prisoners arrived, Robinson and Black made contact and exchanged biographical information and details about prison policy. In May 1967 Navy Lieutenant Commander Charles Stackhouse, who was shot down a few weeks earlier, on 25 April, joined the gang at the Office. After Stackhouse and his cellmate announced how long they had been in captivity, they asked Robinson and Black the same question, to which they answered, 20 September 1965. A brief pause in the conversation ensued before the new guys responded, "Great! Fuck!"[64]

Sometimes the prisoners had little choice but to accept the absurdity of their situation, such as the time Robinson and Black announced the birth of a new arrival in their cell. The *bo* bucket that Robinson and Black used in their dimly lit cell included a lid. When one man or the other was let out of the cell to dump the bucket, the North Vietnamese ordered the POW to leave the lid inside the cell. This requirement led to the unexpected discovery of an eighteen-inch-long worm about three-eighths of an inch in diameter. Neither POW knew "who had fathered the worm," but the prisoners in the adjacent and surrounding cells received the news excitedly and inquisitively. Robinson and Black dipped the worm out of the bucket and displayed it in the community shower. The onlookers marveled, and some wanted to hold a contest to name the offspring. "You know you are bored at this point," Robinson observed of the momentary respite at the Zoo in 1967, "but at that particular time the older guys were being left alone, although all hell was breaking loose" at other camps in North Vietnam. It would not remain that way for Robinson and Black for very long. A new season of torment lay on the horizon, one requiring the same selfless commitment to one another that the two enlisted men exhibited at Briarpatch, but they were afforded a noticeable advantage this time, an additional cellmate.[65]

Joining the two enlisted men was Air Force Sergeant Art Cormier, who, like Black, was a PJ, but unlike either Black or Robinson had reached a greater level of maturity, one achieved by different life experiences. Born in 1934, Cormier was ten years older than Robinson, had been in the Air Force ten years longer, was married with four children, and had previously served a tour of duty in Vietnam. Just forty days after the shootdown of Robinson and Black, Cormier and a crew of air rescue men boarded a CH-3C, a Jolly Green Giant helicopter, to attempt the rescue of a downed A-1E pilot. As the Jolly Green approached the scene, small arms fire crippled the helicopter, forcing the crew to bail out. Cormier managed to evade capture for eight days before the North Vietnamese corralled him. As he and two other Americans made their way to Hanoi, they drove into a village and stopped at a stadium. Cormier estimated that "there must have been hundreds of people there . . . they had movie cameras and were taking pictures of us . . . then they gave us the sign." The POWs interpreted the sign to be instructions to be seated. When the prisoners took their seats, however, their guards admonished them to rise. After standing and sitting five or six times, the Americans learned that they were expected to bow as a sign of humility. Cormier remembered that the "crowd was getting out of hand," and as the guards escorted them out of the stadium, "they were punched and beaten" before making it to the bus for the trip to Hanoi. Later, Cormier was forced to participate in the Hanoi March of July 1966. At the start of the march, he was handcuffed to Navy Lieutenant Jerry Coffee, who instructed him, "Hold your head high and be proud that you are an American tonight." Once the march was under way, the North Vietnamese ordered the prisoners to bow their heads, and Cormier was pummeled by three or four crazed Vietnamese before Coffee could drag him away and the two raced to the safety of the downtown sports stadium.[66]

Robinson and Black quickly realized that Cormier "had gone through the [torture] circuit," just as they had. They welcomed their fellow rescueman at a time when they were eager for new companionship. Cormier added his personal narrative to their collective memories. Although Black and Cormier, as PJs, shared similar military backgrounds, Robinson insists that he "was never tag-teamed" by his two cellmates. Robinson also believes that the three men "strengthened each other" and never looked to criticize one another. Of course, the three enlisted men did not always agree, but they "had respect for one another." The fact that Cormier was married with children and Black and Robinson were bachelors did not divide the cellmates. It made them closer. "His family became our family," Robinson felt. "We shared in his pain" of being separated from his wife and kids. As their time in captivity increased, "there was always something" that they "could learn from each other." Of the three cellmates, Robinson was the only one who had not undergone survival training and "depended on their guidance . . . in dealing with certain situations." Cormier had "a calming effect" because of his greater experience, although Robinson and Black "had grown up pretty quickly during their first year and a half in captivity."[67]

The burgeoning population at the Zoo required structural changes to the compound. The North Vietnamese constructed the Zoo Annex in October 1967 in the "southwest end of the main compound." It "was so distinct in character and so segregated physically and administratively that most [POWs] considered it a separate camp." The Zoo Annex included its own indoctrination-interrogation rooms and "a cluster of cellblock buildings . . . surrounded by a drainage pond which the Americans unaffectionately dubbed 'Lake Fester.'" The North Vietnamese portioned each of the individual cellblocks "into two large rooms that measured 17 feet by 20 feet and held four to nine prisoners." For whatever reason, the communists designated the Zoo Annex a facility for junior officers of the rank of 04 or below, meaning Air Force captains and Navy lieutenant commanders.[68] Robinson, Black, and Cormier moved to the Zoo Annex in March 1968 and were joined by the Navy aviators Lieutenant (j.g.) Read Mecleary (shot down 26 May 1967), Lieutenant James Bailey (28 June 1967), and Lieutenant (j.g.) Dave Carey (31 August 1967) and Air Force flyers Lieutenant John Borling (1 June 1966), Lieutenant Darrel Pyle (13 June 1966), and Lieutenant Harry Monlux (11 November 1966). The association of the three enlisted men with the six junior officers created a new dynamic. Previously, Robinson had shared a cell with only one other officer, Captain Kile Berg, when the two were held together at the Zoo before Robinson's transfer to the Briarpatch. Borling, a torture-tested veteran, served as the cell's senior ranking officer. The 1963 Air Force Academy graduate endured the Outhouse, a torture chamber at the Zoo so named for its noxious odors and resemblance to a sewer, shortly after his capture. As the men shared their stories of what they had been through up to that point, several of those shot down more recently realized they had not yet seen the worst of what the North Vietnamese had to offer. The first major event for the group of nine was President Lyndon Johnson's decision to halt the bombing over North Vietnam in the spring of 1968 and to accelerate peace talks. The change in policy tempted the prisoners to believe that "gee whiz, the end was finally here." Their optimism quickly vanished when the guards "came in and slapped the [POWs] around" and launched a new round of torture.[69]

In previous years, the North Vietnamese had tortured prisoners to obtain incriminating confessions of war crimes or coerced antiwar statements, but in 1968 camp officials at the Zoo concentrated on indoctrination and individual biographies, to include details of their respective military missions. The POWs learned to distinguish the interrogators' intent by identifying the type of stool used in the sessions. "You could always tell what kind of interrogation it would be. If it was a concrete stool, you knew you were in trouble; if it was a wooden stool, it was basically a friendly type of interrogation," observed Art Cormier.[70] The indoctrination consisted of berating the prisoners, calling them pawns or agents of the war-mongering imperialist United States and accusing them of causing pain and suffering to the Vietnamese people. The North Vietnamese pointed to the economic inequalities and the racial strife in America as examples of capitalism's exploitation of the masses. The POWs sat for hours listening to this verbal abuse, and they were expected to pay close attention and be respectful. If they failed to do so, the guards would punch, slap, or kick them until they showed the proper deference. The pursuit of biographical and military information took on a more serious tone and carried more severe consequences. By forcing the prisoners to sit on a concrete stool or cinderblock, the guards subjected the POWs to a simple but painful torture. For a big man like Robinson, remaining in this contorted position for hours at a time over a succession of days caused considerable misery and left him in a weakened state, barely able to walk. The guards sent him back to his cell to recuperate, where he slept on a concrete bunk. Not wanting to dishonor himself or appear weak in the eyes of his peers, Robinson refused to answer certain questions about his family and where he had grown up and withstood the punishment to the best of his ability. When he returned to his cell following one particularly abusive session, Robinson reported the details, via tap code, to his SRO, who had requested a briefing on the session. The SRO responded that answering biographical questions was not worth the risk of bodily harm. He told Robinson "not to worry about it": absolute silence or name, rank, and serial number were not going to be accepted by the North Vietnamese.[71]

POWs, however, knew to withhold vital military information despite the costs. What constituted vital military information? A pilot might know flight schedules, bombing patterns, or evasion tactics, but Robinson, Black, and Cormier were enlisted men who served on rescue helicopters, and they attempted to use their rank to their advantage when dealing with the North Vietnamese. For example, they tried to deceive the interrogators by claiming ignorance. The "game" that Cormier "played" was that he "didn't know anything" because he was a medic "and just went where the helicopter was going." When the North Vietnamese scoffed at Cormier's explanation, he followed up with a question of his own: "Do you tell your medics where you are going?" The strategy did not always work, but the evasive replies offered by the enlisted men probably reduced the number of times that they were questioned.[72] Whatever information the POWs provided, they needed to remember their exact responses: the North Vietnamese were writing them down and periodically checked the consistency of the answers, sometimes waiting as long as a year before verifying a POW's account or claim. For Robinson, this meant not telling "them the whole truth, just something we could remember."[73]

Physical torture was just one of the ways in which the North Vietnamese dehumanized American POWs. The food consumed by the POWs was of a poor quality and lacked nutritional value, leaving them susceptible to a variety of ailments and in a constant state of weakness. The two meals each day consisted of a bowl of rice for breakfast and a type of soup for supper. The men often ate "the vegetable of the season," which for a large portion of the year was grass boiled in water. Pumpkin season generally lasted about five months, during which the prisoners dined on a steady diet of a watery pumpkin gruel before they returned to "more grass." The North Vietnamese provided no vitamin-rich fruit and only the occasional potato; "meat was limited if at all." As Robinson explained, "By the time you cut a chicken up to share with seventy people," your portion was minuscule. The one element of the diet that Robinson looked forward to was a form of French bread. Although the bread was offered infrequently, he described it as "quite good." Because the guards delivered most meals to a prisoner's cell, they possessed the power to turn a meal into a type of harassment or punishment. They often sat hot meals outside the cell doors and waited until the food became cold. Robinson remembers watching the steam rise and disappear from his food as it sat outside his cell, an unnecessary torment on a brisk winter morning. Sometimes the guards allowed ants or other insects to cover the plate or fill the bowl before they actually delivered it to the prisoner. Dealing with the guards was a difficult matter from Robinson's perspective because "most of [them] had experienced a direct loss" as a result of U.S. military actions—"a brother, mother, father, a child, or close friend." They "actually came to the prison hating" the Americans, holding them "responsible for their personal losses." Some guards realized that the POWs hadn't intentionally hurt them, but some of them remained angry and vengeful. In retrospect, Robinson knows some guards were just doing their jobs during a difficult time. Others, however, went above and beyond the conventions of war and maltreated the prisoners. Robinson burns with anger to this day when recollecting their abusive deeds: "I could disassemble them in a heartbeat. I would do it slowly because that would make it hurt a little bit."[74]

Robinson estimated that during his first five years in captivity, he averaged "less than fifteen minutes a day of outside time," meaning time outside his cell. The North Vietnamese allotted time for showering, emptying the waste bucket, and retrieving water, but "the rest of the time we were locked up," Robinson maintains. Under these restrictions, the POWs had to create a harmonious and supportive environment in which to battle the daily grind. A religion infused with patriotism united the prisoners of Robinson's cell. On Sunday mornings the POWs stood in unison, faced east, toward the United States, and recited the Lord's Prayer and the pledge of allegiance to the American flag. Afterward, some prisoners participated in religious discussions, reflecting on certain passages of the Bible, or sang quietly. Most of the services and observances were "done in secret," although they were "not completely secret"; the POWs knew the guards were not entirely unaware of what was going on, but they tended to overlook religious activity unless the prisoners were loud or defiant in their tone.[75]

The prisoners tolerated, even appreciated in some instances, differences of personal opinion within their own cells, but they moved quickly to quash any perceived threat to the group's solidarity. The pranksters in the cell found occasions to make light of those who were overly sensitive or irrationally fearful of group discord. One such instance of badgering occurred around the time that the North Vietnamese increased the cigarette ration from three to six per day. Robinson's cellmates had laid out an exercise track in their seventeen-by-twenty-foot cell. While two men were walking around the track, one turned to the other and out of the blue said, "That's a deal," and they shook hands to confirm the agreement. Another prisoner interrupted and asked, "What's the deal?" But he was promptly told, "This doesn't include you." Perplexed by the lack of openness, the offended POW exclaimed, "What do you mean, we are all over here locked up together—there shouldn't be any secrets." As Robinson recalls, "That went on for a while" and prompted a larger discussion about the negative effects of secrets, which convinced the two POWs to announce their deal. One POW would exchange all his peanut brittle for the other's cigarettes. The peanut brittle was a valuable commodity that came in some of the Red Cross packages the prisoners received. The inquisitive POW, a heavy smoker, protested the arrangement, and he offered some of his personal items for a portion of the cigarette ration. The two POWs declined the offer. Then the debate shifted to whether there should be "private negotiations" in the cells. This lasted an additional day or two. Finally, after the mood had gotten a little dour, the two POWs confessed that they had been playing a joke on their fellow POWs the entire time. The cell erupted: "Oh, Jesus," Robinson remarked in characterizing the initial response to the caper. The men then spent several days discussing how they shouldn't deceive one another. For more than a year Robinson and his cellmates at the Zoo Annex had managed to cope with the daily grind of captivity, and they had accumulated a reservoir of trust and mutual respect. In the summer of 1969 the group would call on all their available resources as they faced an unrelenting challenge to their faith and courage.[76]

Summer of Hell

Although Article III of the Code of Conduct imposes a challenging proviso, "I will make every effort to escape and aid others to escape," there were only a handful of escape attempts in North Vietnam, none of which was ultimately successful. Bill Robinson thought that escaping the building did not present a substantial challenge, but once a prisoner escaped from his cell and the compound, where did he go? It was more complex than simply "making it to the river, floating down to the Tonkin Gulf, and getting picked up," although that was a beautiful scenario. There was no realistic possibility of blending in with the native population or receiving aid from an underground network of sympathizers. In addition to the unlikelihood of reaching friendly lines, the prisoner had to consider the residual consequences. Would a successful escape improve morale for those who remained behind? Would it provide vital intelligence to U.S. authorities? Would there be retaliatory actions against those who assisted the escape? With so many variables to weigh, the POWs routinely debated the efficacy of escape attempts, and these discussions were not simply abstract debates.[77]

On 12 October 1967 Air Force Captain George McKnight and Navy Lieutenant George Coker escaped from a makeshift prison at the Yen Phu power plant in northern Hanoi known as Dirty Bird to the prisoners. The North Vietnamese, in effect, used the prisoners as hostages at Dirty Bird in hopes of deterring U.S. bombing of the power plant. It was hardly a remote or unsecure location, but Mc-Knight and Coker still managed to escape and traveled approximately fifteen miles before being detected by local peasants who turned the two airmen over to the North Vietnamese Army. Surprisingly, McKnight and Coker did not receive any retaliatory punishment for their escape attempt. Apparently, during their interrogation McKnight convinced the North Vietnamese that they had no prison collaborators, and no chain of command had designed or authorized the plan. In the aftermath of the escape attempt, the power plant prisons closed, security tightened at other prison sites, and news of McKnight and Coker's exploits spread throughout the prisoner grapevine, boosting spirits and generating admiration.[78]

Inconsistency characterized the North Vietnamese treatment of American prisoners of war in early 1969. Those held at Hoa Lo and Alcatraz, a punishment camp in north central Hanoi, "were in the throes of renewed terror," while those at the Plantation and Zoo lived "in the midst of a jittery intermission." Against this backdrop, Air Force captains John Dramesi and Edwin Atterberry hatched a highly complex and controversial escape plan from the Zoo Annex. The controversy centered on the proper interpretation of the so-called escape mandate in Article III of the Code of Conduct. The SROs throughout the various prisons had generally agreed that on the issue of escapes, as well as public statements, "unity and obedience to the chain of command" superseded "doctrinaire adherence" to the Code of Conduct. Within the chain of command, the SROs did not wield dictatorial powers. In fact, prisoners of all ranks contributed to the decision-making process, and various commit-tees, including an escape committee, were created within individual cells to replicate an authentic chain of command and to foster unity. At the Zoo Annex, SRO Air Force Captain Konrad Trautman sided with those who viewed escape attempts as having greater potential for risk than for reward. Trautman expressed his personal objections to the Dramesi-Atterberry plan, but he neither sanctioned nor of-ficially prohibited their actions, although he "attached conditions relating to time, consensus, and other constraints."[79]

On the night of 10 May 1969, after meticulous and lengthy prep-aration, Dramesi and Atterberry began their escape. Dramesi and Atterberry, with the help of their fellow prisoners, had accumulated a cache of provisions. Perhaps most important, the men needed to disguise themselves or conceal their identities and to that end car-ried masks, civilian clothing, which they made from their prison wear, conical hats, iodine pills to be used as a cosmetic for dark-ening their skin, and even baskets and a bamboo pole. They also saved food and gathered wire, string, and any miscellaneous items that could be used as tools or weapons. The involvement by other prisoners in the escape attempt extended even to the nine men in Bill Robinson's cell. His cell drew the assignment of knocking out the lightbulb outside the cell, right above the door. It appeared that every conceivable measure had been taken to ensure the success of the escape.[80]

Assisted by their cellmates, the two Air Force flyers were boost-ed into the attic above their cell. After some three hours of staging in the attic, where the men put on their disguises and waited for what they deemed the right moment, Dramesi and Atterberry quickly ex-ited to the roof, navigated the Zoo compound, and climbed over the prison's ten-foot wall. Traveling most of the night, they logged four or five miles before an armed patrol discovered them around sunrise. Shortly thereafter, they were back at the Zoo. Robinson de-scribed what followed as "Hell Summer." Dramesi and Atterberry had been "gone for a few hours, then they were brought back, and then we heard the screams," recalled Robinson. The North Viet-namese quickly went after Dramesi and Atterberry. For his part, Dramesi endured thirty-eight straight days of torture. During this stretch, he was placed in the ropes fifteen times, placed on starvation rations of bread and water, beaten mercilessly with a fan belt, which was actually a long strip of tire rubber that functioned like a whip. If anyone suffered a worse fate during Hell Summer than John Dramesi, it was Ed Atterberry. No one knows for sure what ultimately happened to Atterberry. He certainly faced the same torture and beatings that Dramesi encountered. Rumors circulated through Robinson's cell that the guards had beaten him so severely that "he had open wounds and then they poured salt into those wounds." The North Vietnamese claimed that Atterberry died in captivity on 18 May from complications stemming from a case of pneumonia. Officially, the U.S. government lists Atterberry as having died in captivity. Robinson disputes such claims and classifications. As far as he is concerned, Ed Atterberry was murdered by the North Vietnamese.[81]

Before Hell Summer, "we had a basic philosophy that you would take torture [to the point] that you wouldn't lose control—that way you could control what you said," Robinson explained, but this time "they didn't slow down until they had complete submission, until they found out everything that we were doing as far as communicating between rooms, between buildings, between different sections of camp." Because of this unrestrained pursuit of information, some of the top POW communicators received particularly harsh treatment, including Konrad Trautman, George (Bud) Day, Larry Guarino, and Red McDaniel. Some men were tied to trees and whipped, others, such as Air Force Colonel Bud Day, felt the destructive force of the four-foot-long so-called fan belt. To generate momentum, the guards pushed off from the wall and sprinted across the room holding the strips of rubber high above their heads before delivering their ravaging blows to his buttocks, thighs, and lower back. During one session Day received three hundred lashes, and the beatings continued into August. Day's flesh was shredded, his limbs swollen, his testicles oozed "a watery fluid," his scrotum had been sliced, and he vomited "a mixture of blood and bile" and excreted a bloody diarrhea.[82]

Practically everyone at the Zoo compound, including all nine members of Robinson's Annex cell, experienced torture as a consequence of the Dramesi-Atterberry escape. Robinson thinks extra guards were brought in so that the prisoners went through the torture sessions simultaneously, rather than sequentially, as before. Aside from the basic security concerns and the potential negative publicity stemming from an escape attempt, the guards and camp officials at the Zoo suffered great embarrassment, and therefore there was some personal vindictiveness in their retaliation. In retrospect, Robinson admits, "I don't think we dreamt of this much repercussion" from the escape attempt. "We thought through the glory of escape but not the trauma if it failed." In reassessing the longest period of sustained torture during his first four years in captivity, Robinson concluded that "a lot of it had to do with pure beatings. It had nothing to do with questions and answers. It was just a daily reminder of the wrongs that they claimed we had committed." The punishment went on long enough that it exceeded the point at which the North Vietnamese gained any useful information. In short, "there was nothing left to tell," and the tormentors "just wanted to make sure" that an escape attempt never happened again. The length of Hell Summer varied for each prisoner at the Zoo, from several weeks to two months. When the brutality finally came to a close, it ended a season of terror that few prisoners would ever experience again. Robinson recalls there being "an occasional slap around after that, but it was nothing, it wasn't organized. You pissed a guard off or something, and he might take a personal swing at you, but as far as the door swinging open and three guys coming in and grabbing you and holding you down and beating the shit out of you, it did exist, but it didn't happen to me."[83]

3

After Ho

On 2 September 1969 Ho Chi Minh, who more than any other individual symbolized the North Vietnamese war of national liberation, died at the age of seventy-five after battling chronic health problems stemming from tuberculosis and malaria. The international community paid tribute to the revolutionary leader by sending more than 22,000 messages of condolence to the government in Hanoi. The state funeral was held on 8 September at Hanoi's Ba Dinh Square, where twenty years earlier Ho had read the Proclamation of Independence of the Democratic Republic of Vietnam. The demonstration of national mourning drew more than one hundred thousand people.[1] In contrast to the dignified yet emotional observances in the capital city, the reaction to Ho's death among the guards and officials stationed at North Vietnam's prisoner-of-war camps was quite different. At Alcatraz, in the heart of Hanoi, Navy Commander Jeremiah Denton remembered that a camp official warned him not to offend the guards, given their highly charged state of mind; they "would be very irritable and unpredictable." Denton heeded the warning and "passed the order to cool it" to his fellow inmates, and wisely so. The guards at Alcatraz broke into a storage cell and took drugs and wine, and while messages of condolence from other countries were being read endlessly on the camp radio, they wept and got drunk. Even the officers appeared "badly shaken" to Denton, who studied their movements. They "wandered through their duties in a daze."[2]

Denton also noticed, "almost immediately," that "subtle changes began to take place . . . the camp administration was less harsh, and the [torture] purge petered out"; soon no one "was tortured for propaganda or military information." Although some prisoners continued until the very end of the war to be abused for disciplinary reasons, the pattern of behavior described by Denton extended to the other camps in North Vietnam as well. What caused the change? It seems unlikely that Ho Chi Minh had a personal hand in directing the torture of American POWs or their inclusion in North Vietnam's propaganda program.[3] From 1955 to 1969 Ho "had played a largely ceremonial role in the affairs of the country," according to his acclaimed biographer William J. Duiker. In fact, Ho delegated his authority to senior party colleagues. They deferred "to his experience in world affairs and in the strategy of revolution," but otherwise "his influence had declined."[4] Coinciding with Ho's death was a more aggressive approach by newly elected President Richard Nixon to achieve a successful conclusion to the war. In the spring of 1969 he advocated the "Go Public" campaign, which placed more emphasis on the plight of American POWs, and in early November 1969 he announced his Vietnamization plan, which outlined his program for withdrawing U.S. combat troops from Southeast Asia. With the possibility of a fast-approaching peace, North Vietnamese leaders had to be aware of international perceptions of its treatment of U.S. prisoners of war. Indeed, at a press conference on the exact day of the death of Ho Chi Minh, three recently released prisoners, Air Force Captain Wesley Rumble, Navy Lieutenant Robert Frishman, and Seaman Douglas Hegdahl, detailed the numerous atrocities committed by the North Vietnamese, and Frishman continued to recount the abuse as the group's unofficial spokesman in follow-up interviews.[5] Whatever the reason, most POWs marked the end of the torture era of captivity with the passing of Ho Chi Minh.

Emergency Appendectomy

In the fall of 1969 Bill Robinson faced a medical emergency that could have resulted in fatal consequences. At the time he felt "very fortunate" that the one major health crisis of his seven and a half years in captivity occurred after the death of Ho Chi Minh. Other than dysentery or an occasional boil, Robinson's health had been fairly good. After a weight loss of fifty or sixty pounds, his weight had stabilized at around 170 to 180 pounds, down from his capture weight of 240.[6] Fortunately for Robinson, his two roommates,

Neil Black and Art Cormier, were both PJs, and the two men "had a certain amount of medical training; they certainly weren't doctors, but when it came to their medical training versus what the doctors in the prison camp had, they were probably pretty well qualified." For several days Robinson had been experiencing lower abdominal pains, and because someone else in the prison camp had earlier experienced appendicitis, Black and Cormier concluded that Robinson probably had appendicitis. The diagnosis seemed logical, but convincing the North Vietnamese that Robinson needed medical treatment was a different matter altogether. The only way to get medical attention was to stop eating. "We were treated like dogs," a frustrated Robinson recalls. "If you think about it—you have friends who have dogs—when do they get concerned about the dogs? When they don't eat. That's the same way the Vietnamese felt about us—as long as we would eat the damn food, then there wasn't anything wrong with us." To convince the guards that something was seriously wrong, the men set one uneaten serving of food outside their cell after each meal, pretending that Bill was incapable of eating. The three men shared the remaining two meals for a period of three or four days. Sharing the remaining two rations "was tough, considering that under normal circumstances, the three rations were enough for one person; and now two rations had to feed three men." The uneaten meals caught the attention of the North Vietnamese, who sent in the camp doctor, but after looking at Robinson, he was not convinced that the POW had any type of illness and left, which forced the three men to continue their original idea another day or two. Then, one night, the North Vietnamese appeared without prompting, gathered Robinson, and escorted him to a bus to take him downtown.

At the time Robinson was barely able to walk and was hunched over and in severe pain, having received no medication of any kind. The windows in the bus had been blacked out. They loaded him behind the rear wheel, which meant that during the bus ride Robinson's stricken body absorbed every bump and shock caused by the cobblestone road and bomb craters. They arrived at what Robinson assumed was a hospital, where, still in the bus, he was examined by someone who he assumed was a doctor. The individual examining

Robinson held a flashlight and pricked the patient eighteen times in an attempt to draw blood. Robinson questioned the competency of his examiner, while conceding the difficulty of drawing blood in the back of a bus at night with only a flashlight for illumination. After his examiner finally drew the blood samples, several medical attendants had a discussion, and they started to remove him from the bus, but another patient arrived on the scene and they left Robinson on the bus so they could deal with their new case. Suddenly, the bus driver started the vehicle and, with Robinson still in the back, drove off to another hospital. This turn of events left Robinson in a state of concern and astonishment, and his outlook changed very little when he left the second hospital after the so-called doctors reviewed his case, only to send him to a third hospital. By this time a couple of hours had elapsed, but Robinson was eventually admitted to the third hospital. He was placed in "an old hospital bed with wooden slats on it, and basically a sheet over the slats, they didn't even have a mat" under the sheet. As Robinson lay on the bed, the attendants drew blood and went out and locked the door. After a rectal exam, Robinson received what he believed to be a massive dose of penicillin. Previously, someone had asked Robinson in broken English if he was allergic to penicillin. The following morning they returned and drew blood once more. Robinson was then told, again in broken English, that the doctor needed to operate. They actually solicited Robinson's permission. He questioned whether the operation was really necessary. The doctor replied, "Very necessary. If we don't operate, you don't live." With that choice, Robinson agreed to the operation.

He received a razor to shave himself. Once he completed this task, they walked him out of the room, into the hallway, and laid him on a stretcher. They apologetically covered his entire exposed body with a blanket; but the blanket was so small that they had to use two of them to cover him. Their justification, according to Robinson, "was that they didn't want anyone to know that an American was in the hospital." Robinson considered the obvious, the unlikelihood of any Vietnamese body requiring two blankets to cover it. At any rate, they wheeled Robinson to the operating room, pausing once along the way for a discussion before coming to a dead halt.

"As it turned out, they just couldn't wheel the stretcher [directly] into the operating room." There was a lip on the floor at the entrance to the operating room about six or eight inches high. To get Robinson into the room, the attendants had to carry the patient and the stretcher through the door. Four or five North Vietnamese were now involved in the process. They started to push him through the door when suddenly the man inside the room started screaming because he was the only attendant in the room and was saddled with bearing the weight of the patient alone. Additionally, the stretcher would barely fit through the door. So they reversed the process to place more attendants inside the room. In what was becoming a comedy of errors, the North Vietnamese, "after going through all of that trouble, placed the stretcher on the floor" and instructed Robinson to crawl up off the stretcher and onto the operating table on his own.

The insanity continued when they attempted to secure the patient to the table and discovered that the straps were about a foot short. The North Vietnamese decided to wrap Robinson in surgical gauze "from one end of the table to the other." The ensconced Robinson, while lying on his back, looked up to see a light fixture with a broken globe and "a bunch of dead bugs lying up beside the light." Robinson's imagination began to run wild, and he envisioned bugs falling from the light into his incisions and being sewn up inside him by inattentive doctors. All the assistants as well as the doctor were barefoot, except for the one female handling the surgical instruments. She wore wooden shoes. After administering a local anesthetic, the so-called medical team began the operation. For unknown reasons, the attendants rotated the table to such an extreme angle that Robinson feared he would be jettisoned onto the floor. To stabilize himself, he freed one arm and one leg from the gauze binding and supported himself during the operation. The local "had reduced the pain level to where it was tolerable," but Robinson could feel the doctor making his way to the appendix. When the doctor prepared to remove the appendix, he said, "Now you will feel pain." Robinson felt "a real strong blast" of pain—and that was it. After the doctor stitched up the patient, the attendants slid Robinson off the operating table onto the stretcher, backed out through the door, covered him with two blankets, and rolled him back down the hall. When they reached the recovery room, they deposited the patient and stretcher on the floor and instructed him to get up and get into the bed when he felt he was sufficiently strong.

After a couple of hours, Robinson had regained a little strength but still required some help to make it to the bed. The attendants brought Robinson a bowl of soup, "real thin noodles and a lot of water." To recover properly, he needed more nourishment, especially when several postoperative complications developed. As soon as the medication began to wear off, Robinson developed considerable pain, and he had trouble relieving himself. Apparently, his kidneys had shut down, and so a catheter was inserted to provide relief. Robinson began to improve, and a series of medications, albeit limited by most modern standards, allowed Robinson to discharge an intestinal worm about the diameter of his pinkie finger and eighteen to twenty-four inches long. Robinson's stay in the hospital lasted eight days. When he rejoined his roommates, he considered himself to be "in pretty good shape." He could move around, but only slowly, and he did need help with things such as hanging his mosquito netting and other activities that required stretching. His roommates washed his clothes for him two or three times and wanted to make sure that his health concerns remained a short-term rather than long-term problem. Despite the meager rations and poor diet, Robinson's age (he had just turned twenty-six) and his previously good health aided his recovery. His roommates gladly offered their food, but Robinson ate only his portion, which for him included a serving or two of fruit. The Vietnamese did not offer any fruit to Black or Cormier at that time, and when Robinson offered to share they declined, believing their friend needed the additional vitamins and nutrients more than they did. His total recovery took a few weeks, at which point Robinson felt "everything was back to normal." He suffered no long-term repercussions from the monthlong ordeal.

Families in Waiting

In response to the prisoner-of-war issue in Vietnam, the administration of President Lyndon B. Johnson believed that the humane

treatment and the eventual release of POWs would be more easily achieved if the North Vietnamese government was not publicly
condemned. Conflicted and uncertain over America's war aims and
military strategy, Johnson struggled with the press, suffered some
intense criticism, and never fully marshaled the country behind the
war effort. One specific consequence of his general failure with the
media was that he never rallied public support for the POWs. The
administration of President Richard M. Nixon abandoned Johnson's
"quiet diplomacy" and initiated the Go Public campaign in the
spring of 1969. The goals of the Go Public campaign were to obtain
a complete list of POWs in captivity, the release of infirm prisoners, third-party inspections of prison camps, and compliance with
the Geneva Convention. The Nixon administration also encouraged
individual citizens and private organizations to promote the objectives of the Go Public campaign.[7]

The largest of the family-led organizations to champion the cause
of POWs was the National League of Families of American Prisoners
and Missing in Southeast Asia (NLOF). The group, consisting primarily of the wives and parents of prisoners, formed in June 1969,
incorporated in May 1970, and opened a national headquarters in
Washington, D.C., in June 1970. Local branches in military communities such as Norfolk and Virginia Beach on the East Coast and San
Diego on the West Coast were vital hubs in the NLOF's network.
The original leaders of the NLOF were Sybil Stockdale, the first
chair of the Board of Directors, and Iris R. Powers, the first full-time
national coordinator. Louise Mulligan and Jane Denton were very
active members, as was Doris Day, Anne Purcell, Maureen Dunn,
Phyllis Galanti, and Valerie Kushner. NLOF representatives met, or
attempted to meet, with North Vietnamese representatives in Paris
on several occasions. The Texas businessman and U.S. Naval Academy graduate H. Ross Perot sponsored one of the largest NLOF
delegations in December 1969, "when fifty-eight wives and ninety-
four children boarded *The Spirit of Christmas*, bound for Paris. Only
three wives were allowed to meet with a four-member North Vietnamese delegation; they produced no concessions. Members of the
NLOF also testified before the US Congress on several occasions."[8]
In May 1970 Voices in Vital America (VIVA) joined the public rela-

tions campaign. VIVA developed one of the most enduring popular culture symbols of the entire war, the POW bracelet. Each bracelet contained the name, rank, and date of loss of a POW or MIA. People wore them as an expression of concern and commitment and vowed not to remove the bracelet until the POW was released or the MIA accounted for. Celebrities who wore the bracelets included Billy Graham, Bill Cosby, Bob Hope, Cher and Sonny Bono, and Princess Grace of Monaco. They sold for $2.50 for a nickel-plated bracelet and $3.00 for a copper bracelet, and VIVA raised millions of dollars for the POW/MIA cause.[9]

Under the umbrella of the national organization, state and local chapters of the National League of Families waged companion drives in behalf of POWs and MIAs, and the Robinsons joined the efforts in North Carolina. Ginger Hux, Bill's sister, remembers traveling to Raleigh each year to attend the North Carolina State Fair, where she and members of the Robinson clan met with other POW families to offer support to one another and to educate the general public. They sold buttons, bumper stickers, and VIVA bracelets to raise money for the NLOF, and they distributed leaflets and news items pertaining to POWs and MIAs. Jackie, Bill's older sister, Ginger, and his stepmother, Jessie, formed the core group making the annual ninety-mile pilgrimage to Raleigh. Other family members participated as their work schedules permitted. In addition to the state fair, Robinson's father, William, and his stepmother traveled extensively to the various POW/MIA meetings. They knew a lot of the POW families, especially in North Carolina, and they attempted to connect their nuclear family to the extended family of the POW community. The Robinsons were particularly close to and attended several events with the family of a fellow North Carolinian, Air Force Lieutenant Colonel James Hiteshew, who was shot down on 11 March 1967, leaving behind his wife, Billie, a thirteen-year-old son, Mike, and a ten-year-old daughter, Susan.[10]

In mid-April 1970 William and Jessie Robinson and Billie Hiteshew joined the family of Air Force Captain Norman Wells, a POW, and the family of Army Private First Class Darrell Johnson, an MIA, in the state capital to promote a letter-writing campaign. Not all North Carolinians possessed a basic understanding of the

POW situation, as Billie Hiteshew painfully learned during a visit to her grocery store in Goldsboro earlier in the month. When she informed a fellow shopper that her husband had been shot down in North Vietnam and had been a prisoner of war for three years, the woman expressed surprise and then asked, "Well, how long is his sentence?" Billie responded, "There are no sentences in North Vietnam." The exchange underscored the need to educate the American public about prisoner treatment and camp conditions. The families called for impartial inspections of prison facilities, assurances of adequate food and medical care, improved lines of communication between prisoners and their loved ones, and guarantees that prisoners would not be used for propaganda purposes. With public support, the families believed they could influence North Vietnamese treatment of the POWs. "We just want letters asking that these men be given their rights as prisoners of war under the Geneva Convention," pleaded William Robinson. "We don't care how short they are, either." The families intended to turn the letters over to the POW activist H. Ross Perot. "If Mr. Perot has any future conferences with officials from Hanoi or other governments, he'll be able to point to the letters as proof of Americans' concern," explained Jessie Robinson, referring to the Christmas mission to Paris sponsored by Perot the previous year. The four families that gathered in Raleigh supported the government's efforts to obtain information about their loved ones, but they said Perot's attempts offered "an extra bit of hope." Pressed by a 1 May deadline, the group intended to enlist Governor Bob Scott of North Carolina to help publicize their project.[11]

Jessie Robinson and Billie Hiteshew appeared together again in New Bern, North Carolina, in 1972 to hear a proposal from a Republican candidate for the U.S. Congress, Mack Howard. They were joined by John E. Davis, whose son Air Force Major Edgar F. Davis had been missing in action for four years; the senior Davis had been a prisoner of war himself in World War II. Lynda McGarvey, whose husband, Marine Lieutenant Colonel James McGarvey, had been missing since April 1967, was the final member of the party. The McGarveys had four children. Howard, a former Army major who served two tours in Vietnam, was proposing the formation of a "Tar Heel MIA-POW Family Report." Basically, "selected journalists from all over the state" would team "with the free world press of Japan, Canada," and similar nations to visit prison camps in Vietnam. They would deliver "news reports from the U.S. on the families and hopefully return with recorded news interviews" of Americans held in captivity. All four families expressed their gratitude to Howard for making the challenge to the news media, and as Jessie Robinson commented, "We will never give up trying to find some channel to improve contacts and to work for their return." The four families also desired that the issue "should be and remain one of total non-partisan concern." Additionally, they all agreed that the U.S. government should not make special concessions or bow to the demands of the North Vietnamese to secure the release of the POWs, saying that "their husbands or sons would not want America to take this course of action."[12]

The Robinsons had been more fortunate than others when it came to hearing from their son, Bill. For example, the wife of Captain Norman Wells, who partnered with the Robinsons on the Perot letter-writing campaign, had received only "eight letters from her husband in more than three years—and these were censored to about six lines each."[13] Before 1969 the families of American prisoners received a total of 620 letters written by 103 POWs.[14] From 20 December 1965 to 15 December 1969 Robinson wrote a total of seventeen letters to his parents, five in 1966, one in 1967, three in 1968, and seven in 1969. The first seven letters were written before the compulsory six-line, postcard-style format was instituted, which Robinson first used in July 1968; the earlier, less restrictive policy allowed him to ask a wide range of questions about life in North Carolina as well as to convey some measure of assurance about his own well-being. Beginning with his 18 July 1968 letter, Robinson was limited in what he could communicate, and his letters from July 1968 until December 1969 often repeated what became his standard refrain: "Dear Mom and Dad, [writing] To say I'm well in good health and doing just fine, hope same for you. Give my love to all and may we be together in the near future."[15] Also, Robinson always tried to comfort his family and remind them that his faith in God was strong. He longed for home and to be reunited with family and friends.

One exception to the postcard-format letters occurred on 3 December 1969, when Robinson sent instructions regarding Christmas packages. He informed his parents that "the D.R.V. [Democratic Republic of Vietnam] Government will again allow families . . . to send Christmas packages." To ensure the package arrived "fast and in perfect condition," he included a very specific and detailed set of procedures that had to be scrupulously followed, or the packages would not be delivered.

1. Everyone is allowed to receive only one package and not exceeding 3 Kg (appo. 6.6 lbs).

2. Following items are allowed: Dried food stuff, tonics in pill, tablets or capsules, tobacco together with pipes (no cigarettes). Personal articles. Soap, tooth brush, pastes, handkerchiefs, wash towels, underwear, scarf, pullovers, gloves and socks.

3. Food and medicine stuffs must be packed in hermetic and solid containers. Tonics must be packed in original containers from manufacturers.

In this letter Robinson acknowledged receipt of packages on 30 January and 29 September 1969.[16] Preparing the packages was a family activity coordinated by Bill's parents. It seemed to Bill's sister Ginger that they met once a month to gather pictures or personal items to send, and she believed that these items would help her brother stay abreast of happenings in North Carolina and in some way keep him connected to the family that he had left behind.[17]

Although the Robinsons received a considerable number of letters, they encountered periods when communication was infrequent or ceased altogether. After five letters in 1966, they received only one in 1967. From 7 December 1966 to 22 November 1968, they received a total of four letters. The pace picked up again in 1969, and the North Vietnamese even allowed Robinson, on two separate occasions, to mention his appendectomy, but he commented simply that he had undergone the surgery and suffered no complications. He gave no additional details. Once in a while the Robinsons received updates through various media outlets, such as the *Life* magazine spread in April 1967 and an Associated Press (AP) story in March 1970 that was carried by their local newspapers. The AP story, written by Daniel De Luce, who had just completed an eighteen-day tour of North Vietnam, was accompanied by a photo of Robinson. The photo, showing a young girl armed with a rifle escorting Robinson through the jungle, was actually the one taken a few days after his shootdown and capture in 1965. At the time the Robinsons had no idea how important the photo had become to North Vietnam's internal propaganda campaign. De Luce reported that the North Vietnamese admitted to holding 320 prisoners, 100 fewer than the number given by the U.S. Department of Defense, and that officials in Hanoi maintained that "prisoners have been treated humanely . . . [and] that agitation to try prisoners as 'war criminals' is a closed chapter." When questioned about the emotional pain and suffering of POW families, North Vietnamese spokesmen quipped, "We understand the concern of mothers and wives. Perhaps Vietnamese mothers should go to the United States and ask for their children and husbands killed by U.S. bombs and shells, and the return of their homes and schools, bridges, and roads." De Luce gave no indication of ever having met Bill Robinson.[18]

The Robinsons did, however, catch a glimpse of their son in a television news show on American POWs in early 1970. The rare film footage was obtained by Roger Zion, a Republican congressman from Indiana during a visit to Paris, where he met with North Vietnamese representatives and delivered a letter signed by 406 members of the U.S. Congress, demanding the humane treatment of American prisoners of war. Analysts counted about seventy-five POWs in the film and identified twenty whose names had not appeared previously on any POW list. U.S. government officials notified the Robinsons that the film would be shown nationwide. A Greenville television station intended to broadcast the film in northeastern North Carolina on one of their nightly news programs, and the station invited the Robinsons to Greenville to review the footage "as many times as they wished." Technicians played the tape at slow speeds for the Robinsons so that they could examine every individual prisoner and inspect every detail in the group scenes. With this advantage, they easily recognized their son. "We knew it was Billy as soon as we saw a close-up of him singing" at a Christmas service, Robinson's father explained. "He looked exceptionally well, as if he were holding his normal weight, a fact that makes us feel much better about him." Jessie agreed. "He had a pleasant expression on his face," she declared. "This delighted us because the picture we had seen of him was taken over there and used in a *Life* magazine article in 1967. It was just an individual head shot, but to us he looked dejected. And he appeared so thin at the time, too." The Robinsons had been particularly concerned about their son's health after hearing the news of his appendectomy several months earlier. "Although he assured us he was fine, we have been fearful ever since that he had not received good care," Jessie Robinson revealed in a newspaper interview. "The way he looked [on TV] eased our minds somewhat." The film reassured Robinson's father as well. "I just can't describe the wonderful feeling having seen it," William said; "I get chill bumps every time I think or tell about it. We just have more hope than ever that he will get home yet." Jessie attributed the release of the film to recent efforts "to use worldwide public opinion to prevail upon the North Vietnamese," and she challenged concerned Americans "to sign petitions . . . and to write letters to anyone who has influence." The Go Public Campaign launched by President Nixon and the activism of the National League of Families brought some measure of comfort to the hurting POW families and on some level diminished their feelings of helplessness. They continued to wait, however, and they faced an uncertain future.[19]

The Pigsty and OCS

Although the families had no way of knowing, the Zoo compound, "the most volatile of the Northern camps during 1969," was transformed into one of "the quietest during 1970." Among the changes was the North Vietnamese transfer of a number of prisoners to a new camp at Dan Hoi, nine miles northwest of Hanoi, and reorganization of the Zoo. The Zoo had always possessed the character of a distinct set of camps within a larger compound, and the renovations preserved that identity. The prisoners remained "segregated by a labyrinth of walls and screens that in effect formed separate" facilities; at the same time the Pigsty, one of the Zoo's original buildings, was enlarged to include four rooms holding twenty POWs. Joining Robinson at the reconfigured Pigsty were the naval aviators Everett Alvarez (shot down 5 August 1964), Jerry Coffee (3 February 1966), Dick Ratzlaff (20 March 1966), Robert Woods (12 October 1966), and Air Force flyers Richard (Pop) Keirn (24 July 1965), Tom Browning (8 July 1966), Norm McDaniel (20 July 1966), Mike Brazelton (7 August 1966), Norm Wells of North Carolina (29 August 1966), Mike Lane (2 December 1966), John Davies (4 February 1967), Gary Sigler (29 April 1967), and Harold Johnson (30 April 1967). Robinson's longtime companions, Neil Black and Art Cormier, were also part of the group as well as Dave Carey, Read Mecleary, Harry Monlux, and John Borling, who had been with him at the Zoo Annex. They enjoyed nearly unprecedented freedom of movement, and their captors permitted them to mingle inside or outside their building.[20]

The new setting allowed the group to revisit an issue that originated at the Zoo Annex in 1968: battlefield commissions for the three enlisted men, Robinson, Black, and Cormier. One participant in the ongoing conversation remembered, "Once the commissioning idea was hatched, it consumed a lot of time." The discussions centered on the Air Force regulations covering battlefield commissions. The officers of Annex cell no. 3 agreed wholeheartedly that the three enlisted men, by their behavior and actions, had earned the promotions. Robinson, Black, and Cormier had "kept faith in America during four long brutal years, from 1965 to 1969," explained Air Force Major Leo Thorsness, a member of cell no. 3 whose actions before his capture later earned him the Medal of Honor. All three had "withstood individual torture, kept their integrity, and served honorably in terrible living conditions with inadequate food. Despite all of this, they had kept their dignity intact." The officers of cell no. 3 were united in their belief that the three enlisted men "exhibited heroic qualities." No one could recall a battlefield commission for an enlisted airman during the Korean War. The Navy officers were asked for their opinions, since the Marines fell "under the Navy . . . and have had a lot of battlefield commissions." While the question was under review, some POWs worried that if the North Vietnamese found out that Robinson, Black, and Cormier had been promoted, the new officers would be exposed to more torture. The three enlisted men addressed that concern by stating: "We have been tortured already; we have nothing to lose." Having reached a consensus in cell no. 3, the POWs needed the approval of the Zoo Annex's SRO, Air Force Captain Konrad Trautman. Trautman was located in cell no. 5, a fair distance away, which presented some communication obstacles. The prisoners passed a message written on toilet paper through a small hole in the wall separating cell no. 3 and cell no. 4, and then the note was attached to a stone using rice paste as glue and "airmailed" across the compound by a strong-armed prisoner, whereupon it reached cell yard no. 5. Trautman reviewed the proposal and, in consultation with his staff of eight officers, gave his approval. Upon receiving confirmation, the members of cell no. 3 administered the oath of office. "Never had the oath been taken more seriously—nor, likely taken in prison pajamas," recalled Thorsness. "Cormier, Black, and Robinson each repeated the oath standing at attention and proud. It was a solemn, memorable occasion." The newly commissioned officers then embarked on an "in-cell Officer Candidate School."[21]

When Robinson arrived at the Pigsty in summer 1970, he, Black, and Cormier underwent additional officer candidate training. Everyone involved took the process seriously. Political and military topics covered a wide spectrum, from Adlai Stevenson to Douglas MacArthur. But lighthearted discussions surfaced, too. Robinson jokes that one initial topic covered the differences between the officers' club and the enlisted men's club, and the three candidates had to decide whether they were "going to sit around in the officers' club and drink martinis and sing college" fight songs or "sit in the enlisted club and drink beer" and tell dirty jokes. Each of the Pigsty officers contributed to the curriculum, but the Air Force Academy graduates Tom Browning and John Borling and Naval Academy graduates Dave Carey and Read Mecleary assumed leading roles. Some of the sessions were structured and some were not; most of the course content focused on military professionalism and the proper deportment of officers. A top priority for the officers was to pass along the accumulated wisdom that they had gleaned from past experiences, whether personal or professional. And some of the older officers pulled the two younger enlisted men, Robinson and Black, under their wings for one-on-one conversations. At the time it seemed as though the OCS went on "forever." Every time Robinson turned around, someone had a lesson or advice to offer. In reality, it lasted about six months. Robinson benefited greatly from the mentoring his cellmates provided.[22]

Robinson's first stint at the Pigsty coincided with North Vietnamese aspirations to produce propaganda in the form of film footage, photographs, paintings, or drawings. They wanted "to impress a still skeptical public" with their humane treatment of American POWs. Robinson's group had access to a basketball court, a Bible, and a guitar, and they learned that adjacent buildings had Ping-Pong equipment, volleyball, and other offerings. To some degree their captors succeeded: exhibitions in Moscow and Paris displayed paintings and drawings by several POWs that suggested that they had recreation outlets available. Inducements were offered throughout the Zoo compound, and the North Vietnamese extended special favors to encourage cooperation.[23] Robinson and his Pigsty cellmates discussed the appropriate responses to the North Vietnamese gestures. The rules agreed on by Robinson's cell were that the POWs could participate in sporting activities and use the amenities for a reasonable period, provided those privileges were available to the rest of the camp. Otherwise, they decided they would cease all activities. Satisfied that the opportunities had been shared throughout the camp, Robinson and his cellmates began to play basketball. The restrictive environments of the past and the prisoners' prolonged immobility had caused a deterioration in their muscle fitness and coordination. In describing some of the first basketball games at the Pigsty, Robinson admitted that the POWs looked "spastic" and "out of place" as their bodies relearned the game that many had played as kids. Rather quickly, they regained some dexterity, and then suddenly cameras appeared on the scene.[24]

The POWs immediately returned to their cells and sat on their bunks. Their response confused and upset the North Vietnamese, and the guards came and slammed the cell doors shut and put the

prisoners under lockdown, which led to "a couple of days of negotiations of what would and would not happen." During the discussions, the prisoners contemplated two realities. First, the North
Vietnamese had furnished the sporting equipment and other materials without subjecting the POWs to any recent mistreatment, and
they did not require or compel public or recorded statements. The
items in question improved the standard of living for the prisoners.
Jerry Coffee identified the rejuvenating effect of the various games.
"After a closely contested volleyball game," Coffee "was struck
with the realization of the importance of fun" in the prisoners' lives.
Until that moment, he had forgotten how much he "had missed just
plain fun." Putting the situation in this context, Robinson declared:
"We can't deny the truth. If we deny the truth, then we are no better than they are." Second, and what Robinson viewed as "the most
important" variable, "some of the guys were still listed as missing
in action and had not even been allowed to write a letter home."
Their families had no proof that they were still alive. One photograph contained the potential to grant a family a measure of relief
by supplying visual evidence of a particular POW's well-being. Personally, Robinson believed a "loved one knowing not only that [his
or her POW] was alive but was in good health" superseded any potential propaganda value the North Vietnamese might derive from
a photo. Not everyone agreed. Ultimately, the cell's senior ranking
officer issued a rule of wide latitude in the event that North Vietnamese photographers returned to the basketball courts. Individual
POWs could exercise their own prerogative and allow themselves
to be photographed or not. Once the POWs resolved the impasse,
they resumed the basketball games. The photographers reemerged,
snapped some pictures, and the North Vietnamese proved their
cunning by "coming and taking the basketball away."[25]

The Son Tay Raid and Camp Unity

In late May 1968, the North Vietnamese opened a prison camp some
twenty miles northwest of Hanoi, near the town of Son Tay. It was
a small camp, never exceeding more than fifty-five captives, with
very primitive physical conditions, but the spacious cells that ac-

commodated as many as eight prisoners apiece helped inspire the name Camp Hope. The prison camp is best known as the site of one of the most daring and sophisticated rescue raids of the Vietnam War.[26] The U.S. military began a feasibility study on 5 June 1970, and two months later a task group was formed to plan and carry out the raid. Training commenced on 20 August 1970 at Eglin Air Force Base, Florida. In short, Army Rangers were to be ferried to Son Tay by five Air Force rescue helicopters, supported by five A-1E Skyraiders and two C-130E Combat Talons. The plan called for one of the five helicopters to crash-land inside the compound and to neutralize the guard detail. The Rangers in the other four helicopters were to be dropped outside the prison with orders to force their way into the compound to complete the operation. Training concluded in mid-November, and the team quickly assembled at Takhli Royal Air Force Base, Thailand. To arrive before an approaching typhoon, the U.S. military launched Operation Ivory Coast on the night of 20 November 1970. It would become known as the Son Tay Raid. The carefully scripted operation drifted slightly off course when three of the four helicopters mistakenly attacked a North Vietnamese sapper (fortifications and demolitions) school just one-fourth of a mile from the prison. Approximately fifty Rangers penetrated the site and engaged in a firefight with the enemy. The rescue force realized their mistake within a matter of minutes and reboarded the helicopters and advanced on the actual target. In their wake, they "left scores of People's Army of Vietnam (PAVN) troops dead or bewildered and so confused they could not interfere with operations going on nearby." At Son Tay, the fourth helicopter had already successfully inserted its team of Rangers and the search was under way. Simultaneously, the Navy conducted diversionary maneuvers, including the simulation of the mining of Haiphong Harbor, in what constituted the largest night carrier operation of the entire war. The Navy jets "completely befuddled" the North Vietnamese air defense system: several radar operators erroneously reported B-52 attacks, and one confused operator reported that "an atomic bomb had been dropped on Hanoi."[27]

Despite months of preparation, training, and the successful tactical execution of the plan, no prisoners were found at Camp Hope.

What happened to the POWs? In explaining the absence of prison-ers, two primary theories have emerged. Some analysts conclude that intelligence leaks alerted the North Vietnamese to the impend-ing raid, which allowed them to relocate the prisoners. Other ana-lysts believe that poor preraid air reconnaissance prevented the U.S. military from discovering that the prisoners had been moved. The latter explanation purports that the camp's well water had become contaminated, which forced the relocation of the prisoners. Also, bad weather in the days leading up to the raid combined with the eagerness to launch the mission and resulted in the erroneous re-connaissance reports.[28] Despite the failure to recover any prisoners, the Son Tay Raid clearly raised security concerns for the North Viet-namese. Almost immediately after the rescue attempt, an explosion of construction activity commenced at the Hoa Lo prison. Within a matter of weeks, the North Vietnamese moved more than 340 POWs, including Bill Robinson and the residents of the Zoo, to the reconfigured Hoa Lo prison. The transfer occurred with no warning or explanation.[29]

Most of them were moved in one night, and "the only thing we left the Zoo with were the clothes on our backs," Robinson re-called. "The rest of it [their belongings] was left behind." With un-precedented security concerns, the North Vietnamese meticulously searched the POWs' few possessions for contraband and later re-turned all approved items to the prisoners. According to Robinson, "They went through everything we had and we got back what they wanted us to have, and what they didn't want us to have, we didn't get back." News of the Son Tay Raid reached the American POWs in a fragmentary fashion. When prisoners who had been held near Camp Hope were moved as part of the consolidation process, they could report to their new campmates only that "something had hap-pened over there." New shootdowns, numbering fewer than twenty in 1971, added a few details to the accumulating knowledge of the rescue attempt, but Robinson did not hear a complete or workable story of the raid until after his release in 1973. Nevertheless, the res-cue attempt immediately affected Robinson and his fellow POWs. Not wanting to stand by passively, they made contingency plans in the event of another rescue attempt. The prisoners assumed that if American forces landed in a prison compound again, the guards "would kill everybody they could rather than let them be rescued." In fact, the prisoners realized that their consolidation made them "much more vulnerable . . . sort of like shooting fish in the barrel," when "compared to being in isolation and small groups." After evaluating their situation and surroundings, the POWs determined that in the event of a subsequent rescue effort, they had "the responsibility to remain alive for five minutes" once an operation was under way. Lacking offensive weapons, the prisoners devised a defense strategy, and each cell member received an assignment. One group of prisoners was tasked with collecting the bed boards and barricading the doors to keep the guards out. Another group would monitor the windows on the cell doors or cell walls in case a guard inserted a rifle through the opening to spray the room with bullets. Their job was to grab the weapon or obstruct the shooter's line of fire. The prisoners considered every possibility to improve their chances of survival. They even decided they would wrap themselves in a "blanket or layers of blankets to form a makeshift body armor that might deflect a ricocheting bullet."[30]

The Son Tay Raid caused an immediate improvement in prisoner morale, and for many prisoners the transfer to the Hanoi Hilton marked a turning point in their captivity more dramatic than the death of Ho Chi Minh. Indeed, the changed atmosphere coaxed the prisoners into renaming the Hanoi Hilton Camp Unity, signifying the dawn of a new era in the former place of horrors. "From that December day 1970 until the day we were released we lived in a world that was as different from that in which we lived before as day and night," commented Commander James Stockdale. "We still had guards. We still had communications problems. I spent a few weeks in irons as did several others, and all that jazz. But it was really a different emotional and environmental situation." Senior ranking officers such as Stockdale, who spent years in solitary confinement or prolonged isolation, welcomed the new arrangements, and for a time the atmosphere at Camp Unity resembled that at a high school reunion. The men greatly appreciated the accelerated lines of communication. It had sometimes taken forty-eight hours to traverse the chain of command by tap code to ask and answer a question, but now they reveled in the face-to-face interaction.[31] The changes were somewhat less dramatic for Robinson, who had eight cellmates at the Zoo Annex in March 1968 and nineteen when he moved into the Pigsty in mid-1970. Despite the improvements, the POWs knew that they were not on the verge of being released. Therefore, they continued the familiar practice of exchanging their personal biographies with the prisoners they were meeting for the first time. Each POW worked to mentally compile a list of prisoner names to be able to assist in a full accounting of missing American servicemen once the war was over and the POWs were released. When the list reached an unmanageable number, the POWs shifted to familiarization rather than memorization. The goal was to be able to pick a name off a list instead of reciting the complete list verbatim. Additionally, one memorization strategy involved the year of a POW's shootdown date. Those shot down in 1965, for example, learned the names of all others who had been shot down during that year, and so on. This technique lightened "the burden of having one person remember" the names of every POW. Thus, at Camp Unity Robinson and his fellow prisoners busied themselves with a critical intelligence assignment.[32]

The larger cells at Camp Unity necessitated careful planning and cooperation to avoid chaos, confusion, and contention. Sometimes simple matters such as bathing and sharing toiletries required mediation. The North Vietnamese, looking to avoid predictability, alternated the bathing schedule of the POWs, allowing half of Robinson's cellmates to bathe at one time on some occasions, and at other times they permitted the entire group to go in a single session. The first time half of the group bathed, the second half discovered when their turn came that all the water had been used, and the POWs called a mandatory meeting. Because there was a limited amount of surface water at Camp Unity, Robinson's cell decided that, in the interest of fairness, each prisoner "got one bucket to get wet and two buckets to rinse off." Everyone was encouraged to follow the terms of the rationing agreement or face the wrath of angry cellmates. Once this problem was solved, another surfaced. Despite his having lived under the authority of the North Vietnamese communists for more than five years, Robinson's one forthright attempt at "the socialist way of doing things" failed miserably. Sufficiently supplied with toiletries, Robinson and his cellmates threw all their soap and toothpaste into one of the cell's corners. The rules were simple: "When you wanted to brush your teeth you would get some toothpaste, and when you wanted to take a shower you grabbed a bar of soap." An astonished and dismayed Robinson soon discovered the entire cell was "out of soap and out of toothpaste." What ensued next "was one of the most interesting room meetings" to occur during his entire time in captivity, as a group of hardened and torture-scarred prisoners stepped forward to express their dissatisfaction with this turn of events. Speaking as one of the old-timers, Robinson interjected: "I know how to make my soap last. I know how to make my toothpaste last." It was the first time in three years that he had been without toothpaste because he, like many others, had learned to survive during the periods of scarcity. The conference ruled that from that point on there would be no further collectivization of soap and toothpaste, and they would revert to the principles of private ownership: "what's mine is mine, and what's yours is yours."[33]

Most historical accounts of Camp Unity stress the innovative and wide array of classes organized and conducted by the POWs. They compiled a list of traditional topics such as history, political science, foreign languages, mathematics, music, art, and literature as well as hobby-oriented offerings such as chess, beekeeping, poultry farming, skiing, and auto maintenance.[34] Robinson marveled at "how many people couldn't describe how to change a tire on a car," so he lent his expertise on mechanical things, such as where the jack is located, finding the spare tire, how to remove the lug nuts, and the use of tools. His favorite group, however, was the toastmasters' club. Very popular among the POWs, the toastmasters' club provided tips and training on the practice of public speaking. Robinson often sat in on the sessions and found them interesting, but the fractious or contentious tone of some of the speeches, coupled with his own lack of confidence in his public debating skills, made it difficult for him to be a regular participant. Robinson preferred low-key, personal discussions with his cellmates or other POWs.[35]

Lost Souls

Robinson and several of his roommates left Camp Unity in October 1971 and returned to the Pigsty building at the Zoo compound. There they faced an unusual challenge, one that, strangely enough, was led by two of their fellow POWs, Marine Lieutenant Colonel Edison Miller and Navy Commander Walter Eugene (Gene) Wilber. Miller and Wilber had earned reputations as renegade senior officers "who had embraced their indoctrinators' concept of the war and were disseminating it in return for favorable treatment."[36] On 4 July 1971, while at Camp Unity, the two turncoats made an antiwar tape in which they classified American involvement in Vietnam as illegal, referred to themselves as war criminals, denounced the Code of Conduct, and asked for parole in order to return home.[37] The North Vietnamese broadcast the message publicly as well as throughout the prison network, which caused American POWs "to recoil" in anger and astonishment.[38] Miller and Wilber continued their divisive behavior at the Pigsty into the fall of 1971. Robinson's cell was in the same building as the two collaborators', and he and his cellmates dealt directly with their attempts to manipulate the POWs. The North Vietnamese gave Miller and Wilber keys to each of the cells and allowed them to function as turnkeys, or guards, meaning they would unlock the cell doors when the prisoners were permitted to go outside and relock them upon their return. When Robinson and the others learned that Miller and Wilber had been designated as turnkeys, they refused to leave their cells and informed the North Vietnamese that they would not tolerate such treatment. The frustrated North Vietnamese "got mad and locked the doors" and "stormed off and came back a few minutes later and unlocked the doors," at which point the Americans went outside. This outcome was exactly what the POWs hoped for, and they felt that they had won a "major battle" with their captors.[39]

Not long after this incident, another occurred that resulted in a renewed test of wills. The customary procedure when a POW returned to his cell was to turn and face his captors before the door was closed and locked. One day, as the normal routine played out, Miller and Wilber prepared to shut the door. The closest prisoner to the door used his foot as a wedge and pushed back, stating, "This ain't happening." Everyone in the cell was "just taken aback by the whole scene." Tempers flared and Robinson's cell was "ready to kick ass and not take any names." This second attempt at humiliating the Americans also failed. From that point, the North Vietnamese and their two conspirators adopted a less confrontational approach, although the two still raised the ire of the prisoners. Waiting until after the North Vietnamese guards had secured the POWs for the night, Miller and Wilber would select a particular cell and stand by its window and attempt to persuade the other prisoners that they "were taking the wrong approach" and that "the Vietnamese people were good people." They accused the prisoners of being unnecessarily antagonistic and unruly toward the North Vietnamese, who were justified in punishing them. They further suggested that if the Americans condemned the war publicly, they would be rewarded with better treatment. Robinson and his cellmates were not convinced. "We tried to be respectful of their rank [as senior officers], but we didn't have anything to do with their propaganda," Robinson explained. The actions and rhetoric of Miller and Wilber overstepped the principle of freedom of speech in the minds of the POWs. Within Robinson's cell there were men who "disagreed with the war, with the conduct [of the war], disagreed with a lot of things that were going on" at the time. They expressed their opinions freely, and the differences of opinion were "totally acceptable." By contrast, Miller and Wilber were not simply expressing their opinions. Their public statements were being used to help the enemy in a time of war. Moreover, the two served as informants for the North Vietnamese, and their reports led directly to the punishment of several individuals, actions "totally unacceptable" to Robinson and the other prisoners.[40]

Undeterred, the duo of defectors remained steadfast in their efforts, and the POWs resiliently resisted their appeals. "It was almost a daily thing for weeks on end, talking about the same things over and over again," recalled Robinson, "even though we were convinced we weren't going to change their minds, and we knew damn well they weren't going to change ours, but we still felt like we had to try." Throughout the process, the prisoners of the Pigsty did not "belittle" Miller and Wilber; in fact, they "referred to them as Lost Souls" and worked desperately to bring "them back into the fold."[41] What drove the two collaborators to take such extreme measures? Robinson's cellmate Navy Captain Dave Carey has pondered this question in the years since their release and has reached very different conclusions about the two Lost Souls. "I think the Colonel [Miller] was the only totally amoral person I've ever known," Carey bluntly stated. "As soon as he was shot down and captured, he recognized immediately that the game had changed and decided to cooperate with his captors." Although he disagreed with Wilber's message and methods, Carey was a bit more sympathetic toward his fellow naval aviator. It was widely believed that Wilber had suffered a mild stroke immediately after his capture in June 1968, and in his "weakened condition and intensive exposure to propaganda," he fell victim to "something close to brainwashing." Wilber's vulnerability stemmed in part from "carrying a terrible load of guilt for the death" of his radar intercept officer, Lieutenant Bernard Rupinski, who was killed by a missile during their shootdown. Carey also suspected that Wilber worried that if he were tortured or severely punished, he would surely die. Thus, he chose self-preservation above all else.[42] Regardless of their motivations, neither Edison Miller nor Gene Wilber recanted his statements or repented his deeds.

A Maturing Servant

When given the chance to participate in the educational activities at Camp Unity, Robinson opted for more intimate conversations with other POWs, especially those who demonstrated a high level of maturity, experience, and common sense. By his own admission, he coveted their counsel on personal and professional matters and intended to apply what he learned from them once he had the opportunity to resume his life as a free man. The letters he wrote home between late 1970, following the Son Tay Raid, and November 1972 indicate that he was thinking of the future and his eventual release, and he resolved to pursue his goals in an honorable manner. In a rare note to his grandparents, just before Christmas 1971, Robinson expressed his thanks to Gene and Geneva for their love and support over the years. Reflecting on what he had endured as a prisoner of war, he confidently informed his grandparents, "I can shoulder a lot." Stronger, but still sentimental, Robinson confessed, "I hope I can make you very proud of your oldest grandson."[43] Robinson's correspondence reveals, in addition to his hopes for reuniting with family and friends, his expectations for financial success and his guarded approach to marriage. He received guidance on money matters from the more senior POWs and began to quiz his parents as early as August 1970 about how they were managing his money for their collective benefit. Nearly a year and a half later, Robinson offered specific counsel to his parents regarding investments: "I hope all my funds are in the Ten Percent Program [military savings deposit program] or better and that we are all getting maximum allowances, most important, sit tight." Robinson's "sit tight" remark did not mean that he viewed his release as imminent, which would have placed him in a position to direct his own affairs, but reflected a modicum of concern about his parents' fiduciary choices. Several months later he learned that his father had used some of the account funds to start a successful service station. He felt reassured by the news and recognized their efforts by appreciatively remarking, "Thanks a million about my funds."[44] After his release, Robinson became aware of a different version of his parents' handling of his assets.

In addition to serving as financial overseers, William and, in particular, Jessie assumed the role of matchmaker for their imprisoned son. From their home in North Carolina the two parents filtered information to Bill about potential romantic partners. Beverly, Robinson's girlfriend at the time of his deployment to Vietnam, continued to express her concerns for him immediately after his capture by staying in touch with his family. Robinson wrote five letters to her between June 1966 and December 1967, but by late summer 1966 she had ceased to communicate with Robinson's parents, and he was left to assume that she had moved on with her life.[45] Out of the blue, Jane's name appeared in three letters sent by his parents in mid- to late 1968. Robinson and Jane had dated seriously before his enlistment in the Air Force. It was Jane who had broken off the engagement because she did not want to be married to an enlisted man. Now Robinson had apparently gained some form of enhanced status in Jane's mind by becoming a POW, and she seemed willing to overlook his lowly rank.[46] In November 1970 Jessie mentioned Jane for the first time since 1968. "Fill me in," he asked his stepmother, and "extend my holiday [Christmas] and birthday greeting to Jane." Apparently, Robinson remembered her birthday from their previous involvement. An unexpected word from a young woman would lift the spirits of any POW, and Robinson was no exception.[47]

The earlier breakup with Jane still troubled Robinson, however, and her renewed attention confused him. Therefore, he proceeded cautiously. "I would like to hear from her, with pictures," he told his stepmother, but only on the condition that "it can be made clear that it's been a long time and may be longer. I feel I should not commit myself at this time." Still, he did not close the door completely, instructing his stepmother, "Do what you think right, ok?" For the next seven months, Robinson communicated very little with his parents, writing a two-line letter in February 1971 and a one-line note in April. When the tempo of letters picked up again in June 1971, Robinson casually referred to Jane in a greeting to include friends, but a month later, after receiving a photo, he added a note for Jane in a letter to his parents: "Hi Jane, you look great, been a long time."[48] Robinson did not refer to Jane again until 4 December 1971, and at that time he stated to his parents his future intentions toward her in unmistakable terms: "I don't know what is happening at home as far as Jane is concerned. I may be worried about something that doesn't even exist. But just in case, I want to make myself clear. I've been away a long time and have changed very much. I have many plans for the future none of which include Jane. Please don't let her count on something that doesn't exist. I want to start anew, day one beginning when I come home."[49] The 4 December letter was the last time he mentioned Jane, but he certainly did not lose his interest in women. "I hear there is a new crop of girls around," Robinson remarked to his parents in response to news from home. "Send some pictures," he requested. A few months short of his seventh anniversary in captivity, Robinson joked with his parents, who were preparing for summer vacation, that he also had plans for "a long vacation . . . with lots of dear hunting," but he did not "plan to close in for the kill" any time soon.[50] Despite the playful banter, Robinson spent countless hours with his fellow POWs discussing the keys to a successful romantic relationship.

To cope with the uncertainty, some prisoners debated all aspects of their status as single or married men. One mindset held that "young marriages were going to be in trouble" because the bonds of love were still forming and would not survive the separation. Others disagreed, arguing that "old marriages were going to be in trouble because the young were still in love," whereas an older partner desired stability and security over romance, especially if children were involved. No consensus among the POWs was ever reached, and a large segment of the prison population felt it would be easier on them if their status were simply reversed. Single men believed married men held the advantage, while the husbands and fathers deemed the bachelors to have the advantage. As the months and years in limbo passed, the prisoners "learned to read between the lines" of each arriving letter, and some were able to prepare themselves for bad news. When Robinson's parents explained that Beverly was no longer communicating with them, they did not offer an explanation. By then Robinson had sensed "a coolness" between himself and his former girlfriend that should not have existed in a committed relationship. Robinson observed firsthand the heartbreak that some POWs encountered while in captivity. On Christmas Day 1971 his cellmate Everett Alvarez read, in a letter from his mother, that his wife Tangee had left him; he subsequently received word that she had remarried. "I think Everett was prepared" for the news, Robinson postulated, "but I don't think he accepted it" at the time. In fact, Alvarez held onto hope until his release. Robinson believed that some POWs operated under the mindset that nothing was final "until all avenues had been exhausted." The POWs realized that when dealing with the matters of the heart, the issue was not "the adversity that you were dealt but how you dealt with it that made a difference." In the end, there would be happy reunions and tragic betrayals, but the mills of time ground excruciatingly slow for all the POWs.[51]

From December 1970 to February 1973 Robinson was moved back and forth between Camp Unity and the Pigsty. Over the years, some POWs became known for their communication skills, some for their daring escape attempts, and some for their ability to withstand torture and long stints in solitary confinement. Bill Robinson developed a reputation for servanthood. His actions were manifested in subtle and not-so-subtle ways. Smoking became an important ritual for the POWs. Even during the torture era, when rations were meager, the North Vietnamese consistently supplied the POWs with cigarettes three times a day. By the time of the consolidation at Camp Unity, the allotment had doubled. Though some bartered their tobacco for other commodities, many POWs found smoking to be cathartic and a crucial segment of their daily routine. For military men, establishing and maintaining a routine was an essential coping mechanism during the ordeal of captivity. The prison schedule, which deviated little throughout the course of the war, aided the prisoners in this regard: wake-up occurred at 6:00 A.M., morning meal between 10:00 and 11:00, afternoon meal between 3:00 and 5:00, lights out at 9:00 P.M.[52] On Sundays, however, the North Vietnamese did not "ring the gong" to roust the prisoners at 6:00 A.M., and some POWs, including Robinson, opted to sleep in occasionally. Straying from this pattern proved problematic for a prisoner accustomed to or dependent on an early morning cigarette, a situation Robinson faced at Camp Unity. As he understood, the United States had bombed one of the major cigarette factories in North Vietnam; although the prisoners still received their tobacco ration, they now had to roll their own cigarettes. Robinson mastered the rolling technique and often rolled ten or twenty cigarettes at a time so that he would have them available for those five-thumbed POWs who had trouble rolling their own. One Sunday morning the cache of cigarettes had been exhausted; it also happened to be a morning on which Robinson decided to sleep late. Rather than wait until Robinson arose, one impatient prisoner woke him and asked him when he planned to start rolling cigarettes. Instead of responding in anger, Robinson groggily but good-naturedly obliged the request.[53]

This seemingly small gesture illustrates the way Robinson dealt with the individual needs of his fellow prisoners, and some appreciated his sensitivity and discretion, among them Air Force Major Fred Vann Cherry. A Korean War veteran and the first and highest-

ranking African American shot down and captured in North Vietnam, Cherry commanded the respect and admiration of virtually
every POW who encountered him. He embodied raw courage and
quiet dignity, and his ability to withstand pain and torture had become legendary. He sustained numerous injuries—a severely dislo-
cated shoulder, a broken left wrist, and a broken left ankle—when
he ejected from his plane on 22 October 1965. The North Vietnamese
operated on Cherry's shoulder in January 1966 and put the pilot
in an upper body cast, but complications led to a potentially fatal
infection. Multiple surgeries followed; the North Vietnamese doctors poured gasoline in his wounds during one operation, believing
it contained antiseptic properties. Cherry's white cellmate, Navy
Lieutenant (j.g.) Porter Halyburton, tended to his every need during
his long recovery in a remarkable display of solidarity that thwarted
the North Vietnamese' plan to promote racial tensions among the
prisoners.[54]

Robinson befriended Cherry "sometime after the Son Tay Raid"
when they bunked next to each other at Camp Unity. The two men
had grown up a mere eighty miles from one another, Robinson in
northeastern North Carolina and Cherry in southeastern Virginia,
at a time when white and black worlds were separate and unequal.
But men like Fred Cherry, Porter Halyburton, and Bill Robinson
did not acknowledge a color line in the prisons of North Vietnam.
Late in the war, Cherry and Robinson developed a special bond,
one that continued after their eventual release. At Camp Unity the
effects of Cherry's injuries still lingered. He could not raise his left
arm above his shoulder, and he struggled with routine tasks such as
washing and hanging up clothes. All the prisoners in the Unity cell
offered to help Cherry with any task, and Cherry readily accepted
help when he needed assistance, but he also wanted to do things for
himself. Some prisoners, however, became impatient with Cherry's
slowness. They preferred just to do all the work for him rather than
wait until he had made as much progress as possible on a chore
before intervening when he absolutely needed help. Their irritation
frustrated the proud and independent Cherry. Robinson recognized
Cherry's predicament and stepped forward to assist on terms more
to Cherry's liking. Robinson allowed Cherry to work at his own

pace and lent a hand only when Cherry had reached the limits of his physical strength and mobility.[55]

Whether prompted by propaganda needs or moved by humanitarian impulses, the North Vietnamese generally granted more liberties to the POWs during the Christmas season, provided a special meal, permitted religious services (but only under their direct supervision), and delivered holiday packages to the POWs sent by families and loved ones. At Camp Unity as well as the Pigsty, Robinson and his cellmates took advantage of the holiday reprieve and exchanged Christmas gifts. The gifts, of course, were fictional, but the sentiment was real. "There were so many of us in the room," Robinson remembered, "it was hard to come up with gifts for everyone." So each POW drew one name out of a hat and created a personal, albeit imaginary, present. One Christmas, Jerry Coffee pulled Robinson's name and decided to give his cellmate "a five-mile spool of cadmium-plated high-tensile no. 9 bailing wire (trailer mounted to place behind his Lincoln), complete with a gold-plated pair of lineman's pliers and holster." The amusing gift and accompanying card actually conveyed a genuine sense of gratitude for Robinson's devotion to his cellmates. Individual images on the Christmas card included a clothesline, leaky faucet, cigarettes, and mousetraps, which alluded to Robinson's work as the cell's handyman.[56]

As far back as his days at the Zoo Annex, where larger cells and more roommates became the norm, and continuing at the Pigsty and Camp Unity, Robinson took it upon himself "to fix things up as best" he could in the cramped and ill-furnished cells. Through their senior ranking officers, the POWs frequently requested materials from the North Vietnamese that they could use to improve their living quarters and make conditions more palatable. One such request was for additional clothesline. After numerous rejections, the guards appeared, unannounced, with the clothesline and set it inside the cell door. Robinson, eager for some task to occupy his time, jumped to grab the wire and started working. Surprisingly, Air Force Captain Richard (Pop) Keirn, the cell's SRO, instructed Robinson to put the wire down. Keirn, who had also been a POW during World War II, wanted to see if anyone else would take the initiative and hoist up a new clothesline. The wire lay on the floor for "about a week" without anyone showing an interest. The test worried Robinson "half to death." Finally, Keirn informed Robinson that he could hang the clothesline. Robinson grabbed the wire and, just as he began to work, "there were five instructors" providing supervision and guidance for the project. The clothesline episode is not a story about lazy POWs versus active POWs. Quite the contrary: it illustrates the role that Robinson assumed among his fellow POWs. In many ways, he had become the crew chief of his cell, and Coffee's Christmas card heralded his efforts. Whether he was hanging a clothesline, repairing leaky faucets, making ashtrays out of canned chicken containers, rolling cigarettes, or using his imagination to build a better mousetrap, Robinson placed the needs of others above his own self-interest. He clearly did not want to be a burden to anyone, either in North Vietnam or North Carolina.[57]

Throughout his captivity, when given the opportunity to write home, Robinson attempted to raise the spirits of his family members. He did not want his situation to deprive his loved ones of life's joys, particularly during the holidays. He always extended Mother's Day, Father's Day, and birthday greetings, and he encouraged everyone to maintain family traditions. In so doing, they would be comforting one another, as he intimated in a Christmas letter in 1970.

> I can see the tree now with all of its bright lights and gay colored packages underneath, with all of you gather[ed] around, with wrapping paper all over the floor, kids playing with their new toys, and you can hardly hear yourself think for all of the noise, lots of laugher and lots of cheer. You can say for sure that Old St. Nick has made a stop here. Sorry I can't get in on all the fun but remember there will be another time, another year. All of you rest for sure my thoughts will go with you during the holiday season and into the New Year . . . I'm well and full of Christmas spirit, hope you are too.[58]

A year later he urged his parents to "keep smiling!" But his letters never avoided the reality of their separation. In December 1971 he wrote, "The holiday season is here once again and finds us separated by miles but not in mind and heart . . . remembering we must always remain understanding and patient and that our burdens will never be more than we can stand." They overcame their sadness by clinging to a faith in a future reunion. Just before Christmas 1972, his eighth in captivity, Robinson repeated his familiar words of hope: "Another year is coming to an end and it finds me still here, least you know where I am. . . . I hope all of you have a very fine Christmas with lots of the good life. Leave a place for me, you never know when I might show up. Any way I am hanging in there and standing on the first team, hope you are too." Christmas 1972 was the last one Robinson spent in North Vietnam.[59]

4

Coming Home

The signing of the Paris Peace Accords on 27 January 1973 formalized and prescribed an exact timeline for the withdrawal of the U.S. military from Vietnam. The agreement also set the conditions for the release of American prisoners of war. On that same January day the North Vietnamese and Viet Cong representatives in Paris released the names of 577 American prisoners of war; of that number 555 were U.S. military personnel, including William Andrew Robinson. Repatriation planning, dating back to December 1969, had been coordinated under the code name Egress Recap. The antiseptic moniker was actually a part of the military's extensive and utilitarian lexicon: Returned, Exchanged, or Captured American Personnel. Just before the release of the POW names, Melvin Laird, the outgoing secretary of Defense, ordered that the repatriation operation be officially called Homecoming. Operation Homecoming, as it became popularly known, consisted of three distinct phases. For prisoners being held in South Vietnam, Laos, and China, the initial points of release varied, but for those prisoners being released by the North Vietnamese, Phase I began at Hanoi's Gia Lam Airport with the actual transfer of custody.[1]

The first phase of repatriation was limited to an identity check and a brief medical evaluation before departure to Clark Air Base in the Philippines, where Phase II commenced. At Clark the POWs would undergo more thorough medical examinations, but any routine medical procedures were postponed until the men returned to the states. Meanwhile, they would establish contact, usually by phone, with family members, and would complete a preliminary intelligence debriefing that would focus on MIAs or those unaccounted for. The men also received updates on their career status, back pay, and personal affairs. Most POWs would stay at Clark for only seventy-two hours. Phase III entailed the most extensive and intensive medical examinations and information-gathering sessions. During the third phase, the POWs were assigned to one of thirty-one military hospitals, one that would be relatively close to their hometown so that family reunions could occur as soon as possible. In addition to reuniting with family, the men received further medical treatment and dental care, completed comprehensive intelligence debriefings, and underwent psychological evaluations. Finally, the former prisoners reviewed their career and assignment options. The duration of Phase III varied from man to man, but it was not unusual for a prisoner to spend a month or more at the hospital or with family members before receiving a final clearance and being declared fit to return to duty.[2] Beginning on 12 February 1973, the first group of 116 prisoners left Hanoi for Clark Air Base. Subsequent releases resembled the first in terms of procedures and the number of prisoners repatriated; the last major release occurred on 29 March. Navy Lieutenant Commander Alfred Agnew, who was shot down on 28 December 1972, earned the distinction of being the last American to board the final plane.[3]

First Freedom

On 12 February Bill Robinson was among the first 116 prisoners to begin Phase I of Operation Homecoming. Transported in buses still painted with camouflage, the men arrived at Gia Lam Airport at midmorning in groups of twenty.[4] As Robinson's bus approached the airport, he saw "devastation all around." He later learned that the U.S. had bombed both ends of the runway to prevent fighter jets from taking off, but at the same time they had left enough room for transport planes to land and take off.[5] In addition to North Vietnamese and American military officials, Canadians, Hungarians, Indonesians, and Poles from the International Commission of Control and Supervision were on hand, as well as "some 120 Vietnamese and foreign journalists—none, however, from the United States." As the men arrived and disembarked from the buses, each busload formed into two lines of ten. At 12:30 P.M. Hanoi time the transfer began as, one by one, the prisoners passed before Lieutenant Colonel

Nguyen Phuong of North Vietnam and Colonel James B. Bennett of the United States, who were "seated at a small table under a canopy of green parachute cloth installed in case of rain. The table was in a grassy enclosure surrounded by a wrought-iron fence." After passing the table, each repatriated prisoner was met by an American serviceman who escorted him "about seventy-five yards to one of three C-141 Starlifter transport planes." Of the 116 men, "three were carried aboard their plane on stretchers, two were using crutches." Amazingly, the entire process took just more than an hour to complete, and all released prisoners were airborne by 1:45 P.M. As one North Vietnamese official sardonically remarked, "They were released as rapidly as they were captured."[6]

The C-141, which had been introduced in 1965, was a novelty to many of the men who had been shot down early in the conflict. Robinson had only seen pictures of the plane before his capture. While stationed at Nakhon Phanom Air Base in Thailand, he had received the emergency evacuation plans for the C-141. Back then, imagining the massive aircraft making an emergency landing on a jungle runway produced a hearty laugh of disbelief from the helicopter crew chief. Now Robinson viewed the C-141s, which the prisoners would christen the Hanoi Taxi, as his passage to freedom. The men approached the planes somberly because they "didn't want to show any emotions that could be seen by the Vietnamese" and used for propaganda purposes. Consequently, they "were very careful in that regard . . . [and] made sure there wasn't anyone hanging around the back of the airplane" with a camera or any type of recording equipment. Robinson felt that "it was sort of like there were two countries there. Everything on one side of the line was American and everything on the other side was Vietnamese. Once we got inside [the plane], we could let our guard down a little bit."[7]

As Robinson's plane, the second to leave Gia Lam Airport, prepared for takeoff, he noted a humorous juxtaposition. The forty POWs were seated in order of shootdown, which placed Robinson near the front, along with Colonel Robbie Risner, whose exploits in Vietnam would make him one of only four airmen to receive more than one Air Force Cross, and Commander James Stockdale, a Gulf of Tonkin veteran, the senior ranking naval officer held in captivity, and a soon-to-be recipient of the Congressional Medal of Honor. These were some of the most senior-ranking and experienced pilots in the American military, and yet the plane was being piloted and copiloted by a couple of junior officers. They "looked like kids," Robinson recalled, although he was now not yet thirty years old and probably not more than five or six years older than the young airmen. His seven and a half years in Vietnam had obviously given him a unique perspective on life, one that would color, in significant ways, his postrelease adjustment. The plane taxied briefly, and as it "broke ground, there was a small amount of emotion, but nothing compared to when we got over the water and the fighters joined our wings. I think that is when we knew freedom had finally arrived." Interestingly, Robinson to some extent associated freedom with the safety of the fighter escort: "The excitement rose to a complete peak—there was like a silence—and then there was this great big roar . . . [and when] the fighters joined us, we were out of the range of anything the Vietnamese had."[8]

Once the former prisoners were beyond the range of North Vietnamese missiles and the realization of freedom had begun to sink in, all sorts of conversations and activities ensued. According to Navy Lieutenant Commander Milton S. Baker, who accompanied the men on the second plane, "Medical treatment on the flight was limited to two aspirins and some nosedrops. The men drank coffee, tea, and the nutrient drink, smoked, read, and asked dozens of questions on subjects ranging from sports to women's liberation."[9] Anticipating an appetite for news, Homecoming planners had prepared *In Brief for the P.O.W.: A Catch-up on News from the Missing Years.* Beginning in 1965 and concluding with 1972, the magazine covered tidbits of news on such topics as Vietnam, aerospace, world and domestic news, deaths, sports, and awards. The compilers incorporated a modicum of popular culture features, but they did not promote a sanitized version of noteworthy events. For instance, the antiwar riots and race riots of the mid- to late 1960s, the murders committed by the followers of Charles Manson, and the shooting of college students by Ohio National Guardsmen at Kent State University all received coverage, as did international events in the Soviet Union, Greece, and Czechoslovakia. The twenty-four pages of news and photos certainly depicted a world and nation in turmoil.[10] Robinson remembered one on-board conversation with a nurse who said that the POWs "would have culture shock" because "women had thrown their bras away." Never bashful and always eager to interject humor into a discussion, Robinson replied, "We are used to that." The retort perplexed the nurse momentarily, until he followed up: "We have been seven years with the breastless look. We shouldn't have too much trouble introducing ourselves to the braless look." The euphoria of release temporarily overshadowed the depth of transformative change that had occurred in America during the previous decade. For that moment, the men aboard the planes were simply glad to be free.[11]

As each plane arrived at Clark Air Base, the senior ranking officer on each plane exited first and made a brief statement. The first to do so was Navy Captain Jeremiah Denton, and his words have been forever associated with the Vietnam-era prisoner of war: "We are honored to have the opportunity to serve our country under difficult circumstances. We are profoundly grateful to our Commander in Chief and to our nation for this day. God Bless America!" The second plane to arrive included Bill Robinson and carried Colonel Robinson Risner as its SRO. Risner, who had welcomed Robinson to the Hanoi Hilton seven and a half years earlier with a dire warning that he might be required to pay the last full measure of devotion in service to his country, now expressed relief and thanksgiving: "On behalf of all the other men who have been prisoners, I would like to thank you all. I would like to thank our President and the American people for bringing us home to freedom again. Thank you ever so much." Navy Captain James A. Mulligan, the SRO on the third plane, echoed these thoughts of privileged service and thanksgiving and added that during the long years of captivity "our faith in our God, our country and in our families has never wavered. Today I'd like to thank the President of the United States and our families for maintaining their faith with us and making this wonderful day possible." A fourth plane arrived at Clark around eleven o'clock that night carrying prisoners released from South Vietnam. The delay stemmed from "a dispute over an exchange of Communist prisoners." Still, a crowd of well-wishers waited, and Army Major

Raymond C. Shrump, the SRO on the final plane, made a simple statement: "It has been a long time. I want to thank each and every one of you for such a very, very fine welcome."[12] These foundational themes of duty and honor undergirded by faith in God, country, and family encapsulated the historical memory of the former prisoners of war.

When Robinson arrived at Clark Air Force Base in the Philippines, enthusiastic and excited crowds turned out to greet the returning prisoners. Large in number, the crowds "seemed like half the world" to Robinson. Although willing to show their admiration and appreciation, the general public did not have access to the released prisoners. A few POW family members had made the trip to Clark, and some of the base's military personnel joined the celebratory reunions, but everything was closely monitored and tightly restricted. Robinson attributed the caution to the fact that the military was not completely sure of the mental state of the released prisoners and so it shielded them from the crowds, to protect them until proper evaluations were completed and they were ready to handle the spotlight. He deemed Operation Homecoming "a long-thought-out plan; it wasn't something that just happened overnight. It was to ensure a positive return, and to make sure we were treated with the utmost respect." Once the military determined that the former prisoners seemed ready, they were given a little bit more freedom.[13]

Robinson, however, did not consider it complete freedom, because they "just didn't allow people to get to us." The press "was in the go position" and desperately wanted their stories. Captivity had limited his access to news and information about the war. Nevertheless, the constant influx of new prisoners in the later stages of the war had tinted Robinson's perceptions. He viewed the media as "98 percent liberal," an opinion fairly common among the military during the Vietnam War, and he thought that maybe the "press was more interested in doing us harm than doing us good." He recalled hearing a false story about an individual who "had presumably stolen a uniform" and infiltrated the base hospital area. Afterward, the imposter filed a news report claiming that nurses and other women were willing to have sex with the former prisoners in order to make them happy. Several stories of this nature actually appeared in well-known dailies such as the *Chicago Tribune;* additionally, the *Omaha World-Herald* carried a story under the headline " 'Bunnies' Await the POWs," suggesting that the former prisoners were in store for "a sweet taste of femininity." Understandably, the story "didn't sit very well with the families" of the prisoners and ironically led to a relaxing of press restrictions as a way to promote fact-based reporting of the POWs' return. The attempts to create sensational and titillating stories, even false ones, placed a tremendous burden on those who worked in the hospital as they labored to protect the privacy and reputations of the former prisoners. The former prisoners greatly appreciated the dedication and professionalism of the hospital staff.[14]

During their brief stay in the Philippines, the former prisoners had access to culinary delights and material items that they had been denied while in captivity. Navy Lieutenant Commander Charles Plumb, whose six years in captivity had exposed him to some of the worst of prison fare, described the homecoming menu succinctly: "Food ranged from hash to lobster and drink from buttermilk to champagne." Few former prisoners dined in a manner to surpass Robinson's former SRO Pop Keirn. When Keirn entered the cafeteria at six o'clock in the morning on his second day at Clark, he ordered "six eggs over light, a couple strips of bacon, a couple of pieces of sausage, a piece of ham, some hash browns, and some grits." Before he left the chow line, a cook gave him two three-ounce steaks, and Keirn grabbed a couple pieces of toast and a quart of milk. After consuming this smorgasbord, Keirn had a bowl of ice cream, and he then returned to his room and slept "for about eight hours."[15] As Bill Robinson recalled, "I had never been to a banquet like that before. They had everything laid out from A to Z, with made-to-order chefs. Whatever you wanted they could fix it right there." Looking back, he considers it "kind of funny. I've listened to what others have said—one wanted ice cream, one wanted eggs and bacon—I guess in reality we wanted a little bit of everything." At that moment, however, Robinson was willing to settle for very simple pleasures when it came to food: "my craving . . . was a salad that didn't give me dysentery." In the later years of the war, when the food was noticeably better in the northern prison camps, the prisoners still had to deal with dysentery, caused in part by the Vietnamese' use of human feces in vegetable gardens. "It was nice to eat a salad that would not haul you off to the bathroom," Robinson explained. Naturally, there was some overindulgence, and, of course, "we all had a little bout with sickness, because we weren't accustomed to the rich food" and their digestive systems had not yet recovered from years of nutritional deficiencies.[16]

As the former prisoners satisfied their gustatory appetites, they also enjoyed shopping at the base PX. To prevent spending sprees or buyer's remorse, clerks in the PX provided catalogs and allowed the men to order items for a period of ninety days, along with free shipping to the states. Robinson did not make any expensive purchases. It seemed, though, that everyone held an interest in one particular category of items: watches. As prisoners, the POWs had lived a regimented life of sorts, and now, as they looked to acclimate themselves to postrelease military life, the watch symbolized a new type of order. The desire for dress uniforms had a similar basis. Colonel Robbie Risner relished the opportunity to wear his uniform "mounted, fixed and ready to go" with all the medals and ribbons that he had earned. "When I got everything on, I felt like a new man," Risner explained. "It had been so long since I had had any decent clothes on. Besides being dressed, I was in a uniform that reflected something of which I was very proud—the United States Air Force." Many POWs shared this sentiment, among them Bill Robinson. Although their Vietnamese captors had attempted to strip the American prisoners of their dignity and self-worth, the vast majority of POWs had remained faithful to their oaths of enlistment and the values expressed in the Code of Conduct. By donning their military uniforms, medals, and ribbons, the former prisoners reclaimed one personal signifier of their loyal service to the U.S. military and to their nation.[17]

Until reuniting with his family, Robinson, like most POWs, occupied his time with an assortment of activities, "getting fitted for uniforms, getting physicals—we had hundreds of things going on." They also dealt with news from home. To help the men navigate the appointment docket and bureaucratic processes, the military assigned to each former prisoner a serviceman from the same branch of service who held an approximately equal rank. Sometimes the escorts were the bearers of bad news. Sadly, amid the excitement, some men learned that "things weren't so well at home." In these instances, the former prisoners turned to one another for advice and consolation. As Robinson made clear: "Just because we were free, we hadn't stopped looking after each other . . . making sure" that everyone was dealing with his situation as best he could. Robinson feels strongly that this level of brotherly commitment "exists to this day." As prisoners, they had been somewhat aware of potential problems at home. They received bits of news while in captivity, and they read between the lines of odd or detached notes from loved ones, but release brought confirmation of bad news and betrayal. Few faced a more difficult set of circumstances than Robinson's friend Major Fred Cherry. The extraordinary details of Cherry's case "sent alarms through the Pentagon, which had a thick file about his family: the death of his mother, Shirley's [his wife's] living with another man and having a baby, the depletion of his savings account [from $147,184 to $4,720.98], and the legal troubles of his oldest son." The Air Force assigned Colonel Clark Price, a personal friend of Cherry, to be the POW's escort officer, and dispatched Major General Daniel (Chappie) James, a widely respected African American soldier who had a strong rapport with POW families, to brief Cherry on each of these heart-wrenching circumstances. The ever-resilient Cherry received the reports with a confident stoicism, responding to each revelation: "I can handle that. I can handle that. I can handle that." Having survived the ordeal of torture and captivity, men like Fred Cherry and Bill Robinson firmly believed that they could manage and overcome any form of adversity.[18]

Just before leaving Clark Air Base, Robinson, his former cellmate John Borling, and Jeremiah Denton visited approximately four hundred children at the Virgil I. Grissom School for U.S. military dependents. The occasion marked the first public appearance of the three men and, for that matter, the first appearance by any of the 142 POWs at the base. Their intentions were straightforward. They merely wanted "to meet with the children and to say thank you." Robinson had seen them from a distance but had not "been up close and personal." Because of the intense media scrutiny, the military kept the POWs and the adoring Americans separated. As part of the visit, the three men returned "greeting cards and posters that the pupils had [previously] drawn and sent to the base hospital," which had subsequently been autographed by the released POWs and were intended as repayment for the various acts of kindness directed toward the returning heroes.[19] The three former POWs who went to the Virgil I. Grissom School did not deliver formal talks or presentations; they simply spoke from the heart. "I have seven children of my own just like you," Denton said to the assembly. The veteran Vietnam War correspondent Peter Arnett noted that Denton's "voice choked as he talked to the rows and rows of children." Borling, another family man, told the kids, "I have a 7-year-old just like you, but I have not seen her the last 6½ of those seven years." When Robinson appeared before the school group, his message, as a bachelor, was different: "I am not married yet, but when I do, I want a lot of kids like you." These notions of lost time, reconnecting, and beginning life anew appeared frequently in the journalistic coverage of the released POWs, as did a focus on the POWs reasserting the sexual dimensions of their manhood. And Arnett's coverage of the very first public appearance confirmed this mindset. In describing Robinson's exit following the end of the school visit, Arnett wrote: "Robinson was also embraced. He walked out of the gymnasium and back along a path crowded with children, arm in arm with the assistant principal, Joan Shelter of New Hartford, N.Y., and another third-grade teacher, Nancy Graham of Gainesville, Fla. Asked what it felt like to be so close to an American woman again, Robinson said, 'Beautiful, just beautiful.'" Despite the media's presence and persistence, Denton, Robinson, and Borling had not been allowed to talk to reporters. In fact, when one newsman posed a few questions to Denton, a military official stepped in and quipped, "You're not playing the game."[20]

Despite the media's frustration, the military could not have been more pleased with the initial success of Operation Homecoming. The size and efficiency of the operation at Clark was indeed impressive. More important than the logistical success, however, was the "generally excellent physical condition and high level of morale" of the former prisoners. In fact, spokesmen for the Joint Homecoming Reception Center admitted that "the rapidity with which the necessary processing is being accomplished" was a function of the "returnees themselves." The former prisoners also recognized the significant role played by Clark Air Base's entire community. Navy Captain Jeremiah Denton expressed these sentiments publicly in a statement he delivered upon his departure from Clark on 14 February: "I would like to express our thanks to you people here at Clark. You have shown us that your feeling is as deep as ours, and that is the highest compliment I can pay for the wonderful welcome we received here. I would like to thank President Nixon and everyone associated with this project for an experience we will never forget."[21] On many levels, the gathering and celebration at the Virgil I. Grissom School and Clark Air Base served as precursors to larger displays that awaited the former POWs in the states and in their hometowns. For the Robinson family, the celebrations had already begun.

Family Reunions

POW families received news of their loved ones' announced release of 12 February with joy and excitement, but the outlook of those who had waited more than seven years was tempered by a degree of caution. The Robinson clan gathered at the family patriarch's home in Roanoke Rapids to watch on television the arrival of the first POWs at Clark Air Base. The anticipation weighed differently on each family member; Ginger, Bill's younger sister, remained guardedly optimistic, needing visual proof. The large group of immediate and extended family included Bill's grandparents, Gene and Geneva, his father, William, and stepmother, Jessie, his sister Ginger, her husband, and their two children, Pam and Tim, and Jackie, Bill's older sister, her husband, and their four children, Mike, Debbie, Teresa, and Brian. They all gathered around the television and watched as the former prisoners departed the plane one by one. As Bill stepped down, Ginger recognized his leg and gait and shouted, "It's Billy!" Then the "whole room exploded" with excitement. Geneva, who was rocking in her chair, almost spilled over onto the floor. Gene, who had waited all those years for this moment to arrive, had his view of the momentous occasion obstructed by the jubilant celebrants. As the first wave of emotional energy subsided and as the television network prepared to rebroadcast the event, Gene Robinson took command of the room and announced that "he didn't see it the first time, but he was going to see it the next time." He then warned, "If you can't be still and quiet, then you will have to leave the room." No one dared deny him the chance to witness the release of his grandson. Once the replay had finished, the entire household resumed their rejoicing and awaited an opportunity to hear Bill's voice once again.[22] When members of the local community heard the news, they quickly joined the celebration. A small group stopped at the home of Bill's parents "with candles aglow to sing the 'Battle Hymn of the Republic.'" Afterward they quietly set the candles in the snow and departed.[23]

At Clark, the military placed few restrictions on POWs when it came to communicating with family members and loved ones. "It was pretty much open," Bill Robinson recollected. He spoke with his parents and grandparents "pretty much anytime" he chose to and with no delay.[24] The first conversations covered a variety of topics. Bill informed everyone that his health was good and that he was "looking forward to just getting home and just living again." The family asked how much advance notice and how many details he had received about his release, to which Bill replied, "They just closed up shop," and the men were on their way. The airman also told his parents, "I'm smiling now, but it won't be complete until all the MIAs are accounted for." The Robinson family could not contain their excitement. All their daily routines ceased as the reality of Bill's release began to set in. Coffee flowed continuously from a thirty-two-cup percolator and a ten-cup percolator operating around the clock. No one had time to sleep. Friends and town folk delivered food and other gifts to the Robinsons, and some even stopped by their house to wash the dishes.[25] The passage of time has folded those phone calls from Clark Air Base in the Philippines to rural North Carolina into a single memory for Bill. He does not differentiate between the first call and the last call he placed to his family, nor does he divide those phone calls into the traditional increments of time. To him, "it just seemed as if we [his family] were in constant contact over that period of time." That period was relatively brief. Robinson arrived at Clark Air Base on 12 February and left on 14 February. He accompanied Captain Denton and eighteen other former prisoners on the sixteen-and-a-half-hour trip from Clark to Travis Air Force Base, just outside San Francisco. From the Philippines they went first to Guam, where they had a short layover, then on to Hawaii, and then to Travis. There was an official welcome at each stop, and Robinson jokingly remarks that he was able to celebrate Valentine's Day at three separate places.[26]

At Travis, family reunions became part of the celebration. Three former POWs, Air Force Lieutenant Colonel Alan Brunstrom, Air Force Captain Terry M. Geloneck, and Air Force Lieutenant William Arcuri, greeted their wives and loved ones. Geloneck and Arcuri, the pilot and copilot of a B-52 bomber, were returning ahead of schedule because of injuries they had sustained when their plane was shot down during the Christmas Bombings of 1972. Geloneck "hugged his pregnant wife, Jane," and Arcuri, who had just "limped down the ramp," embraced his wife, Andrea, and as they "walked to a waiting car, she slowed her stride to match his halting walk." Nothing could temper the emotion and intimacy of these individual reunions, but Travis officials "had prepared a warm but subdued greeting," in part because the former POWs were not the first American servicemen to return to the high-profile base. As the reporter Steven V. Roberts, who covered the events at Travis, wrote: "Over the years, Travis has been the homecoming point for thousands of plain metal caskets, covered with American flags, and in the midst of the joy and relief that marked this day, many found the memory of what the war had cost the nation hard to erase." In addition to the 58,000 deaths in Vietnam, "hundreds of thousands had been wounded, physically and mentally, by the longest war in America's history." And the longest war in American history was still not over. That very day servicemen crowded the terminal as they waited to board planes for Okinawa, Guam, and Thailand. As one bystander noted, "They're sending out just as many as come back." Fortunately for Robinson, he had survived his ordeal in reasonably good health, and it was finally his turn to come home.[27]

From San Francisco the POWs would disperse to the bases

nearest their hometowns. Robinson's group, now totaling around ten, stopped next at Scott Air Force Base near Belleville, Illinois. At Scott, Robinson made a spontaneous decision to join the excitement: "I looked out there, and all of these people were standing there, and I went over to Captain Denton and said, 'All of these people came to see us; they didn't come to see this airplane. You think we ought to go out there and meet them?' He said, 'If you want to, go ahead.'" So Robinson excitedly left the plane and "shook hands and hugged and kissed and had a great time." As he walked through the crowd, someone presented him with a bottle of Champagne. Walter Cronkite, who was covering the event for CBS, commented on air that it seemed as though Robinson had a lot of friends and relatives in attendance. Later the media icon learned that Robinson "didn't know a soul there," which prompted him to label Robinson "the kissing Carolinian." Valentine's Day 1973 would always hold special meaning for Robinson. After a brief layover at Scott, Robinson boarded another aircraft that arrived at the Norfolk Naval Base in Virginia, where Denton gave one final speech. During the speech Robinson remained on the plane, and afterward "the Navy guys" departed the plane, and Robinson and his fellow members of the Air Force headed to Andrews Air Force Base, just outside the nation's capital. Even though the former prisoners would for the most part remain a close-knit group, each man would travel a separate path to freedom, and the initial period of readjustment proved especially difficult for some former prisoners.[28]

Before Bill's arrival, William, Jessie, Jackie, and Ginger traveled the two hundred miles from North Carolina to Andrews and met with Air Force officials, who briefed the families on the protocols, procedures, and expectations for reuniting with the former prisoners. Family members were placed in a receiving area on the runway cordoned off to allow the returning prisoners to disembark ceremoniously from the plane. The formalities were soon succeeded by a groundswell of jubilation. As Ginger recalled, "One of the wives broke through the line," and the others followed her lead, snapping photos on their way to find their loved ones.[29] In the pandemonium, Bill "with his arms spread like wings . . . caught four women in an embrace—one a total stranger." In addition to his stepmother and two sisters, he grabbed Mrs. Benjamin Black, the mother of his crew-mate Neil, who he incorrectly assumed was his aunt. Unable to free herself, Mrs. Black exclaimed, "Let me go, let me go, you're not my son." Realizing his mistake, Robinson allowed her to escape. After a short period of spontaneous celebration, the participants calmed down. Each family huddled together on the runway before retiring to private quarters. The years of separation were finally over, and for a brief instant nothing else seemed to matter.[30]

The Robinson family stayed together that first night, talking into the wee hours of the morning. They were all eager to discuss personal events, and Bill received updates "on family affairs, including the deaths of two uncles and an aunt, two of whom died at age twenty-three." The family had written to Bill concerning these matters, but "the letters must have been misplaced or misunderstood." They made a collective decision "not to talk about his captivity, and he did not talk about his experiences" in the various North Vietnamese prison camps. At one point the family attempted to persuade Bill to go to sleep, but to no avail. He could barely contain himself, and it was obvious to everyone that he was ecstatic about finally being free. And yet he made a remarkable admission to everyone, which his father succinctly explained during a press conference the following day: "If they told him tomorrow morning that he was going back over there [to] Vietnam," he would go. "There was no implied criticism of the North Vietnamese in anything" that Robinson shared with his family. Jackie was really surprised that her brother was not bitter or angry over the way he had been treated in Vietnam, nor did he seek sympathy from anyone. "I have never seen anyone with a more positive attitude or outlook," said an impressed sister. "I admire him for that. I really do." Only seventy-five hours had elapsed between Robinson's release in Hanoi and his arrival at Andrews Air Force Base. The next contingent of American prisoners still had nine days to wait before their scheduled release, and nothing could be taken for granted. As Robinson's stepmother explained to reporters, "We still have a lot of work to do to get our missing men back."[31]

When Robinson arrived at Andrews, his parents and two sisters were there waiting, but not his grandparents. Robinson did talk to

them by phone, and he asked his grandfather, "When are you going to come see me?" Gene Robinson replied, "You will be coming
home in a couple of days, I will wait here." By then Bill had learned
that he would need several surgeries before he would be medically
cleared to leave Andrews. When he informed his grandfather that
he would be recuperating in Washington, D.C., for some time, the
elder Robinson reversed his earlier decision and promised, "I will
be up there in the morning." The Air Force provided Robinson's
family with quarters on base so that they could maintain some privacy during their emotional reunion. During his first two weeks at
Andrews, someone from Robinson's family was always with him,
although members of the family alternated in and out because of
work obligations and because they had to care for and tend to their
own families. But someone was always there.[32] And two men who
had been stationed with Robinson in Thailand stopped by for a visit. His stepmother described that scene as something "you've never
seen" before.[33]

Robinson's family immediately recognized that he had changed,
but it was not his physical appearance that struck them. In fact, Robinson's father thought his son "looked great," although he was obviously a little tired from the nearly twenty-four-hour flight from
Clark to Andrews. Still, "at 219 pounds the airman weighed nearly
the same as when he completed basic training." What impressed his
family the most was how much Bill had matured during his long
confinement. Speaking like a proud parent, twenty-six-year-old Ginger announced assuredly, "He was a boy when he went away, but
now he's a man." She attributed the transformation to her brother's
"faith in God and the wonderful men who were with him" in North
Vietnam. Bill's father echoed this sentiment, calling the POWs "the
finest Americans in the world." The family also noticed Robinson's
intellectual maturity. "Billy has done a lot to improve himself while
he's been there," concluded his stepmother. "He's read extensively
and has studied diction, vocabulary, and the like. He says he wants
to go to college now, though whether he'll do it in or out of the service we don't know yet." Bill's sister Jackie even detected a change
in Bill's speech patterns, marveling at all the new words her brother
had incorporated into his conversations. "You've gotta see it to be-

lieve it," she confided to reporters. "They even changed his accent and he picked up someone else's." With a laugh and a sly smile, she told reporters, "We'll fix that when we get him back home."[34]

While at Andrews from 15 February to 2 March, Robinson went through a series of "mental evaluations and physical evaluations and dental work" as well as an assortment of routine medical procedures that had been neglected for the previous seven years. He also went through a debriefing with an intelligence officer "who wanted to know everything . . . about everything." At this point in the repatriation process, only a portion of the POWs had been released, and they had not been "cleared to speak to anyone about anything without going through" the intelligence officer first. "Of course," as Robinson maintains, "we had already made it clear to everybody that we weren't going to say anything—we were the first group—and we made it clear we would not say anything publicly . . . that would jeopardize the release of others."[35] Although a carefully scripted and scheduled release had been agreed on by the United States and North Vietnam, Hanoi officials surprised everyone when they announced on 14 February "a special release of 20 men . . . as a goodwill gesture coinciding with the visit . . . of a U.S. delegation" headed by Secretary of State Henry Kissinger. The sixteen Air Force and four Navy officers, dubbed the "Kissinger 20," were released on 18 February, reinforcing the need for caution and restraint until the final prisoner was released.[36] Nevertheless, the journalists covering the Homecoming events and the editorial boards of the nation's leading newspapers accused the Department of Defense of imposing "an invidious form of censorship, not in the interest of the P.O.W.'s or of national security but for obscure and self-serving political reasons."[37] The decision to remain silent, however, had been made by the POWs themselves before their release from Hanoi, and as an enlisted man Robinson himself had no intention of breaking the chain of command that he had followed for seven and a half years while in captivity. Moreover, he felt duty-bound to honor his commitment to his brothers who had not yet reached American soil.

Robinson actually took this position to rather unusual lengths when he challenged the person conducting his "psych eval." During the interview, a number of questions were posed to Robinson to which he responded: "You are going to have to call my [intelligence] debriefer—he hasn't told me I could talk to you." This led to an argument of sorts, as the questioner persisted and Robinson offered some answers, but there were certain questions that he simply would not answer. Looking back, Robinson says, "It was relatively easy because I didn't have on any leg irons or handcuffs." In the face of Robinson's opposition, the questioner tried a different tactic and explained that "colonel so-and-so" had cooperated, which prompted Robinson to assert his own rank: "I am a master sergeant, not a colonel. He can make his own decision." The interview lasted some thirty minutes before the questioner finally relented and contacted the intelligence officer. The intelligence officer told Robinson that he could answer the questions, and "the conversation went great from that point on."[38]

But even the military realized that they could not maintain a wall of silence between the POWs and the media. Consequently, Robinson and the rest of the former prisoners at Andrews had to meet with the Washington press before they could talk with any representatives of their local media. In short, the POWs had to participate in a press conference, of some sort, before they left Andrews for the final leg of their trip home. Robinson was not eager to enter the spotlight generated by the unfolding story of returning American POWs. To fulfill his obligation, but to serve as a mere backdrop to a larger story, Robinson chose to do his press conference with Colonel Fred Cherry. Aside from their obvious difference in rank, Colonel Cherry was the first African American captured in North Vietnam and the highest-ranking African American held during the Vietnam War. The choice was a calculated one; Robinson certainly did not want to face the press alone, and he knew attention would be focused on Cherry.[39] But if he simply wanted to fade into the background, he could have done so by choosing to appear with almost any officer. He selected Cherry because he shared a special bond with him and he respected him. In early April, after the two men had been officially released from Andrews, Robinson made the short trip from Roanoke Rapids to join Cherry in his hometown of Suffolk, Virginia, for a parade and welcome-home ceremony. During a dinner at the National Guard armory, Cherry thanked the attendees and delivered a forceful statement on patriotic devotion: "I am a fighting man, and I wear this uniform to protect you and your way of life. I would have given my life if necessary, proudly and honorably. I was tortured severely. . . . I had faith in God, in my country—and in you. If necessary, I will do the same thing again because I want America to be what you want it to be."[40] These words reflected the beliefs and feelings of Bill Robinson as well, but when he participated in his own welcome-home ceremonies, he often struggled to express himself. At times the events and emotion of coming home were simply overwhelming, not just for Bill but for everyone involved.

Robinson's grandfather sensed the mounting pressure and worried that the family would be engulfed by the throngs of spectators turning out for the celebrations planned in Roanoke Rapids and Robersonville, North Carolina, for early March. On the eve of the Roanoke Rapids welcome-home event, Gene Robinson arranged for the family to spend the night in a hotel in a small town a few miles away, so that close family members would have a chance to spend time with Bill before the community-wide celebrations began.[41] Some of the first to see him before his grand arrival in Roanoke Rapids were Ginger's kids, Tim and Pam, and Jackie's children, Debbie, Brian, Mike, and Teresa. Bill's Uncle Harold brought his kids, Robbie and Timmy, and Aunt Hazel brought her four, Steve, Forrest, Katherine Gail, and Randy. In the hotel the children gathered on the floor and Bill sat in the middle of them for nearly two hours and kissed them one by one. Being reunited with his nieces and nephews filled him with joy. For Tim the reunion process was seamless. His mother had spent so much time telling her children about her brother that Tim genuinely felt that he already knew his uncle, although he was only one year old at the time of Bill's capture. The next day the Robinson family shared their long-lost son with the rest of the local community.[42]

On the morning of 3 March, Roanoke Rapids Police Chief Drewery Beale met Robinson at the North Carolina welcome center on Interstate 95 on the Virginia–North Carolina border to escort him to a hometown celebration. On the way, they stopped at the Roanoke Rapids Holiday Inn just off the Interstate 95 interchange. The changes to the city shocked Robinson. "It's beautiful," he exclaimed, as he surveyed the vibrant business corridor that had been "nothing but peanut fields and woods" when he last saw it. Approximately fifty well-wishers had gathered at the Holiday Inn to greet Robinson. He paused to exchange "kisses with several women in the motel lobby and was presented a traditional lei of flowers" by the city's Diamond Jubilee queen, Sherry Elliott, before joining a ten-car motorcade for the final few miles to the heart of the city. In addition to family members and city officials, the motorcade included representatives from the local chapters of the Disabled American Veterans, the Veterans of Foreign Wars, and AMVETS. Despite a steady rain and temperatures in the low sixties, around five hundred people assembled in town to honor and pay tribute to the city's war hero. The high school band performed several musical tributes, the Boy Scouts provided a banner and flowers, and tricolored streamers served as the backdrop. After the "Star-Spangled Banner" had been played, Mayor Kirkwood Adams delivered the official greeting.[43]

"We are here to show our respect for you and our appreciation for what you have done," the mayor announced, "we thank God that our prayers for your return have been answered." Speaking on behalf of the local community as well as "all Americans," Adams welcomed Robinson home. He suggested that Robinson stay in Roanoke Rapids and pledged through individual and collective efforts to provide Robinson with "a place . . . to work and a place . . . to play and an opportunity for a meaningful future." The mayor also stressed the importance of the sacrifices that Robinson had made in Vietnam. "You provided an example of sacrifice and dedication to the interests of this nation at a time when such an example was badly needed," Adams declared. "What you and others like you did in Vietnam will have a profound and lasting effect on the young people of this land." Adams compared the former POW to the country's forefathers, who had transformed a wilderness into a great and powerful nation. The mayor concluded with a heartfelt thank-you and expressed great pride in proclaiming Bill Robinson "our friend and neighbor."[44]

When Robinson replaced the effusive mayor at the podium, he uttered only a simple, albeit sincere, thank-you, nothing else. The mayor then presented Robinson with a key to the city. Reverend John M. Walker, pastor of the city's First Presbyterian Church, offered the benediction, praying for the safe return of all prisoners held in captivity and expressing a desire for "peace in the world." When the ceremony ended, Robinson "was mobbed for 20 minutes by old high school buddies and friends." Among "personal friends and acquaintances" Robinson held sustained conversations, but when he stood before large crowds, he rarely managed to say more than a few words.[45] He seemed able "to wave and say thank you" and an occasional "God bless America," but that was about it. On one level, he was not prepared to present his personal story or assign some type of meaning to the American prisoner-of-war experience in Vietnam, at least not publicly. Despite putting thoughts to paper and writing "a couple of things down" when called on to speak in public, Robinson "couldn't utter a word." The situation clearly "overwhelmed" him. He tried to prepare for these events, but he became too emotional. Lumps rose in his throat and he just froze up, unable to speak.[46] Eventually, Robinson developed the ability to convey his story to larger audiences, sharing the pain and scars of his captivity experience, but only after a series of personal tragedies, a personal transformation of sorts, and a new national perspective on both the Vietnam War and prisoners of war in general. In the interim, Robinson turned to his family.

The night after receiving the key to the city, Bill spent a quiet evening at his grandparents' house in preparation for the next day's festivities at nearby Robersonville, where his father and stepmother lived. After things quieted down somewhat, he was able to spend more time with his family. "He wanted to do for everybody when he got home," Jackie remembered. "He frequently disappeared with his nieces and nephews. For example, he and several kids drove to the Carowinds amusement park in Charlotte, North Carolina, where they ate to excess, played games, and enjoyed the rides. These excursions became routine. Sometimes they followed a plan, such as the time they went to a family member's house in Concord, North Carolina, a four-hundred-mile round trip, just to spend the night. Other times, Bill just took the kids for a ride," only to call his sisters a few hours later and say: "We are in Norfolk and are going to spend the night. We will see you tomorrow." He did not seem to care that no one had packed an overnight bag or carried any extra clothes. It was easy to see how happy Bill was among his family, and they too were glad to be with him. Jackie was simply grateful that her brother came home alive, when "so many had come home in boxes."[47]

Ginger shared her sister's sense of relief. Although speaking from her own heart, she captured the prevailing mood of the family when she penned a poem, "The Return of a Son."

Bells are ringing and my heart is singing!
A heart of peace, as the war doth cease.
Seven years of tears, uncertainty and fears.
Will be o'er, as he reaches this shore.
A time of joy for a very dear boy.
Out of that land comes a giant of a man.
The return of a son, only God could have done.

In some ways, the family's rejoicing masked the pain they had suffered during this long ordeal. Moreover, the future seemed uncertain, and Ginger worried about the potential for more sorrow. Regarding Bill's commitment to the Air Force, she believed that her brother would resign, return home, and "settle down with us, even though he was more or less promised that" he would not receive an assignment that carried the possibility of capture, or worse. Ginger just wanted him to stay near; she wanted the family to be whole again. But it was not meant to be.[48]

When not with family and friends, Robinson had an opportunity to read the hundreds of letters and packages that had been sent to him since his return, some of which contained his VIVA POW bracelets. Many individuals had purchased the POW bracelets at county fairs or shopping centers and worn them in an effort to raise awareness about the captured and missing soldiers in Southeast Asia. These concerned citizens returned the bracelets, often with an accompanying letter, to the former prisoners once they arrived home safely. Their gestures were a small token of their support and admiration. Initially, Robinson had hoped to answer all the letters that he received, "but it got so overwhelming" that the family drafted a form letter and Robinson added a personal note at the bottom of each one. Also, "the phone was constantly ringing off the hook." Not all the calls were from patriotic well-wishers; sometimes a caller wanted to tell Robinson that he was a "bastard and he got what he deserved." It troubled Robinson that the calls had to be screened, but fortunately he had family members to assist him in dealing with this newfound attention. They often took notes when the calls came in, which allowed Robinson to read through the notes and make follow-up calls when he desired.[49]

Lieutenant Robinson

The news of the battlefield commissions, or "Hanoi commissionings," that Robinson, Black, and Cormier had received while in captivity broke shortly after the men arrived in the states. Initially, the Air Force opposed granting the promotions to the three enlisted men, having informed them at Clark Air Base that the commissions were subject to review. A personnel officer explained publicly the Air Force's position: "The secretaries of the military services have authority to tender commissions, but that authority has not been delegated to the senior ranking officer in a prisoner-of-war camp. . . . Once these men and the senior officer have been returned, all the facts in the case will be carefully considered in making a final decision in the best interest of the men involved and the Air Force." Privately, the Air Force took a much harder line, called in each of the enlisted men "individually, and basically said nice try," and implied that the men should not expect to receive promotions. The rejection disappointed and concerned Robinson. Without the promotion, he would be a "senior NCO with zero experience" instead of a junior officer who did not need experience but only "the ability to learn." Complicating the matter was the absence of Colonel John Flynn, the highest-ranking Air Force officer held during the Vietnam War. Flynn had approved the commissions at Camp Unity in his capacity as the service's senior ranking officer, but his shootdown date, 27 October 1967, meant that he was not among the first wave of POWs released on 12 February 1973. The question lay dormant until Flynn's release on 14 March. Upon his return, Flynn "made it a personal priority" to make Robinson, Black, and Cormier's battlefield commissions official, because he "made a commitment to three enlisted men in the bowels of a prison camp in North Vietnam . . . and 'no' was not" an answer he intended to accept. Flynn sought the assistance of the former POW James Stockdale, who now held the rank of admiral. The two men prepared a formal document "explaining the rationale, process, and training for the battlefield commissions," which they submitted to the Air Force. Despite their push, the Air Force balked and denied the request, but Flynn and Stockdale persisted and presented their case to Secretary of Defense Elliot Richardson, who passed the final decision on to the White House. After receiving a briefing on the commissioning request, President Richard Nixon reportedly exclaimed, "Hell, yes!" The president's decision satisfied a number of former POWs, including Leo Thorsness, who had been present at the original commissioning. The Medal of Honor recipient proudly stated, "Commissioning the three enlisted POWs in prison was one of the few positive events during those long years. It was the right thing to do for them, and the right thing for all of us."[50]

During the relatively quick-paced deliberations, Robinson's admiration of and respect for Flynn grew deeper, because Flynn sacrificed time with his family so soon after his return to go to Washington, D.C., and lobby for the three enlisted men. It would not be the last time that Flynn intervened in Robinson's behalf. The agreement the general brokered, however, did not accept the commissioning in the prison camp. Instead, the Air Force established 9 April 1973 as the official date of the commissioning. As part of the deal Flynn negotiated, other enlisted men received opportunities and avenues that could expedite their becoming officers, but Robinson, Black, and Cormier were the only three who received "direct commissions based on conduct" as prisoners of war. When the commissioning occurred at Andrews Air Force Base, Robinson had the option of selecting who would participate and administer the oath for commissioned officers. Although Flynn was an obvious choice, Robinson did not know that he was available and in the area, so he asked his friend Colonel Fred Cherry to administer the oath.

A Visit to the White House

Shortly after all the POWs returned to the United States, President Nixon invited them to the White House for an elaborate welcome-home celebration. The Hilton Hotel in the nation's capital provided accommodations for the former prisoners and their guests, and a story circulated that because the POWs had used the Hilton designation in Hanoi, the hotel chain now wanted them to live in luxury in Washington, D.C. The Hilton staff made a number of arrangements, including assigning roommates to all the unmarried POWs. Robinson soon learned that his assigned roommate was none other than Neil Black. After more than seven years together in the same cells in North Vietnam, the two men mutually agreed to make their own lodging arrangements. Robinson gave the room to Black and continued to use his quarters at nearby Andrews Air Force Base. On 24 May 1973 more than 1,280 guests assembled under a massive yellow and orange tent on the White House lawn. The weather did not cooperate for the august group, as a hard rain fell. At the time Robinson still had both of his feet in casts because of recent surgeries and was practically barefoot as he stood in water surrounded by electrical cables. He waited for approximately one and a half hours in the receiving line to meet the president. He described his conversation with President Nixon as very cordial, and when the president learned of Robinson's foot problems, he asked the airman why he had not just jumped to the front of the line.[51]

The lavish evening included fine dining and a star-studded slate of entertainers. The menu consisted of Seafood Neptune, served with hearts of palm, a main course of roast sirloin, and ninety quarts of puréed strawberries for dessert. More than two hundred butlers used two aluminum canoes filled with ice to chill the Champagne. The president called on several of Hollywood's top celebrities to pay homage to the former prisoners. John Wayne, the cinematic metaphor for the American warrior, sat at a table with Larry Guarino, one of Robinson's former SROs. At one point during the evening, Guarino leaned over and said, "Duke, I tried to think about how you might have handled the interrogators," which quickly garnered Wayne's undivided attention. Guarino then explained, "So when they asked me to do something, I told 'em to stick it up their asses. ... And do you know what, Duke? They beat the shit out of me!" As Guarino recalls, John Wayne "shook with silent laughter, but there were tears in his eyes. He knew that the Hollywood solution never works for us mere mortals." Bob Hope, the unsurpassed stalwart of the USO, provided the after-dinner entertainment, and only he possessed the credentials and the nerve to address the POWs with the line "This is the first time I've played to a captive audience." They, of course, responded with a good-natured chorus of boos and cat-calls. Other celebrity participants included Sammy Davis Jr., Phyllis Diller, Joey Heatherton, Jimmy Stewart, Ricardo Montalban, the composer Irving Berlin, and a *Playboy* playmate who had accompanied one of the returning POWs.[52] There were more than 125 tables at the reception, and Robinson's seat was a considerable distance from the head table and the center of activity. In some ways he felt more an observer than a participant. "We were so far away from the stage," Robinson explained, "we had a gist of what was going on" but were somewhat removed from interaction with celebrities and dignitaries. Of course, Robinson thought that everyone involved did a terrific job, the "meal was excellent," and it was an amazing evening.[53]

Despite all the glitz and glamour of the White House reception, the next day's news coverage focused on a speech President Nixon delivered to a group of former POWs just before the reception. When the commander in chief appeared before the former prisoners, they greeted him with an extended standing ovation. He expressed pride and thanksgiving in sharing the spotlight with them and then called them back to action. "We need you," the president pleaded, "the nation needs you." Nixon explained that the return of the former prisoners, the withdrawal of American combat troops, and the signing of a peace agreement meant the successful "end of the American involvement in Vietnam." Nixon suggested that two recent developments could potentially "have even more meaning to the world and to peace" than the return of the former captives and the end of the war in Vietnam. The first development was significant progress in U.S.–Chinese relations. In fact, on 1 May 1973, just three weeks earlier, the United States Liaisons Office had opened in

Beijing, operating as a de facto embassy and working toward the goal of full diplomatic relations between the two countries. The second development had occurred a year earlier, on 26 May 1972, when the United States and the Soviet Union signed the Strategic Arms Limitation Treaty (SALT I), a major accomplishment in slowing the nuclear arms race. In his remarks Nixon cautioned that this "doesn't mean they aren't still Communists," but he hoped this new era of détente would avert a nuclear confrontation.[54]

Still, he argued, the Cold War continued, and further cuts to the defense budget posed a "mortal danger" to national security. The president then asked the POWs for their "support in helping to develop the national spirit, the faith that we need in order to meet our responsibilities in the world." Nixon urged the POWs to take their stories "to the young of America," because, as the president predicted, "they will believe you. They will believe because you have suffered so much for this country and have proved that you will do anything that you can to do what is best for America, not just yourselves." The process had already begun, Nixon believed, citing the many acts of heroism and defiance exhibited in the prison camps scattered throughout Vietnam, as well as the patriotic statements delivered by the POWs immediately following their release. "You have helped reinstill faith where there was doubt before," the president declared, "and for what you have done by your faith, you have built up America's faith. This nation and the world will always be in your debt." The former prisoners cheered their approval.[55]

The White House reception was an "emotional experience" for Robinson, but it was only one aspect, and probably the least intimate, of some of the early homecoming ceremonies. Before the White House reception, the American Legion held their national convention in Washington, D.C., and invited three former prisoners, Ed Davis, Kevin McManus, and Robinson, to attend the meeting. "We got on our blues," Robinson recalled, "but they really didn't even tell us where we were going." Unaccustomed to any type of elaborate banquet setting, Robinson relied on small-town common sense to navigate the dining etiquette. "I can remember sitting there, the plate in front of me, and the silverware went in both directions." Looking for a little consolation, or perhaps a quick etiquette lesson, Robinson turned to the "young lady" seated next to him, whose husband was still listed as MIA, and said, "I have been eating with one spoon and one plate for so long—I don't have a clue." She replied, "We don't have this in East Texas, either." And so they decided to eat slowly, and whatever anyone else picked up to eat with they picked up too, "until all the silverware was gone." That was how they "spent their evening." The pomp and circumstance of these events mattered far less to Robinson than did the simple expressions of appreciation. After the meal, the three POWs were introduced and received an ovation that "seemed to go on forever." As the crowd cheered, the first person to jump down from the stage to shake their hands was George McGovern, and then "people around us shook our hands and hugged us." The moment—and especially McGovern's actions—was somewhat surreal to Robinson. In 1970 Senator George McGovern of South Dakota and Senator Mark Hatfield of Oregon had sponsored a congressional amendment requiring the end of U.S. military operations in Vietnam and a complete troop withdrawal by 31 December 1971. The amendment, which was defeated in the Senate, was not contingent on a peace agreement with North Vietnam or the release of American prisoners. McGovern's extreme antiwar positions caused many POWs "to hate" him for his willingness "to negotiate from a point of weakness," and for his failure to demand their release as a condition of any peace settlement.[56]

Ultimately, Robinson's judgment about a man was based on that individual's deeds and actions, not speeches at ceremonies. Not coincidentally, the White House reception for the POWs occurred just one week after the Senate's Watergate hearings began, which had been televised nationally. The very edition of the *Washington Post* that covered the reception contained a small story indicating that the three major television networks were "leaving their options open" on whether to "continue live gavel-to-gavel coverage" after the current recess. There was also a second story naming a White House official as its source, who said the president's POW reception speech "apparently marked the beginning of . . . a counteroffensive to shift focus from the Watergate case." Moreover, just two weeks before the reception, a U.S. District Court dismissed all charges including theft and espionage against Daniel Ellsberg in the *Pentagon Papers* case, which involved the publication of a secret RAND study, a compilation of war memoranda suggesting that both the Kennedy and Johnson administrations had misled the American public about its intentions in Vietnam. During his speech to the POWs, Nixon remarked on the Ellsberg case when he stated, "I think it is time in this country to quit making national heroes out of those who steal secrets and publish them in newspapers." Furthermore, the president claimed in the same speech, secrecy proved to be the essential element in the successful negotiations for the prisoners' release, the China initiative, and the Soviet arms deal. Regardless of the intent of the White House reception for the POWs, the Watergate story continued to hound the president. Roughly three months later, on 4 September 1973, Nixon's operatives Gordon Liddy and Howard Hunt were indicted for burglarizing the office of Ellsberg's psychiatrist, Lewis Fielding. Rather than face impeachment and removal from office, Nixon resigned the presidency in August 1974.[57]

Robinson understands Nixon's misdeeds, but he also considers Nixon from a unique perspective. He sees Nixon as his commander in chief at a time when the young airman was a prisoner of war in North Vietnam, and he credits the president with securing his release. In fact, many POWs see the massive bombing campaigns of Linebacker I and Linebacker II as inextricably linked to North Vietnam's decision to sign the Paris Peace Accords in January 1973. The peace talks had stalled on 2 May 1972, but they resumed on 12 May. Not coincidentally, Linebacker I opened on 10 May, marking the first sustained bombing campaign since the cessation of Operation Rolling Thunder. During Linebacker I, U.S. Air Force and Navy aircraft destroyed more than four hundred bridges by the start of July, including the crucial Thanh Hoa and Long Bien bridges, and dropped more than 150,000 tons of bombs on North Vietnam by 23 October, when the campaign ended. At the time of the bombing halt, a preliminary peace agreement between the United States and North Vietnam had been reached, but South Vietnam rejected it. Peace negotiations resumed in early November but broke down again on 13 December, prompting President Nixon to issue an ultimatum: negotiate, "or else." Nixon gave the North Vietnamese seventy-two hours to return to the negotiating table. When they refused, Linebacker II commenced on 18 December, in which the massive B-52 Stratofortress played a key role. Linebacker I had destroyed virtually all the viable military targets in North Vietnam, and thus the intent of Linebacker II was more psychological in nature. During the eleven days of Linebacker II, also known as the Christmas Bombings, the United States dropped more than 20,000 tons of bombs on portions of Vietnam. The speed and scope of the resulting devastation was unfathomable: "A three-plane cell of B-52s could drop more than 300 bombs into an area the size of . . . [an] airstrip in less than a minute." One unnamed Vietnamese official, who had experienced a lifetime of war, made the spectacular claim that 100,000 tons of bombs "had fallen on Hanoi alone." Nixon called off Linebacker II on 29 December, the day after the North Vietnamese government accepted the president's preconditions for resuming the peace talks. When the North Vietnamese signed the peace agreement a month later, they accepted the same terms Nixon had offered in October 1972. From Robinson's perspective, only one conclusion can be drawn from the chronology of the peace process: that Nixon's forceful resolve during Linebacker I and II led to the release of the prisoners. When it came to waging war against North Vietnam, President Nixon was decisive and focused, and Hanoi responded to his threats.[58]

The White House reception constituted just one example of the special attention and generosity bestowed on the returning prisoners. The cultural commentator Craig Howes suggests that "the POWs came back to one of the largest outpourings of goodwill America has ever lavished on a group of its citizens . . . when corporations, private citizens, and federal and local governments practically fought with each other to supply POWs with the biggest welcome or most expensive gifts."[59] For instance, Major League Baseball Commissioner Bowie Kuhn presented the POWs with a lifetime pass to every major league ballpark. The POWs also received offers for courtesy cars from automobile dealerships, free admission to movie theaters, country clubs, and various recreational facilities, and "an all-expense-paid week's vacation in Orlando, Fla.—including admission to Disney World." Several U.S. congressmen sponsored bills that would have provided "benefits ranging up to $200 a month for life, tax exemptions, extended medical care and scholarship aid for the men and their families."[60] Critics of President Nixon and the war in Vietnam labeled the red-carpet treatment accorded the POWs a type of hypocrisy when compared to the federal government's response to Vietnam-era veterans. The political columnist Tom Wicker observed that some 254,000 Vietnam-era veterans were "unemployed in the richest nation on earth" at that time, and he pointed out that President Nixon had recently vetoed "a veterans health care bill that would have provided funds to bring V.A. hospitals' staff–patient ratios up from less than 2 to 1 to the 2.7 to 1 average of other hospitals." Wicker harbored no animosity toward the returning prisoners. On the contrary, he called on the nation to "honor the P.O.W.'s and be glad their ordeal is ended." But he added, "Let us remember also those who shall have borne the battle, those who need a new Ford less than a decent job, those for whom the only bracelet is a band of needle marks."[61] Even the National League of Families opposed some of the more extravagant gift ideas, arguing that "it is not in keeping with our ideas of what the prisoners need."[62] In the end, some POWs enjoyed a bounty of material rewards,[63] and a small number capitalized on endorsement deals and private-sector employment during their postrelease years, but not Bill Robinson.[64] The two decades following his return home constituted a turbulent period, both personally and professionally, and as he journeyed down the road of life he sometimes found comfort in his own personal creed: forget and move on.

Bill at his junior prom, Roanoke Rapids, North Carolina. (Courtesy Bill Robinson)

Bill in basic training at Shepherd Air Force Base in 1962. (Courtesy Ginger Hux)

Bill and an H-19 helicopter during his tour in South Korea. (Courtesy Bill Robinson)

Bill *(far right)* and maintenance personnel at Nakhon Phanom Royal Thai Air Force Base in 1965. (Courtesy Bill Robinson)

Bill in his barracks at Nakhon Phanom, 1965. (Courtesy Bill Robinson)

An HH-43B like the one Bill was on when he was shot down, 1965. Barracks at Nakhon Phanom are in the background. (Courtesy Bill Robinson)

Bill's pilot, Captain Thomas J. Curtis. (Courtesy Erich Anderson, Veterans Tributes)

Bill's copilot, 1st Lieutenant Duane W. Martin. (Courtesy Erich Anderson, Veterans Tributes)

The famous Guerrilla Girl photo taken three days into Bill's captivity. (Courtesy Bill Robinson)

A photo of Bill taken early in his captivity. (Photograph VA 007971, Malcolm McConnell Collection, courtesy Vietnam Archive, Texas Tech University)

Bill exercising at the Zoo Annex, 1970. (USAF photo, courtesy Bill Robinson)

Left to right: Bill, Mike Lane, Harry Monlux, Harry Johnson, and Tom Browning in the Zoo Annex, 1970. (USAF photo, courtesy Bill Robinson)

Bill in the Zoo Annex, 1970. (USAF photo, courtesy Bill Robinson)

Bill's father reviewing pictures of Bill furnished by the U.S. government, 1970. (Courtesy Bill Robinson)

Bill's stepmother, Jessie *(left)*, and Billie Hiteshew (wife of Lieutenant Colonel James Hiteshew, another POW) selling VIVA POW bracelets, 1970. (Courtesy Bill Robinson)

Christmas card given to Bill by a fellow POW during the later stages of captivity. (Courtesy Bill Robinson)

Side 1 of a postcard-style letter sent by Bill's parents in September 1972. (Courtesy Bill Robinson)

CX 9.11.72

21

GỬI (Addressee)

HỌ TÊN (Name in full):
WILLIAM ANDREW ROBINSON

SỐ LÍNH (Service number): AF 14782798

NƠI VÀ NGÀY SINH (Date & place of birth):
Aug 28 1943 - Halifax County N.C.

ĐỊA CHỈ (Address):

TRẠI GIAM PHI CÔNG MỸ BỊ BẮT TẠI
NƯỚC VIỆT - NAM DÂN CHỦ CỘNG HÒA

VIA MOSCOW, USSR (Camp of detention for U.S. pilots captured
in the DEMOCRATIC REPUBLIC of VIETNAM)

COMMITTEE OF LIAISON
with Families of Servicemen Detained in North Vietnam

NGƯỜI GỬI (Addresser)

HỌ TÊN (Name in full):
Mr & Mrs William Jackson Robinson

ĐỊA CHỈ (Address):
P.O. Box 386
Robersonville
North Carolina 27871

Side 2 of the letter.

Dear Bill: Hope you have packages o.k. Used to get your June letter. You sound good. We are all fine as are those in R.R. Tomorrow is our last day at station. Can't get help & hours to many. I'll going to work in yard just as much money & less hours. Later retire from RCC. Aunt Blanche took her place I misshe. No news. We pray for your safe return home and soon. Love Mom & Dad.

NGÀY VIẾT (Dated): Sept 9, 1972

GHI CHÚ (N.B.):

1. Phải viết rõ và chỉ được viết trên những dòng kẻ sẵn (Write legibly and only on the lines).
2. Trong thư chỉ được nói về tình hình sức khỏe và tình hình gia đình (Write only about health and family).
3. Gia đình gửi đến cũng phải theo đúng mẫu, khuôn khổ và quy định này (Letters from families should also conform to this proforma).

Prisoners on board the Hanoi Taxi. *Front to back:* Ron Byrnes, George Hall, Neil Black, and Bill Robinson. (USAF photo, courtesy Bill Robinson)

Bill deplanes at Scott Air Force Base, February 1973. (*St. Louis Post-Dispatch* photo, courtesy Bill Robinson)

Left to right: Gene Robinson, Bill, and Geneva Robinson at Andrews Air Force Base, 1973. (Courtesy Ginger Hux)

(*Above*) *Left to right:* Jessie Robinson, Bill, and Jackie Robertson at Andrews Air Force Base, 1973. (Courtesy Ginger Hux)

(*Below*) *Left to right:* Ginger Hux (sister), Bill, and Jessie Robinson at Andrews Air Force Base, 1973. (Courtesy Ginger Hux)

Bill after his release in 1973. (Courtesy Bill Robinson)

Colonel Fred Cherry administers the oath for commissioned officers, 1973. General John Peter Flynn is at far left. (USAF photo, courtesy Bill Robinson)

General Cecil Fox awards Bill the Air Force Cross and the Silver Star, 1973. (USAF photo, courtesy Bill Robinson)

Bill after completing a solo flight during pilot training, 1974. (Courtesy Bill Robinson)

Bill with his Lincoln Mark III and Ford Thunderbird before his marriage to Sue Gill. (Courtesy Bill Robinson)

Bill feeding his horses at his home in Florida, 1986. (Courtesy Bill Robinson)

Bill and his fellow POW Ben Rensforth during a reunion of POWs stationed at Eglin Air Force Base, 1988. (Courtesy Bill Robinson)

Bill and Ora Mae on their wedding day. (Courtesy Bill Robinson)

Bill with members of the documentary film team in Vietnam, 1995. (Courtesy Bill Robinson)

Nguyen Kim Lai, the Guerrilla Girl, with her family in a photo taken during Bill's return to Vietnam in 1995. (Courtesy Bill Robinson)

The North Vietnamese produced stamps to commemorate fictitious shootdown milestones. The Robinson stamp *(top, center)* was alleged to commemorate the 2,000th shootdown of an American aircraft. (Courtesy Bill Robinson)

Bill with the woman featured in the documentary who lost her arm and her home in the war, in a photo taken during Bill's return to Vietnam in 1995. (Courtesy Bill Robinson)

Left to right: Bill, Art Cormier, and Neil Black, at a POW reunion in Dallas, Texas, 1998. (Courtesy Bill Robinson)

Left to right: Bill, Bob Lilly, and Art Cormier at the Air Force Enlisted Heritage Hall. All three were POWs and all three were Air Force air rescuemen. In the background is a replica of a prison cell. The writings on the walls are the signatures of POWs who have visited the Heritage Hall. (Courtesy Bill Robinson)

Bill talks with a school group in the Commemorative Courtyard at the National Prisoner of War Museum, 2003. (Courtesy Bill Robinson)

(Above left) Bill's nephew Tim Hux salutes Bill during the Ride Home POW Recognition Ceremony, September 2009. (Courtesy Tim Hux)
(Above right) Bill and his granddaughters at the POW/MIA Memorial, Robins Air Force Base, 2010. (Courtesy Bill Robinson)

5

Forget and Move On

In mid-April 1973 Robinson underwent a series of extensive medical procedures. The first dealt with a foot problem commonly known as hammertoe or claw toe, a contracture or bending of one or more joints in the second, third, fourth, or little toe, which causes the foot and toes to resemble a claw or hammer. The patient's symptoms include pain when wearing shoes and inflamed or burning sensations in the affected areas. Over the years Robinson's weight had placed a strain on his feet, but the seven and a half years of captivity without proper footwear and the prolonged periods of malnutrition precipitously aggravated the condition. The surgery, which at the time was experimental, involved a tendon-relief corrective. In layman's terms, the tendons at the end of the toes "were disconnected from the toes, which would allow the toes to fall back down." Then the toes and tendons were reconnected in an effort to provide some sort of relief. Robinson gained some temporary benefit from the first surgery, but additional surgeries were required. As Robinson's condition improved, he completed several professional military training programs, including one at Maxwell Air Force Base in Alabama, where he attended "an upgrade school to be reintroduced to everything."[1]

Washout

In August 1973 Air Force doctors declared Robinson fit for duty, at which time he received ninety days of leave. Although he was ready to go back to work, he accepted a free trip to Disney World in September, but while there he received word that there would be an awards and decoration ceremony in San Antonio, Texas, at Lackland Air Force Base, and so he cut his trip short.[2] The Air Force was prepared to recognize Robinson's heroism and service during the Vietnam War. These awards were not given because Robinson had been tortured and held as a prisoner of war. In fact, he received the Silver Star, the third-highest combat military decoration of any branch of the U.S. armed forces, for a rescue mission conducted on 17 May 1965, four months before his shootdown. Air Force Captain James L. Taliaferro Jr. "had ejected from his crippled" F-105 Thunderchief after sustaining thirty-seven-millimeter anti-aircraft fire during an armed reconnaissance mission along Route 7 near Ban Kia Na, North Vietnam. Two helicopter crews from the 38th Air Rescue Service responded to the call, and Robinson served as the crew chief or flight engineer on the high-bird helicopter. En route, they encountered heavy rain and clouds and were forced to detour around known flak positions. As the rescuemen reached the scene, U.S. fighter aircraft were aggressively attempting to suppress enemy ground fire. Having located Captain Taliaferro, the low bird descended, but it attracted heavy enemy fire "from a .50-caliber machine gun and small arms," which originated "about fifty yards behind and below the hovering chopper." "It was impossible to move the chopper nearer than about twenty feet from Captain Taliaferro," recalled the low-bird pilot. "Our blades were clearing trees by five feet or less [the bamboo at the site was almost one hundred feet high] and the undergrowth was brushing underneath us." Positioned as best they could, the low bird lowered the hoist cable to the maximum. At this point the high-bird helicopter moved in and orbited the lead chopper, allowing Robinson and Airman Second Class Marvin F. Brenaman to "cut loose with their M-16s at the ground forces firing at them." Because of the dense undergrowth, Taliaferro took more than five minutes to reach the hoist, as the firefight raged above and around him. Once aboard the rescue helicopter, Taliaferro joined the others in answering enemy fire by unloading his .38-caliber revolver. The two-hundred-mile flight to the recovery site and back to Tan Son Nhut Air Base in the ill-equipped HH-43s exemplified the high-risk nature of air rescue during the early stages of the Vietnam War. All eight members of the two rescue teams received the Silver Star for the Taliaferro rescue mission. Robinson was the only one who had to wait more than eight years to receive his medal.[3]

The Silver Star was not the only medal Robinson received at

Lackland's awards and decoration ceremony. For his actions on 20 September 1965 he received the Air Force Cross, a combat medal second only to the Medal of Honor. His citation reads:

> Airman First Class William A. Robinson distinguished himself by extraordinary heroism in connection with military operations against an opposing armed force as an Aircrew Member of a HH-43B helicopter over North Vietnam on 20 September 1965. On that date, Airman Robinson participated in an extremely hazardous attempted recovery of a downed pilot. This mission required a flight of over 80 miles, mostly over hostile controlled territory. Evaluation of the environment in which the downed pilot was located indicated that maximum performance would be demanded from each crew member if successful recovery was to be effected. Though exposed to intensive hostile ground fire, Airman Robinson, with complete disregard for his own safety, performed with courage and professional precision in the supreme effort to rescue a fallen comrade. Airman Robinson's courageous action and devotion to duty are in keeping with the highest traditions of the American Fighting Man under Attack by an Opposing Armed Force. Through his extraordinary heroism, superb airmanship, and aggressiveness, Airman Robinson reflected the highest credit upon himself and the United States Air Force.

Both Robinson and his crewmate Neil Black received the Air Force Cross for their actions during the Forby rescue mission. Although the awards were presented eight years after the fact, the actual date of action, 20 September 1965, meant that Robinson and Black were the first enlisted men to be awarded the Air Force Cross. Since the beginning of the Vietnam War, the Air Force has been very selective in bestowing the Air Force Cross on enlisted men. As of 1 January 2013, only twenty-four enlisted men have received the Air Force Cross.[4]

The newly minted and highly decorated officer decided to finish his Air Force career as a pilot. Neither these distinctions nor his status as a POW guaranteed Robinson an easy path to success. At

Lackland he went through an abbreviated officer training school, and he completed a pilot training course. Typical candidates for pilot training were younger than the thirty-year-old former prisoner, and Robinson sought advice from a variety of individuals and learned of a pilot training program at Sheppard Air Force Base in Wichita Falls, Texas, which at the time was also training South Vietnamese and West German pilots. Robinson had been told by one of his advisers at Andrews Air Force Base that he would have ample opportunities at Sheppard to obtain his requisite flight training hours. The plan to become an aviator sounded good to Robinson. He completed some training at Lackland, soloing in the T-41, and Sheppard represented the next hurdle toward becoming a pilot. Robinson's arrival there coincided with a fuel crunch and what he termed the "Air Force's bastardization of everything." He soon discovered that the pilot training program at Sheppard was being scaled back for U.S. fliers, although the West German pilots would continue to receive training. "It just turned into a fiasco," Robinson recalls. He had completed the T-37 program and started the T-38 portion, but "unfortunately, having the label of a semicelebrity," he drew the attention of the base's wing commander, who wanted to fly with the former POW. This was in addition to Robinson's assigned instructor and the squad commander.[5]

A week into the T-38 program, Robinson had flown training flights with three men, the instructor, the squad commander, and the wing commander, which presented a potential problem because a candidate could not fly with more than three people before qualifying on a solo flight—no replacements were allowed. When Robinson's instructor received a new assignment, Duties Not Including Flying, the trainee had to complete his training with the squadron commander and wing commander. Robinson knew the wing commander didn't have time to do that, which left Robinson at the mercy of his West German squad commander, and their relationship proved disastrous for the aspiring pilot. It was the squad commander's habit to sit "in the back of the airplane and holler [instructions] in German." Most of the time Robinson "didn't have a clue as to what the bastard was saying." The frustration mounted: "I would get a flight, then I might not fly again for another week. I realized that I wasn't a perfect stick, but there is no way in hell you can learn how to fly this way." The West German was committed to training his own pilots and only occasionally found time for Robinson. Sometimes he might approach the American on a day when the candidate was not scheduled to fly, conduct a "ten-minute briefing, and then go fly." In a four-month period, Robinson logged fewer than ten hours of flying time. He struggled under these conditions; he admits, among other things, that he had "difficulty landing the airplane." And so, as Robinson surmised, "I guess they decided that I wasn't cut out to be a pilot."[6]

Although the Air Force had contributed to the irregularities and problems with Robinson's training at Sheppard, there was a genuine concern about how he would handle his failure. Just a few months earlier, on 3 June 1973, Air Force Lieutenant Edward Alan Brudno committed suicide.[7] Brudno, a Massachusetts Institute of Technology graduate captured on 18 October 1965, spent time at Briarpatch, where he received particularly harsh treatment, and survived the Hanoi March and a stay at Dirty Bird. In many ways Brudno's captivity experience paralleled Robinson's. Because of the Brudno tragedy, the Air Force sent General John Flynn to Sheppard to have "a long conversation" with Robinson. Flynn had already demonstrated his loyalty by fighting for Robinson's commission. Therefore, Robinson had every reason to trust Flynn's counsel. The two friends discussed the situation and agreed that Robinson should accept an "administrative withdrawal" from the pilot training program. Though his record remained clean, Robinson called the administrative withdrawal "the same damn thing as a washout; it just looks better on paper." Aside from the meeting with General Flynn, several other officers, instructor pilots, at least one lieutenant colonel, and two majors came to Robinson and said, "We want you to know that you are being screwed, and we will go to bat for you if you want us to." Robinson appreciated the gesture but told them in unequivocal terms: "Look, I spent seven and a half years as a prisoner of war, and I didn't beg those sons-of-bitches for something and I'm not going to start now. I will just walk away with my head held high, and I will go do something else." Robinson believes that if he had been assigned to a pilot training program some place other than Sheppard, he would have "probably" been a flyer, but "that wasn't what happened."[8]

Robinson's original goal had been to be a "flying" aircraft maintenance officer. When he was an enlisted crew chief, he had noted with pleasure the reaction of pilots when "the guy who worked on the airplane was willing to crawl in and fly in it." Hoping to show the same type of respect, Robinson wanted the people who worked for him to understand that he was "willing to fly what they worked on." He still could fulfill his dream, flying in aircraft serviced by enlisted personnel, but not as a pilot. For the next twenty years Robinson would serve as an aircraft maintenance officer supervising enlisted personnel. Dejected but not defeated, he drew strength from his experience as an enlisted man and his own humble beginnings. He believed wholeheartedly in the adage "You never forget where you came from." As he moved forward, he intended to rely heavily on his own sense of leadership. In his Air Force career he observed people who moved up the ranks with the attitude "I toughed it out, so they can tough it out." Those who held this attitude disappointed Robinson because he felt they missed a chance to solve problems and make things better. "A lot of times you solved more problems by listening rather than doing," suggests Robinson. People sometimes "just needed a chance to vent their frustration," and once they received an opportunity, they often moved on whether the circumstances changed or not. It was important to Robinson that he be "a good ear," listen to his colleagues, and show respect to everyone.[9]

The Father and Son Saga Continues

Despite the setback of the administrative withdrawal from the pilot training program, Robinson knew he still had a future in the Air Force. The ordeal at Sheppard lasted a little more than a year, from September 1973 to late November 1974. In some ways his career trajectory now slowed, which afforded him the chance to reconnect with his family and possibly get married and raise children of his own. Robinson, however, underestimated the effect of his captivity on his family, especially his father and stepmother. The North Vietnamese formally recognized Robinson as a POW for the first time on 22 October 1968, more than three years after his shootdown date. The letters they received from their son and the images that appeared in various news outlets did not reduce their anxiety or concern. In retrospect, Robinson feels that he was not "up front" with his father and stepmother before leaving for Vietnam, and once he became fully aware of the risks involved, he remained silent, not wanting to alarm or upset his family. Thus, they were totally unprepared for the news of his capture. Moreover, Robinson's last visit with his family before going to Vietnam ended abruptly after an agonizing breakup with his fiancée, Jane. When he left North Carolina, he was angry and his attitude was that there was "no looking back." Those nine years of separation compounded an already strained relationship with his father, one that would not be repaired easily. Indeed, Robinson's captivity added a new source of contention between father and son.[10]

Before his deployment, Robinson had to select someone to manage his affairs in the event of a tragedy. Given all that had transpired with his father while he was growing up, Robinson wanted to appoint his grandfather as his executor. The elder Robinson cited his advanced age as a reason not to assume this important responsibility. Instead, he suggested that his grandson name his father as the custodian of his assets and possessions. Robinson reluctantly agreed. While he was classified as missing in action, the Air Force essentially froze Robinson's pay for a year, after which it forwarded a year's back pay to William Robinson and continued to send him monthly payments. Robinson's father and stepmother took the funds to a local bank and established a trust fund for their missing son. At some point (Bill never has learned exactly when), his father crumbled under the emotional strain of his son's imprisonment and suffered a nervous breakdown. Burdened with a debilitated husband to care for, Jessie decided to quit work. They planned to support themselves by using some of their son's trust fund money. The bank, however, maintained that they could close out the account in its entirety, but they could not withdraw a portion of the balance. Desperate for funds, the couple closed the account, kept part of the account balance, and opened a new trust fund.[11]

Upon his return, Robinson discovered that his father and step-mother had repeated this cycle five or six times before they simply opened a savings account. They justified their actions by blaming Bill: he had been shot down and captured, and the uncertainty surrounding his situation created an unbearable misery for the family. They needed money to survive, for food to eat and clothes to wear, and to repair their home in order to keep a roof over their heads. To Robinson, it was all a convenient excuse: "they were living off" his income while he was a prisoner of war. In addition to his base pay, his combat pay, and the dollar per day he received for a Temporary Duty Assignment, Robinson signed up for a savings deposit program that paid 10 percent interest on deposits up to $10,000; the $10,000 ceiling was later removed for POWs. Before his release, Robinson had an inkling of the financial maneuverings of his parents, and in his prison cell he consulted some of the more level-headed POWs about his dilemma. Many urged him to turn the other cheek, arguing that one day Bill would have kids of his own and he would want his parents involved in the lives of their grandchildren. Reconciliation came with a steep price tag. Over the course of his captivity, Robinson's financial account should have grown to a sum in the range of $150,000 to $160,000, but his parents spent nearly $100,000, leaving Bill with $60,000. Back in the states, Bill swallowed his pride and disappointment, because he really just "wanted to forgive and move on." He had always called his father's second wife Jessie, never referring to her as mother. Hoping to build a better relationship with his family, Bill thought that if he called her mother, "then maybe that would help everything out." His father was up-front about the way they handled their son's accounts and admitted their problems. As a good-faith gesture, Bill's parents offered him the deed to their house, while claiming life-time rights. They intended to live in the house until they both passed away, at which time Bill could sell or rent the house or use it as he pleased. The plan sounded reasonable and fair; the value of the house roughly equaled the sum of the missing funds. But Bill's father was very capable of saying the right thing in the heat of the moment, and subsequently avoiding both his responsibilities to others and the consequences of his actions. Bill witnessed this behavior as a child and as a teenager, but he wanted to believe his father could change and was willing to do anything to facilitate reconciliation.[12]

At Andrews Air Force Base, while Bill was awaiting clearance to return to active duty, the two men discussed their futures. William was approaching retirement age, and even though Bill was committed to the Air Force, he would one day retire from the service and move on to a second career. The senior Robinson had always dreamed of owning his own salvage yard, and now his son possessed the resources to finance a joint business venture. Motivated by a desire for his father's love and approval, Bill agreed to form a business partnership. As soon as he made the first deposit in the company account, they bought a farm together, which they intended to convert into a salvage yard, and his father purchased a $13,000 wrecking truck. Profits appeared to be a sure thing. There were thousands of broken-down vehicles cluttering the landscape of northeastern North Carolina. County officials throughout the region wanted the eyesores removed and were willing to pay a small fee for each pickup. These vehicles represented an inventory windfall for a used-parts dealer. Their agreement named William as president of the company, Bill served as vice president, and Jessie was the secretary-treasurer. An optimistic Bill saw the enterprise as "a win-win situation." He had no illusions, though. He knew from the past that he could not work with his father, but if he underwrote the business, he could take over the company once his father retired. It appeared to be a perfect plan, until Bill "married a woman who was just as deceiving and just as cunning" as his stepmother. The much-anticipated reconciliation proved momentary at best, and they soon headed to the nadir of their relationship.

A Ready-Made Family

When Robinson received his commission in 1973, a picture of him, his grandmother, and his stepmother went out over the Associated Press newswire. The editor of a newspaper in Akron, Michigan, pulled the feed from the teletype and handed it to a young female journalist, suggesting that the information might be suitable for a human interest story. She filed the copy, choosing not to compose an article at that time, but she did write down her feelings in the form of a letter to the young Air Force lieutenant. Because of the national attention surrounding the returning POWs, the journalist decided against sending the letter, fearing that it would simply be overshadowed by the hundreds of cards and gifts received by each returnee. She probably surmised correctly. Months later, while cleaning out her desk, she discovered a yellowed envelope containing the wire story and her letter. This time she mailed the materials to Robinson, who was stationed at Sheppard AFB in Wichita Falls, Texas. They struck up a conversation, and a long-distance romance soon developed between Bill Robinson and Sue Gill. Sue first went to Sheppard on Easter weekend 1974. After spending the week with Bill, she returned to Michigan. Over the course of the next month, Robinson accumulated a $700 phone bill, and the two knew they had a decision to make. During their first encounter, Sue had not been completely truthful with Robinson. She failed to mention that she had a young daughter, and Bill did not learn about the child until after Sue returned to Michigan. He was willing to overlook her deception, conceding that not everyone is immediately forthcoming about his or her past. Or maybe he was just tired of being alone.[13]

By then Robinson had learned the details of Beverly's abandonment. She had explained her decision to Robinson's parents in mid-1966.

Dear Mr. & Mrs. Robinson,

Maybe this letter has been long anticipated by you. I don't know but for quite some time now you couldn't help but notice a change in me. I'm sorry. In spite of all you both have been through now I have to tell you this. I am getting married next month. I don't quite know how to tell Bill. I hate to think of what it might do to him. I loved Bill very dearly. That was fifteen months ago when I knew him, when I could be with him and he made me feel secure. Maybe I didn't love him quite as much as he loved me, but I only met him four months before he was sent to Viet Nam. Then in April he left, and I missed him terribly. I thought about him often and wrote as much as I could. Then when the tragedy happened about the time when he was due home, it deeply hurt all of us. And you were wonderful to keep in touch with me and the bad news we heard about our loved one drew us closer together and I couldn't help but love you for it. I lived in dread and fear and almost hated everyone and everything until Christmas time, when the girls tried to get me out to a party. I did always refuse except this one time I thought I owe it to myself to wake up and live again. I'm young and need more than what I was doing to myself. I went to the party and found myself pouring out all my troubles on this nice boy I met. He listened & gave me some comfort. I continued to see him the duration of our stay in Jamestown where he is from. At first we were friends sharing each other's problems but our friendship grew into love and now we are getting married & living in Jamestown.

My parents aren't too happy with what I am doing to Bill also. I'm sorry.

I find that I am not woman enough to tell Bill in a direct letter to him. I don't know what it might do to him. If you would like me to and think it is wise write back to me & I will compose a letter.

I would rather that you tell him or just keep it from him until he gets home. That will be rather difficult.

As far as the rest of the Robinson family who have been so good to me, I love you all and think of you often and it will take quite some time until I lose all of my guilt feelings. I'm not saying you should accept this graciously, but please don't hate me for it.

I must close now. I truly hope you understand. I hope one day I will be able to adjust to life as well as you have.

Good-bye for now—

Much love,
Bev

I will add here—for Bill—I'm sorry Bill. Please forgive me. I will never ever forget you—

The Dear John letter by proxy, which Robinson did not read until after his release, only confirmed what he had already surmised while waiting in the prison cells of North Vietnam. His record with women, especially Beverly and Jane, was anything but confidence boosting.[14] Would he ever find happiness?

Since returning to the states, Robinson "hadn't met anyone" who shared his values or had his level of maturity. He simply was not on the same "frequency" as the young women he met. Robinson was so uncomfortable with the lack of connection that he had started to date older women because he felt he had more in common with them. He noted that, especially at bars and nightclubs where he went to socialize and savor reality, most of the young women he encountered "were trying to escape reality." It was somewhat depressing to him. "Here I was thinking how fun this was, to be free and enjoying life, and I was with people who were miserable" and could not appreciate the simple pleasures of life, he lamented.

Although disconcerted by her initial lack of openness, Robinson nevertheless decided to invite Sue back for a longer visit. She accepted and joined him in Texas. When Robinson had arrived at Sheppard, he obtained a mobile home to live in to avoid residing on the base in the barracks.[15] Because a young child was involved, Robinson did not deem it appropriate for him and Sue to live together if they were not married. Besides, Sue refused to live in his home because he had shared it with a previous girlfriend. He initially arranged, through a friend, to secure an apartment for Sue and her six-year-old daughter, Dani, and he later acquired a mobile home for them next door to his.[16]

In some respects, Robinson looked excitedly at the ready-made family from Michigan as he contemplated the prospects of marriage. Sue, however, had been married previously and wanted "adventure" not matrimony. The two went through a series of breakups, but Robinson "could put up with no obligation [only] for a short period of time." Meanwhile, he received a transfer to Chanute Air Force Base near Rantoul, Illinois, where he would attend aircraft maintenance officer school. Before he left in early 1975, Robinson agreed to take her back home, but she told him that "it would be a cold day in hell before she went back to Michigan." Able to support herself by working at a local newspaper, Sue stayed in Texas. They remained friends during the separation, but Robinson stayed firm in his desire for a deeper commitment from Sue. Gradually, she consented to the possibility of a long-term relationship. After nearly a year of involvement, Sue relented to Robinson's appeals. On 8 March 1975 the couple married in Champaign, Illinois. Along the road to matrimony, Robinson developed some concerns, but once he and Sue married, he "felt comfortable" with his new family. Yet as time passed he discovered new details about the parameters of their marriage. He had incorrectly assumed—he had not actually asked—that he and Sue would have additional children after they became man and wife. Sue had no interest in raising more children, a painful disappointment to Robinson, but he "accepted it and moved on." Perhaps a change of scenery or a fresh start would help. Their opportunity came when Robinson drew an assignment at Eglin Air Force Base in northwest Florida.[17]

The move south in the summer of 1975 represented a new beginning of sorts for the recently married pair. They purchased their first home in the town of Crestview, Florida, a short distance from the air base. Robinson's career seemed on track, a promotion to captain occurred shortly after arriving at Eglin, and he served as a maintenance officer with the 33rd Tactical Fighter Wing. The assignment also reunited Robinson with a number of former POWs. Colonel Bud Day, a Medal of Honor recipient, was the vice wing commander at Eglin, and he was joined by Major Joseph Crecca, held from 22 November 1966 to 18 February 1973, Captain Kenneth Wells, held from 18 December 1971 to 28 March 1973, and Colonel Rudolph U. Zuberbuhler, whose unusual surname earned him the nickname Z-plus Ten, held from 12 September 1972 to 29 March 1973. This setting seemed idyllic in many ways, but appearances can deceive. Despite the bonds created by captivity, the former POWs rarely socialized in the same circles at Eglin. They had separate careers to pursue; Crecca, Wells, and Zuberbuhler returned to flying status after their release, and they had families to raise, which consumed much of their spare time. Moreover, Bill's wife began to reveal her disdain for the Air Force. Sue had grown up in a military family; her father was a noncommissioned officer in the Army and a post commander, and the rules and structure of that world caused her to reject both its utility and its heritage. Thus, trying to balance an Air Force career against an increasingly hostile counterforce in his personal life created an unwelcome tension in Robinson's life.[18]

When Bill and Sue moved from Illinois to Florida, the school year had ended and there was no pressing need to relocate Dani right away, so she traveled to Michigan to stay with her maternal grandparents until her mother and stepfather settled in to their new surroundings. Robinson had always wanted kids, and soon after arriving in Florida he was eager to have Dani join them. When Sue had divorced her first husband, Dani's biological father relinquished all parental rights, paid no child support, and was not involved in any way in his daughter's life. Robinson wanted Dani to have more than a father figure in her life and desperately wanted to legally adopt her, but Sue "fought it every step of the way." Knowing Sue did not want any more children, Robinson, rather than turn a cold shoulder to Dani, invested himself fully in her life. As she entered her teen years, Dani displayed remarkable talents. The Robinsons purchased several horses, and mother and daughter traveled to shows and competitions where Dani often won trophies for her equestrian skills. Dani also possessed artistic abilities that distinguished her from other children. But Bill never established the type of father-daughter connection that he had dreamed of for most of his adult life. They "had natural disagreements," the kind that all fathers and daughters have, but they seemed to be constantly at odds with one another, their relationship strained by Robinson's marriage to Sue. Though Dani and Sue always got along fine when he was not around, Robinson sensed that "in her mind I was the problem, which created a lot of difficulties." Robinson sometimes felt like the enemy in his own home and the source of friction between his wife and stepdaughter, which prevented Dani and Sue from forging a lasting and meaningful bond. Friends of the family noticed the tension in the Robinson household. Sue erected barriers around herself and had a limited number of friends; she "chose the friends who came into her house; they were the only ones that could come." As time passed, she reached the point where she never wanted to travel as a family, and on those rare occasions when they left together, a close family friend had to stay in their home "at all times" to watch over the residence and tend to their animals. Sue's friends knew that she was a "difficult person to live with" and that she and Bill did not have a loving marriage.[19]

Family Feud

Sometime in early 1977, William Robinson phoned his son, asking for more money to help with living expenses and to prop up their failing salvage business. His sense of entitlement knew no limits, and he expected his son to support him although he lacked any semblance of business acumen or work ethic. There were nearly four thousand junk cars in northeastern North Carolina, but William had managed to pick up a mere three hundred cars, and he compounded matters by making poor business decisions. To the supplication for additional funds, Bill responded, "There ain't no more." Despite the warning signs, Bill had put "just about everything he had into the business," only to have his father deplete it all. William and Jessie tried to bully and shame Bill and Sue into acquiescing, which only served to harden Sue's resolve; the entire fiasco mainly disgusted Bill. He constantly and consistently placed confidence in his father, knowing disappointment would be the result. When Bill married Sue, William and Jessie reneged on their earlier promise to deed their house to their son, and the demand for even more money opened old wounds and intensified existing hostilities among the four family members. To extract himself from this family quagmire as well as any financial liabilities caused by his parents' mismanagement, Bill enlisted the help of a friend and former POW. Colonel Bud Day had earned a law degree from the University of South Dakota in 1949 and at the time of Bill's crisis was a member of the Florida Bar. Thus, his help was more than perfunctory. The vice wing commander could certainly handle himself in a legal proceeding. Among other things, Day's investigation revealed that Bill's parents closed some of their son's accounts more than a year after he returned, proving they had never abandoned their habits of deception and malfeasance. After reviewing the evidence, Day advised Robinson, "We've got to go in there and scare the hell out of those people [his parents]," and force them to admit in writing that Robinson was unaware of and not responsible for the debts they had incurred. Then they needed "to get the hell out of Dodge."[20]

Interjecting her imagined legal expertise, Bill's wife Sue "wanted to put the bastards in jail." Day, attempting to reason with Robinson's mercurial wife, said, "Sue, you're in the South, and that ain't the way things are done. No matter what they've done, and we know it's wrong, no judge in the South" would put a set of older parents in jail over a family financial feud. Day spoke a reality that Sue refused to accept. Bill, of course, did not want to put his parents in prison, but he needed to resolve the matter as quickly as possible. For six months Day impressed on Sue the need to accede to his discretion regarding the case. Finally, she relented. In the end, Sue's deep respect for Day, rather than the logic of his arguments, compelled her to drop her demand for jail time. In all likelihood no other lawyer possessed the gravitas to subdue her determination.[21]

Before Robinson made a decision regarding his legal options, he called his grandfather and "explained what was going on and what was about to happen." Gene Robinson reminded his grandson that he had opposed the business partnership from the beginning but had realized that any opposition at that time was pointless. Gene respected his grandson for not giving up on his father and told him he was proud of his efforts, but he "pretty much knew it wasn't going to work out." As for the matter at hand, Gene advised Bill: "Now you've got to do what you've got to do." Before the resolution of the legal drama, Gene Robinson passed away suddenly and unexpectedly, and Bill lost his childhood role model and a cherished loved one. A malicious William turned the tragedy against his own son. At the funeral he looked at Bill and said, "It's your fault. You killed your granddaddy," not realizing Gene had counseled against the original partnership and approved the current legal strategy to end the business arrangement. Moreover, William did not realize that his own sister was poised to play a key role in dissolving the corporation. Day was able to expunge William and Jessie from their positions within the company. Bill remained as vice president, one of his aunts served as secretary-treasurer, and another aunt assumed the mantle of president. He liquidated some of the company's assets to recoup his losses. He sold the farm along with its peanut and tobacco allotments; these allotments gave growers a type of monopoly that helped bolster prices and determined the value of the property. Bill's top priority was to gain control of the company in order to shut it down and cut his losses. This latest confrontation erected a wall of silence between Robinson and his father and stepmother; he essentially had no contact with them for twenty years. Long after the legal resolution, Bill received calls from people complaining about his father's shenanigans. Through it all, Bill followed his usual pattern; he did what he "had to do and moved on."[22]

The tension among Bill and his father and Sue and Jessie affected the rest of Bill's family as well. And Sue's confrontational demeanor drove the family further apart. "When he married Sue and went to Florida, it didn't seem that she was very family-oriented," Bill's sister Ginger observed. "Personally, I felt he was about as far away as he was in Vietnam." By comparing the family's more recent struggles to the seven-and-a-half-year ordeal of Bill's captivity, the gentle-natured and soft-spoken Ginger defined in stark terms the depth of their separation. On one occasion Sue coldly informed Bill's younger sister that if she "could leave religion out of it," they "could be friends." A deeply devout and exasperated Ginger explained, "If that was the only way I could be friends with her, then I was sorry I couldn't be her friend." Bill's older sister, Jackie, had a similar opinion of Sue. Early in Bill and Sue's marriage, Jackie and her daughter Debbie went to Fort Walton Beach, Florida, for relaxation and on two or three occasions visited the newlyweds. But Sue never made them feel comfortable while they were there, and she once suggested that Debbie leave Bill's great-niece in day care rather than bring the child to their home. In addition to their disappointment and personal pain, the sisters were somewhat bewildered by the estrangement. "We couldn't ever really tell what the situation was there," explained Ginger. "We didn't get to see him a lot," and "there was not a lot of closeness." Jackie agreed. Her brother returned to North Carolina "every now and then," but not very often, usually to attend family funerals. Even on those rare occasions, arguments generally occurred. Bill phoned infrequently, and throughout his marriage to Sue his relationships with his sisters stagnated.[23] Driven by the actions of his father and stepmother, Bill felt that his family gave him a choice: them or Sue. In his mind there was no choice. He had taken a vow and made a commitment to Sue. He refused to run from his responsibilities as a husband and stepfather. He hoped, as they all went on with their lives, that one day circumstances would change and the family would reunite. In the meantime, Robinson stayed in touch with one of his uncles as a way of staying abreast of news and developments in the lives of his siblings and their children.[24]

Eventually, Sue's animosity toward the Air Force and the military facilitated Robinson's retirement. He understood certain "square boxes had to be filled," training programs completed, and particular duty assignments accomplished for him to advance through the ranks. Whenever he received such opportunities, Sue erected "a brick wall," refusing to relocate. She expected promotions and awards to be given on the basis of Robinson's achievements as a POW, an attitude completely at odds with his work ethic and sense of worth. On 1 December 1984, after twenty-three years in the Air Force, one-third of which was spent as a prisoner of war in Vietnam, Robinson retired from active duty. He left under a type of temporary military disability stemming from his "bad knees, bad feet, and back problems." The stipulations of his retirement required an annual evaluation to determine whether his physical condition showed signs of improvement. Of course, there were no prospects of recovering from the toll exacted on his body while he was in captivity. Still, the retirement stipulations effectively precluded him from accepting income-earning employment. Consequently, Robinson joined his wife as a volunteer for the Florida Fish and Wildlife Conservation Commission, through which they assisted in the rescue of endangered animals. Owls became their specialty. The work was rewarding despite the occasional false alarm prompted by transplanted Yankees who could not distinguish a loon from a duck. The typical temporary military disabled retiree waited three to five years before being declared permanently disabled, but Robinson's doctor proved within a year and a half that he met the classification standards. Never one to sit idle, Robinson now sought salaried employment and signed on as a manager of a locally owned independent auto parts store.[25]

Closing a Chapter

Early in Sue's life, her mother had contracted cancer. She completed numerous treatments and went into remission, but the cancer returned. Ultimately, she "went through a slow, agonizing five-year death." Sue vowed that would never happen to her. Tragically, she was never given the chance to keep that vow. In July 1993 Sue complained about a pain in her rib cage. She attributed the discomfort to an accident with one of her horses. Other than pain medication, the standard treatment for a broken rib is to allow the injury to heal on its own. Thus, Sue ignored signs of a more serious ailment. The pain, however, persisted. In late September, as she prepared for a trip to Texas to attend a symposium on the assassination of President John Kennedy, she decided to consult a doctor. Bill believes his wife probably knew she was ill long before she went to the doctor. Sue's doctor informed her that she had lung cancer. She demanded an unvarnished prognosis. The doctor said, "You have less than three months to live." She was clearly taken aback by his pronouncement, and it was several days before she revealed the news to her husband. She was referred to a specialist, who confirmed the first doctor's startling discovery. The cancer had spread to both lungs, and the doctor advised the patient that her only treatment option was chemotherapy. Having witnessed her mother's painful death, Sue with customary flair told the specialist, "Not only no, but hell, no." With no treatment and no hope of recovery, Sue's condition deteriorated rapidly. On a few occasions Bill took her to the emergency rooms of several local hospitals, both military and civilian, but there was nothing that the facilities could do to reverse her inevitable course. She finally agreed to chemotherapy but died two weeks after the first treatment. From diagnosis to death, she lasted only fifty-eight days.[26]

As she did with most things, Sue made perfectly clear her wishes for her funeral. She didn't want one. She chose to be cremated, and her family and friends held a small "celebration of her life." Sue requested that her ashes be spread over the graves of her mother and father. Robinson intended to honor his wife's wishes; however, her father had not yet passed away, so he decided to hold Sue's ashes until the appropriate time. After Sue was gone, he turned his attention to his eighty-seven-year-old father-in-law, William Wayne Gill, who had now lost both his wife and his daughter. Robinson had started looking after Gill before Sue died when he underwent radiation treatments for cancer, driving him to the doctor and back home. Gill appreciated Robinson's assistance, and his health improved, but the loss of his daughter robbed him of some incentive to live, and he began to put his affairs in order. He only had one request, to be cremated; he gave no additional instructions. Once Gill reached a point where he could no longer care for himself, Robinson intervened. He called his father-in-law's doctor and explained how badly Gill had deteriorated. The doctor convinced Gill that he had two options: move in with Robinson or enter a nursing home. Gill chose the former. By then, Robinson had met someone and fallen in love. Gill understood and gave his approval. They formed a "happy threesome" for roughly two months, but Gill's health progressively worsened, and he died on 12 December 1995. Although Robinson did not personally disperse the ashes of his wife and father-in-law, he obtained the assistance of a family friend who transported the remains to Michigan and scattered them according to the requests of the deceased.[27]

After Sue died, Robinson reached out once again to his father. Jessie had died in 1988, but he did not learn of her passing until some time later. Bill convinced himself that it was "the women that we put in our lives" who in many respects had caused the discord between him and his father. Perhaps the loss of so many people in a short period convinced Bill to give his father one more chance. He lost Sue in December 1993, and then an uncle, who Bill considered one of his "best friends," passed away; unfortunately, Robinson was not able to attend his uncle's funeral. In January 1994 his beloved grandmother, Geneva Robinson, died. Because of his own dire financial straits, Robinson had to borrow a car to attend his grandmother's funeral; while in North Carolina, he spoke to his father. They "communicated a little" and agreed to work "toward being around each other" without fighting. The process started slowly, but in October 1994 Bill took his fiancée to North Carolina to see, as he put it, if "she could tolerate" his family and "vice versa." He hoped that a second marriage would lessen the relationship gap that existed between himself and his family. During the visit, Robinson's father handed him an envelope, saying, "I was hoping that it would turn into fifty thousand dollars." William had given his son the records for a savings account that Bill had opened while stationed in Grand Forks, North Dakota, an account the son had long since forgotten about. The balance of $1,500 hardly compensated for the years of deception, but the gesture marked a step in a more positive direction.[28]

After Jessie's death, William Robinson married his third wife, a woman six months older than his son, Bill. When they married, the two signed a prenuptial agreement, which left William as the sole owner of his home, the one he and Jessie had promised Bill long before but had never signed over. His third wife had her own home. Sometime after they married, William's house burned down, and rather than build a replacement, he opted for a lump sum settlement from the insurance company. It was at that point that Bill realized that his father "had no remorse" for any of his actions over the years. He proudly displayed a $47,900 check but never offered his son a dime. Still, Bill would not turn his back on his father, especially when his health declined and his young bride had no interest in caring for him. Because Bill's sister Jackie still lived near her father, she became his principal caregiver, and Bill worked the channels of the Veterans Administration to secure some benefits from his father's service in World War II. After a lengthy illness, William Jackson Robinson died in 1999.[29]

Final Rescue

The passing of Sue and, less than six years later, the death of his father closed a difficult and at times painful chapter in Robinson's life. He had always been more than a mere survivor, and as he turned the next page of his life, he did so with optimism and passion. And this time, he found love, friendship, and companionship awaiting him. When Sue had become ill, she made Bill promise not to tell her daughter, Dani. Their troubles had escalated during Dani's teen years, and after graduating from high school, she moved away from home and had little contact with her parents. Although he thought Dani should know about her mother's condition, Robinson felt an obligation to honor Sue's wishes, and so he remained silent. Dani probably learned of Sue's situation from someone other than her stepfather, but she did not see her mother before she passed away. After Sue died, Bill called Dani, and after they spoke she went to see him. At the time Dani was on her own and struggling to raise a small child, and Bill invited her to move in with him. She accepted.[30]

Sue had opposed Bill's adoption of Dani when she was younger, fearing such a move would give him too much control over their lives, especially if Sue and Bill's marriage failed and he sought some type of joint custody or visitation rights. Now, as a grown woman and mother, Dani had no reason to worry about a meddling or controlling father. Bill desired only a chance to build a relationship, and he took the extraordinary step of formally adopting Dani four months after Sue's death. He wanted her to know that he loved her, he "would always be there for her," and he thought of her as his own child. Dani stayed with Bill for only a short while; however, before leaving, she conspired with a female friend, who had a single mother, in a bit of matchmaking. After the two women coordinated a few prearranged meetings, Bill and Ora Mae Creel unraveled their daughters' plot. Bill had actually known Ora Mae since 1978, when the Robinsons, the Creels, and Dr. Richard Thomas had purchased homes in the De-Funiak Springs community in Florida. They developed friendships and regularly socialized together. In fact, Ora Mae had had a close relationship with Sue and was one of the few people whom Bill's first wife trusted. Ora Mae's world changed forever in the summer of 1985, when her husband, an Air Force noncommissioned officer and a seventeen-year veteran, demanded a divorce. During an assignment at Thule Air Base in Greenland he had become involved with a woman from Denmark, and he decided to marry her.[31] As a single mom with a teenager to raise, Ora Mae frequently found herself confronted with routine situations such as car troubles or home repairs, and for a while she struggled. After Sue's death, Bill stepped forward and offered his assistance whenever she needed help. Following a brief courtship, the couple married in the home of their longtime friend Dr. Richard Thomas. It was a small gathering, "with maybe fifty people there," and a notary public officiated at the ceremony.[32]

Bill added not only Ora Mae to his family, but her daughter, Cyndi, as well. This was not merely a figurative gesture by Robinson. He wanted Cyndi to know "she was just as much a part of" his life as Ora was. He formally adopted Cyndi even though she was a thirty-five-year-old woman. And when she decided to marry an Air Force enlisted man, she asked Bill to walk her down the aisle and give her away. Some reconstituted families have members who fall into one of three categories: "mine, yours, and ours." For Robinson, the adoption of Dani and Cyndi signified his feelings that his "two girls" gave him "a whole family . . . out of two broken ones," and the children of his two daughters "would always have a clear path" to their grandfather.[33]

Having observed firsthand Bill's marriage to Sue, Ora Mae was aware of what he had been through and she knew what type of character he possessed. Ora Mae regarded Bill as "always a very sweet person, willing to help in any way that he could." Despite her familiarity with Bill's life, Ora Mae was not fully aware of the depth of her husband's estrangement from his family, although she knew things were strained. Even before they married, she felt "it was important for him to reconnect with his family, because family is all you have in the end." She especially desired that he repair his relationship with his sisters, and she encouraged Bill to do so.[34] Ginger easily recognized the contrast between Ora Mae and Bill's first wife. "Ora Mae has always seemed willing to share him with the family and not try to keep him away from us," Ginger reflected; she and the rest of the family felt free to call, write, or visit Bill for any reason. Whatever bad feelings had existed in the past dissipated between the death of Sue and Bill's marriage to Ora Mae. In the end, Ginger has accepted that "it wasn't any one particular person's fault. We just allowed circumstances to keep us from being the family that we could have been." Jackie sensed the changes as well, and she believes that her brother "deserves all the happiness in the world. He went through so much. His last years ought to be the best in the world."[35] After so many years of disappointment and heartache, Robinson had been rescued, finally. With Ora Mae by his side, Bill was inspired to renew his ties to a group of men who had meant so much to him during one of the darkest periods of his life.

A Brotherhood of Valor

Just as Bill Robinson wanted to reconnect with his family after his first wife's death, he was eager to reestablish ties with his fellow Vietnam POWs. And as she encouraged him to return to his family, Ora Mae offered her unconditional support when her husband inquired about POW-related activities. "I felt like he needed to keep in contact with those people," Ora Mae said. "Those people were like family to him, and just like he lost contact with his blood relatives, he had lost contact with them." The process started simply when Bill received an invitation from the Department of the Navy in early 1994 to participate in a study on the long-term medical and psychological consequences of torture and captivity at the nearby Naval Aerospace Medical Institute at the Pensacola Naval Air Station.[36] He asked Ora Mae for advice and she urged him to accept the offer, which he did. His first examination revealed that he had a sound mind and heart, but the years of malicious treatment in North Vietnam had exacted a heavy toll on his body. Doctors determined that Robinson would eventually require shoulder replacement surgery to repair the damage caused by the ropes treatment and similar forms of torture. They found numerous other signs of physical deterioration as well. During his initial visit to Pensacola, Robinson noticed a flyer on a bulletin board in one of the medical offices announcing a Veterans Day tribute in Branson, Missouri. The flyer instructed former prisoners of war to contact the P.O.W. Network for additional details about the event. Founded in 1989 to distribute and verify information on prisoners of war and missing-in-action servicemen, the organization also promoted various types of patriotic tributes and in this instance offered to make the necessary travel arrangements for the Branson event for former POWs.[37] After a brief discussion, Bill and Ora Mae decided to attend.

Each year since 1934, Branson, Missouri, had hosted a Veterans Day parade. In 1993, however, the city made a conscious and forthright effort to target veterans groups. Tourism officials called on the well-known entertainer Tony Orlando, who opened the Yellow Ribbon Music Theater in the city that same year, to serve as the grand marshal of the Veterans Day parade, and he emceed the First Annual Yellow Ribbon Salute to Veterans.[38] He was an obvious choice. The recent Gulf War had renewed interest in his 1973 hit "Tie a Yellow Ribbon Round the Old Oak Tree" as millions of Americans displayed yellow ribbons, in a variety of forms, to show concern for American military personnel in general, and those soldiers deployed in theaters of combat more specifically.[39] The 1994 Branson event expanded on the inaugural year's festivities and was still a tribute to veterans, not a POW reunion. By a twist of fate, Robinson met about a dozen former Vietnam prisoners of war in Branson, including Thomas Collins, Stephen Long, Pop Keirn, Harold Johnson, and Gary Sigler. For the first time since their release in 1973, Robinson reunited with his former pilot, Tom Curtis. His fellow North Carolinian James Hiteshew was also in Branson. His wife, Billie, and Bill's parents had worked together in the North Carolina chapter of the National League of Families and played an instrumental role in raising public awareness about the prisoners of war. The former prisoners naturally gravitated to those men they knew best, and Robinson spent quite a bit of time with Curtis, but they all interacted and either renewed old friendships or initiated new ones. The following year a POW reunion occurred in Branson in conjunction with the Veterans Day event. At least sixty former prisoners attended the reunion, including Art Cormier, whom Robinson had not seen in more than twenty years. During those twenty years Robinson had experienced his share of postrelease hardships, but none of them compared to the ordeal of captivity, and the reunion placed things in perspective for him. At one social gathering in Branson with a number of former prisoners, Robinson asked the men, "When was the last time you were in a room where you trusted everybody in it?" Robinson felt he had rejoined a brotherhood of valor.[40]

He regretted that he had not reunited sooner, noting that he had access to the NAM-POWs organization through his friend and mentor Colonel Bud Day. Formed in 1973, the NAM-POWs organization had had a fraternal and patriotic agenda from its inception: "Our objectives are to cherish the memories of the valiant deeds of our members; to promote true fellowship among our members; to advance the best interests of members of the Armed Forces of the United States and to enhance their prestige and understanding by example and personal activity; to stimulate patriotism and national pride in the minds of our youth."[41] Familial obstacles, however, denied Robinson the opportunity to be an active member of this unique group. From this point forward, Robinson was determined to stay connected to his fellow POWs, whether an event was slated to be small or large. The former Vietnam War POWs have held several large reunions at the ranch of the Texas billionaire H. Ross Perot. Few Americans will ever know the full extent of Perot's efforts in behalf of America's prisoners of war, as well as its veterans. In October 1993, when Chief Warrant Officer Michael Durant was being held captive for eleven days following his helicopter crash during the Battle of Mogadishu, Perot managed to call Durant's family "on many occasions," was "decisively engaged" in the pilot's release, and established a special fund to assist with homecoming celebrations after his release. Perot's extraordinary endeavors in behalf of the Vietnam War POWs are more well known than that case, and the former prisoners take every opportunity to thank him. Robinson appreciated what Perot did in the 1960s and 1970s for himself and his fellow POWs, and he respects Perot for what he continues to do for "those we admired." For example, Robinson credits Perot with being the driving force behind a nine-foot-tall bronze statue of Colonel Robinson Risner dedicated on 16 November 2001 on the central plaza of the United States Air Force Academy. In Robinson's words, if Perot "got wind" of something that involved the recognition of POWs, "he put more wind in the sail" and made certain that the project was completed. Throughout their captivity, Vietnam War POWs vowed to "return with honor," to commit no acts or utter any words that would dishonor their nation, the U.S. military, or themselves as individuals. Robinson believed that he fulfilled that pledge during his seven and a half years in North Vietnam, and by reuniting with his former prison mates he intended to celebrate their legacy. Though it wasn't initially the case, he eventually found the Andersonville National Historic Site a suitable stage on which to accomplish his new mission.[42]

6

An Iconic Image

In October 1994 Bill Robinson unexpectedly received a letter from Le Manh Thich, a documentary film director at the Central Science Documentary Film Studio in Hanoi. Thich explained that "ever since the sounds of guns and bombs" had ceased in his country, he, as a filmmaker, had "met many people from both sides who fought in the war," including "some former American soldiers who were visiting the battlefields again." Thich then made a startling revelation:

> I had a chance to visit a small town in Ha Tinh on the central coast the other day. On September 20, 1965 when the Vietnam War was getting fiercer, you were in Huon Khe, Ha Tinh. The first Vietnamese you met there was a little girl who was a guerrilla. I would like to tell you that the girl is still alive. She is currently working at a hospital in Ha Tinh as a medical examiner. She has a dog and three children. Her name is Nguyen Kim Lai and lives at 1 Dong hai-putong Bao Ha, Ha Tinh. She is not wealthy, and her life is still hard for her but, her family is very close. She agreed to meet with me. We enjoyed talking and she talked about you a lot to me. You must have made a strong impression on her. She told me that she would be very happy if she could meet you again. If it happened, she said, it would mean a lot to her and also to other people.[1]

Nguyen Kim Lai was the young Vietnamese militia girl who escorted Robinson in the staged propaganda photo take shortly after his capture on 20 September 1965. Thich proposed that Robinson come to Vietnam and meet with Nguyen Kim Lai, while he, as a documentary filmmaker, recorded the important reunion. Thich had already enlisted the assistance of NHK, the Japan Broadcasting Corporation, and informed Robinson that a representative from the company, based in Washington, D.C., would contact him soon.[2] Two weeks later Robinson received a letter from Rumiko Sakai, the Washington-based representative of NHK. She, too, encouraged Robinson to accept the invitation to return to Vietnam and meet Nguyen Kim Lai; she predicted that "it would be a wonderful opportunity for everyone to look back [on] the history and think about the meaning of it."[3]

NHK's interest in the relatively unknown former POW certainly came as a surprise to Robinson, but he accepted their overtures as "legitimate" and never considered the letter a "hoax." Their emphasis on the capture photo and consistent references to a "human interest" story made sense to Robinson, who was aware that Vietnam was reaching out internationally for new allies following the collapse of the Soviet Union. And Japan would be the documentary's primary target audience, though there was the possibility of a future release in the United States. Nevertheless, this was not an easy decision for Robinson. Ora Mae supported her husband's increased involvement in POW organizations and backed his regular attendance at POW reunions. Returning to Vietnam to face his former captors, however, required Robinson to make a bold, perhaps dangerous, and potentially painful step. Aside from any personal risks to Robinson, the issue of missing-in-action servicemen was an ongoing point of contention between the two countries, and he was sensitive to the concerns of such groups as the National League of Families, which opposed normalizing relations with Vietnam until it was satisfied with the levels of access to and cooperation by the Vietnamese government in its accounting for missing service personnel.[4]

The lack of a precedent also complicated the matter for Robinson. He did not know a single former prisoner who had made the return trip to Vietnam. Additionally, he knew how many of his close POW friends would respond to this type of invitation: "Fuck 'em. Nothing has changed." Such conversations would, in effect, be a waste of time. In the end, what concerned Robinson most was the "bigger diplomatic picture." He did not want to do anything to create an incident between the United States and Vietnam that could interfere with the ongoing dialogue between the two countries. Before he made a final decision, Robinson contacted another former Vietnam POW, Douglas (Pete) Peterson. Held for six and a half years in North Vietnam, the former Air Force pilot won a seat in the U.S. House of Representatives in 1990. Robinson's and Peterson's paths had crossed a few times in recent years; Peterson served in the adjacent second congressional district of Florida. Peterson was a Democrat and was working closely with the administration of President Bill Clinton to improve U.S.–Vietnamese relations. In a very "straightforward" manner, he urged Robinson to accept the invitation. With a third party, the Japanese-based NHK, heavily involved in the project, Peterson did not foresee any problems, and he felt the project was "a good idea" and that Bill's story was worth being told. Satisfied with Peterson's assessment, Robinson also saw the proposed documentary as an opportunity for his sisters to share the emotional strain they suffered as a family during his captivity. Thus, Robinson decided to return to Vietnam, a country that still had not recovered from decades of war.[5]

The Long Road to Peace

The legacy of the Vietnam War for the United States can be measured in many ways. The war fractured the nation's political and cultural landscape. The U.S. military services, most notably the Army, needed reforming in its wake, particularly in the areas of recruiting standards, training guidelines, and fighting doctrines. The generation of combat veterans who had served in Vietnam failed to receive proper recognition for their military service. The price of sacrifice for those who served in Vietnam was 58,000 American deaths and another 313,000 wounded, 74,000 of whom were multiple amputees or quadriplegics. Additionally, the National Vietnam Veterans Readjustments Study determined that by 1983 nearly 34 percent of servicemen and servicewomen had full-blown (25 percent) or partial (18.9 percent) post-traumatic stress disorder.[6] For the Vietnamese, the war's legacy was equally tragic on many levels, but, in contrast to their former foes, their country lay in ruins. Indeed, in the South 60 percent of the 15,000 hamlets had been de-

stroyed, and millions of acres of farmland and forest had been rav-
aged by the constant specter of war. All six of the North's industrial
cities were heavily damaged, and nearly 70 percent of its 5,800 agricultural communes needed substantial reclamation. The human
toll confirmed the war's destructiveness as well, in both the South
and the North. During twenty-five years of fighting, some 200,000
South Vietnamese soldiers were killed and as many as two million
civilians became casualties. The victorious North paid a heavy price
for its triumph, losing nearly 900,000 lives on the fields of battle.[7]
And yet the human suffering and bloodshed continued to sweep
unmercifully through Southeast Asia.

First, the communist takeover of South Vietnam had resulted
in the political execution of perhaps as many as 65,000 South Vietnamese; at least 200,000 South Vietnamese spent years in hard labor camps or reeducation centers, and more than a million South
Vietnamese fled the country to escape political persecution and economic deprivation.[8] By withdrawing militarily from Vietnam and
by refusing to normalize diplomatic relations with the communist
nation, the United States allowed "new configurations of power"
to be unleashed in Southeast Asia, some involving "bitter rivalries
older than the entire history of the United States as a country."[9] A
border controversy between Vietnam and Cambodia sparked a new
round of wanton destructiveness. The communists in Hanoi viewed
Cambodia as a client state of China, and, emboldened by their own
patron, the Soviet Union, Vietnam invaded its Asian neighbor in December 1978. On 17 February 1979 the Chinese retaliated by sending
some 100,000 soldiers into the northern provinces of Vietnam and
occupied the towns of Cao Bang and Lang Son, but they met fierce
resistance, losing more than 20,000 dead, and withdrew after sixteen days of fighting.[10] Predictably, Vietnam's ten-year occupation
of Cambodia and its belligerent relationship with China created an
enormous drain on the nation's limited economic resources.

For some scholars, economic deprivation constituted "the most
pressing legacy" for the Vietnamese people. As the noted diplomatic historian George C. Herring explained, "Thirty years of war
left the country in shambles, and the regime's ill-conceived postwar efforts to promote industry and collectivize agriculture made

things worse."[11] The nation's gross national product (GNP) rose an annual average of .4 percent during the last half decade of the 1970s; the Vietnam Communist Party (VCP) had promised a 13 to 14 percent annual increase in the GNP. Inflation rates soared, purchasing power declined, and the standard of living remained low for virtually all Vietnamese. To compensate for declining purchasing power, state employees raised chickens and pigs in the hallways of their Hanoi apartment buildings or in the apartments themselves. Little changed in the early 1980s, as inflation rates fluctuated between 50 and 92 percent and reached an astounding 775 percent in 1986. The loss of economic aid from its former ally China and the U.S. trade embargo against Vietnam exacerbated the economic "crisis but did not play determining roles" in the failure of the state-run economy.[12]

In late 1986 the VCP launched a reform program known as *Doi Moi,* meaning renovation. The tides of change had been churning in Asia for some time. As early as 1978 Deng Xiaoping, who replaced Mao Zedong as the leader of Communist China, had initiated a series of market-oriented economic reforms and encouraged international investment. By the time of his death in 1997, China possessed one of the world's largest economies. But the pace of political reform and the expansion of civil liberties transitioned at a much slower rate, as evidenced by the tragic outcome of the prodemocracy demonstrations at Tiananmen Square in June 1989.[13] As the anthropologist Hy V. Luong has written, "The Vietnamese state adopted initial reform measures [comparable to the Chinese model] in a piecemeal fashion" that focused on economic development rather than political change. These systemic changes, coupled with the altered geopolitical landscape that came with the collapse of the Soviet Union and the end of the Cold War, accelerated the economic transformation of Vietnam. The number of privately owned enterprises rose from 318 in 1988 to 5,714 in 1998, and "those with foreign capital, from 1 to 830"; the number of state industrial workers declined precipitously. An 8 percent annual economic growth rate between 1990 and 1997 raised the GNP substantially, inflation fell to approximately 3.4 percent annually, and the poverty rate fell from 58 percent to 37 percent during this time. Vietnam's emerging market-oriented economy outperformed the paths followed by the Soviet Union and

Eastern Europe and bore "fundamental similarities to the Chinese reform experiences."[14]

There was a thawing of relations between the communist nation and the United States that corresponded with the economic shift in Vietnam and the end of the country's war with Cambodia. During the presidency of George H. W. Bush, the United States drew a detailed road map for normalization of relations with Vietnam that included U.S. pledges for humanitarian aid. The Vietnamese cooperated in the investigations of several "live sighting" reports of American MIAs, and U.S. humanitarian aid and investment capital followed.[15] From August 1991 to December 1992 a U.S. Senate select committee, chaired by the former Winter Soldier John Kerry (D-Massachusetts) and including the former Vietnam POW John McCain, investigated accusations that the United States had abandoned American prisoners in Vietnam at the end of the war and assessed the process for completing a full accounting of MIAs. The committee reported in 1993 that "there is no proof that U.S. POWs survived, but neither is there proof that all of those who did not return had died. There is evidence, moreover, that indicates the possibility of survival, at least for a small number, after Operation Homecoming." The committee, however, concluded that the U.S. government did not "knowingly" abandon POWs in Southeast Asia.[16] MIA activists, who believed that by withholding formal diplomatic recognition, the United States gained valuable leverage against the Vietnamese in the search for missing American remains, criticized the committee's findings.[17] Nevertheless, the results of the investigation placed the two countries one step closer to normalizing relations and provided the newly elected president, Bill Clinton, with a platform for moving forward. On 3 February 1994 the president ended the trade embargo on Vietnam and diplomatic progress continued. The revolutionary changes in Vietnam had little, if any, direct effect on the life of Bill Robinson, but for Nguyen Kim Lai, the *Doi Moi* reforms literally created a new Vietnam. To be sure, not everyone benefited from the transition to a market-oriented economy, and much of Vietnam remained burdened by extreme poverty, but optimism existed in many quarters. Furthermore, as the communist nation prepared to celebrate the twentieth anniversary of its victory over the Republic of South Vietnam, Nguyen Kim Lai reemerged as a symbolic figure in the unfolding patriotic drama. When the re-union finally occurred, the meeting of Bill Robinson and Nguyen Kim Lai revealed much about the construction and usage of propaganda during the war and how the various parties remembered and assigned meaning to the war and their experiences.

The New Vietnam

The documentary, entitled *Reunion,* opens with a four-part introductory sequence. The viewer sees the fifty-two-year-old at his home in Florida, walking down a dirt lane, tossing feed to his chickens, and talking to his horse, while his dog follows faithfully on his heels. Robinson's simple home, nestled in a wooded area overlooking a small pond, symbolizes the achievement of the American dream. After he returned to the states, Robinson resumed his Air Force career before retiring in 1984. "Now he lives on his pension," the narrator explains, and cares for his animals. Sitting in his home, Robinson reviews the series of letters that he received from representatives of NKP and makes the decision, the documentary reveals, to return to Vietnam so that he can learn what happened to Nguyen Kim Lai and to witness firsthand the changes enacted by Vietnam's political leaders. The filmmakers acknowledge the loss of 58,000 U.S. service members who died during the Vietnam War and how that loss, along with the strain of those still unaccounted for, has disrupted relations between the two countries. Before departing for Vietnam, Robinson visited the Wall South in Pensacola so that he could be filmed standing in front of a replica of the Vietnam Veterans Memorial Wall, which for many has become a vehicle for healing. Whether prompted by sincerity or political astuteness, the narrator reminds viewers, as they see Robinson and his reflected image among the thousands of names listed on the wall, that he "lost many friends in this war."[18]

Robinson and his wife Ora Mae, who was making her first trip to Vietnam, arrived in Hanoi on 25 April 1995; thirty years earlier, as a young airman he had left Grand Forks, North Dakota, on 23 April 1965 for his first tour of duty in Southeast Asia. It took a while for the two to clear customs because they were not handled as high-profile guests. The lack of copyright laws and the fear of cinematographic bootleggers compelled the documentarians to downplay the Robinsons' arrival and use an element of secrecy to prevent a crowd from forming around the former POW. Bill and Ora Mae waited in line for roughly thirty minutes before he realized he needed to slip the passport agents a five- or ten-dollar bill to get them through the checkpoint. During the holdup, the film team stood impatiently on the other side of the security fence, waving excitedly with anticipation. Once they had completed the process, the Robinsons joined the film team and immediately reviewed the itinerary and travel schedule. At the planning session, the director stated that the purpose of Robinson's visit was "not only to ask himself what the meaning of the war was but also to make new bonds with the Vietnamese." The reunion of the former enemies, Robinson and Nguyen Kim Lai, was being cast as an act of reconciliation both between individuals and between nations. Communist party officials in Vietnam supported this dual message as they prepared to lead their country into the community of nations. One of the filmmakers' goals was also to showcase the economic revitalization occurring under *Doi Moi*.

Although the group possessed the technical skills and creative talents to make a high-quality production, language barriers presented some very tangible limitations. The documentary's target audience was the people of Japan, and thus the narrative language was Japanese; English, Vietnamese, and Japanese translators were part of the crew. The documentary's editors cut many conversations and impromptu commentary by the main characters from the finished film, and the narrator often dominates at key points, thereby placing the actual participants in the background.[19]

After the introductory sequence, the documentary resumes with Robinson's first moments outside the Hanoi airport. He boyishly confides to his hosts, "I have never seen Vietnam with my [own] eyes," a reference to the fact that the former prisoner was rarely allowed to venture beyond prison grounds during his years in captivity. As he travels from the airport to various locations around Hanoi, scenes of high-rise buildings, renovated hotels, and scores of European tourists reinforce the message of a transforming Vietnam. The group takes Robinson and his wife to the mausoleum of Ho Chi Minh and to Truc Bach Lake, the site where the North Vietnamese netted their prized captive of the war, John McCain. At the Army History Museum in Hanoi, Robinson observes retired tanks used by the North Vietnamese Army in their war with the United States and South Vietnam, anti-aircraft weaponry, the wreckage of U.S. planes shot down by the North Vietnamese, and other spoils of war. The artifacts of victory hardly impress Robinson. He concedes that the Vietnamese people were entitled to forge their own national remembrance of the war, but the conclusion of the Cold War confirmed, in his mind, the United States' status as the world's lone superpower, regardless of the outcome of the war in Vietnam. The museum also displays assorted handcuffs and restraints used by the French on Vietnamese revolutionaries during the colonial era and the First Indochina War. While Robinson inspected the torture devices, the filmmakers lectured him on French atrocities, but they failed to delete his unsolicited response to their lesson. Although they did not translate his remarks, anyone who speaks or understands English can hear Robinson say, "Those are the tools they used on me, too." One section of the museum was devoted to those who were part of North Vietnam's air defense system. Nguyen Kim Lai was among those honored for dedicated service. As the cameraman zooms in on the Guerrilla Girl photo, the narrator briefly explains its historical importance, but at this point in the documentary the filmmakers turn to a discussion of the North Vietnamese treatment of American prisoners of war, and the setting moves from the Army History Museum to the infamous Hoa Lo Prison.[20]

At the time of Robinson's visit, the Hanoi Hilton was under construction. The outer walls were still in place, but construction crews were gutting the prison cells in order to erect the twenty-five-story Somerset Grand Hanoi Hotel. Thus, no one was allowed to enter. From the adjacent street Robinson describes his impressions of the prison. He recalls that he was placed in solitary confinement for the first time at the Hanoi Hilton and "was not allowed to go outside and was put in handcuffs." There is no discussion of torture or coerced confessions. Instead, the documentary describes the humane treatment the North Vietnamese afforded their American captives. When

Robinson stops at the Zoo, he discovers that the Cu Loc Prison has been converted into a housing complex. Amazingly, the buildings are unchanged, and Robinson literally walks "into someone's living room" when he enters one of his former cells. The building that once was the Zoo Annex is still empty. The documentarians, of course, could not re-create the captivity experience by merely returning to the historic sites, and Robinson does not undergo any déjà vu moments during the filming of the documentary. As he stands in the doorway to the Zoo Annex, however, a feeling of uneasiness sweeps over him. He "honestly [doesn't] want to go in"; the empty building resembles a dungeon. Although curious, Robinson conducts his inspection by straddling the doorway and peering in with one foot firmly on the outside. None of these thoughts or reservations is conveyed in the film. The documentary uses propaganda footage from the Cu Loc Prison showing prisoners in the courtyard area, washing clothes, reading letters from home, and playing volleyball. The cinematic montage even includes scenes of Robinson playing basketball with his fellow prisoners at the Zoo prison compound, where the Americans had debated among themselves the efficacy of accepting the recreational equipment and the risks and rewards of being filmed by the North Vietnamese. In keeping with the humanitarian theme, the film team arranged for Robinson to meet one of the Zoo's former prison guards. The guard, attired in a modern military uniform, recognizes Robinson from the Guerilla Girl photo and remembers giving the American "dishwashing duty so that he could eat what was left over [in the kitchen area] because he was a big guy." The cordial exchange with the former guard and the footage from the final years of captivity conceal the pain and suffering that the early POWs endured during the torture era of captivity.

The Propaganda War

The group spent four days in the Hanoi area touring museums and historic landmarks as well as former prison sites before moving south to Ha Tinh Province, the region where Robinson was shot down and captured in September 1965. Most of Vietnam still lacked modern transportation infrastructure, and the documentary notes that a train ride from Hanoi to Ho Chi Minh City, formerly Saigon, a distance of some seven hundred miles, takes thirty-six hours. The group's two-hundred-mile journey by van to the heart of Ha Tinh Province lasted some four hours. During the war Ha Tinh held great strategic significance, and it still proudly claims a patriotic and martial heritage. The Thanh Hoa Bridge, nicknamed Ham Rong by the Vietnamese, which means dragon's jaw, was a high-value target for U.S. Air Force and Navy bombers from 1965 to 1972. The province also included supply bases and key terminals along the Ho Chi Minh Trail. To protect its considerable assets, the North Vietnamese created an effective air defense network around the bridge that relied on local militias to patrol the area. Having established the province's place within the nation's war narrative, the filmmakers recall, in precise and accurate detail, the events of 20 September 1965, beginning with the shootdown of Willis Forby and the response of Robinson's air rescue team from their base in Thailand. Interestingly, when the filmmakers first approached Robinson in October 1994, they were under the impression, having read various accounts in Vietnamese history books, that he "was a heavily armed airman wandering down a village road" when he came face-to-face with Nguyen Kim Lai. Because she reminded him of his sister, as the tale had been passed down over the years, rather than shoot her, the giant American surrendered to her. Robinson corrected them and explained, "No, it wasn't quite that way; she had one hundred friends with her, armed with anything from machetes to machine guns." The advance team stopped Robinson abruptly and asked if he could verify that.[21]

If they needed additional proof, Robinson suggested that the film crew contact his old rescue mates, Tom Curtis and Neil Black. They agreed and flew Curtis and Black to Florida for an interview. The three men, in separate sessions, recounted how they had been taken prisoner, acknowledging that "females had been present in the capturing party" but maintaining that no one had single-handedly captured any of them. Satisfied that the American POWs had provided an honest depiction of their capture and after additional research on their own, the filmmakers shifted the story line to the role of the local militia; they found three members of the original capturing party to participate in the documentary and enliven this particular perspective. During the war the warrior-farmers worked at Nong Truong, an agricultural cooperative located near the Forby scene, but the rough terrain required a two-hour trek by foot to the rescue helicopter's drop point in the jungle. "When I got to where the pilot landed [by parachute], he had already gone," explained one militiaman, "but just then I heard the helicopter . . . coming. It was the helicopter with Mr. Robinson and other members" of the rescue crew. Because he did not believe he "could shoot the helicopter [with his rifle] from the ground," the militiaman climbed a small tree, which he demonstrated during the interview. He also described how he held on to the tree with his legs, aimed his weapon, and fired. "The helicopter was reducing its altitude little by little as I shot," he remarked. "I missed the first time but the second bullet hit the propeller and it flew out of control . . . and crashed." "When we came up on them they were sitting in the corner of the cave and looked frightened," one militia member testified. "We broke into the cave and captured them." The documentary does not mention Nguyen Kim Lai's role in the capture. In fact, the notorious One-Armed Bandit, the North Vietnamese soldier who had first tortured Bill Robinson in Vinh just a few days after his capture and the man Robinson has accused of murdering several American prisoners, appears in the documentary to clarify the specifics of the capture. According to the One-Armed Bandit, who supervised the recovery effort, Nguyen Kim Lai assisted in the "search operations, but when the [American] soldiers were captured, she was not there. Mr. Robinson was handed over to the military by people from . . . the farm and [later] placed in the village where Nguyen Kim Lai lived." The documentary's revelation about Nguyen Kim Lai's having had no role in the capture of Bill Robinson was startling, given the historical significance of the Guerrilla Girl photo.

To explain North Vietnam's use of the photo in its propaganda program, the filmmakers relied on two of the war's ablest practitioners, Phan Thoan and To Huu. Phan Thoan, a photographer for the Vietnamese News Agency who took the photo of Robinson and Nguyen Kim Lai, "never expected" it "to become so famous." When asked if Nguyen Kim Lai captured Robinson by herself or if others were nearby, Phan Thoan admitted that "there were actually many other people" in the area, but he selected an angle that eliminated them from the picture. He also stated, "At the time, photographers were ordered to not only raise the nation's fighting spirit against America but also to take pictures of people's heroic acts." This philosophy permeated the practices of Vietnamese photographers and journalists, which the anthropologist Christina Schwenkel contends differ from the professed objectivity of Western war correspondents, making people like Phan Thoan "cultural soldiers of the revolution."[22] Their intent was to offer useful lessons on how a revolutionary people's movement could counter "the military advantages of a more powerful adversary."[23]

In that vein, party leaders downplayed the importance of modern weapons and instead celebrated the decisive role of individuals in war.[24] Under this strategic umbrella, the Central Committee of the Vietnam Women's Union in 1965 devised the "three responsibilities," which instructed women on their wartime obligations. Aside from maintaining agricultural production, women defended and repaired bridges and roads, including the Ho Chi Minh Trail, joined militias, and manned anti-aircraft batteries. The extensive recruitment of women was consistent with communist theory on national mobilization and was not merely a propaganda scheme.[25] Moreover, the Communist Party worked aggressively to garner the support of all North Vietnamese people, male and female, military and civilian. On 13 November 1964, less than a year before Robinson's capture, *Quan Doi Nhan Dan*, a People's Army publication, announced that Military-Civilian Unity Days would be held in conjunction with the twentieth anniversary of the founding of the People's Army of Vietnam (PAVN). The initiative, the first of its kind, "was not simply a celebration but an integral part of preparing the population for greater cooperation with the military."[26] The critical role played by the male and female members of the various militia units in Ha Tinh Province demonstrated the success of such communist mobilization doctrines.

To spark the engines of the propaganda machinery, the cultural soldiers of the revolution tirelessly searched for the most suitable materials. The poet To Huu found the Guerrilla Girl photo by chance in a Vietnamese newspaper and added to its evolving legend. Imprisoned by the French for his dissident activities from 1939 to 1943, when he escaped from Dac Lay prison, To Huu became a member of the secretariat of the Vietnamese Communist Party and was appointed deputy chairman of the Council of Ministers, a government agency that regulated, or controlled, the arts. To Huu, however, was best known as a poet who celebrated the ideals of Vietnam's revolutionary struggle and inspired determination and commitment to the cause. In 1965 U.S. air superiority and the intensity of Operation Rolling Thunder produced an adverse effect on the collective psyche of the North Vietnamese population. According to To Huu, the "Vietnamese people were afraid of Americans and thought it was impossible that they could stand up to the American Air Force. So we needed to exert revolutionary heroism over these people." To Huu realized that "what people can see concretely was more effective than listening to instruction in towns." When he discovered Phan Thoan's photo of Robinson and Nguyen Kim Lai, he thought to himself, "This is it." To embolden the Vietnamese people, he composed a poem, "O Young Guerrilla," to accompany the photo.

A Guerrilla Girl will stick a gun into a person.
Big American soldier put his head down.
A brave one cannot back down.
Hero is not always a big man.

In the documentary To Huu provides an interpretation of his own poem: "This poem says even a woman is not afraid of a big guy. Of course big guy means American, and also this poem says that women can be heroes, contradictory to accepted myth." In an aside, To Huu reveals that Nguyen Kim Lai had been chosen as the escort "because she was the youngest and shortest girl in the village."

Communist propagandists frequently used, in a variety of outlets, the images of females, or "long-haired warriors." They appeared in such popular publications as the *Vietnam Courier* and *Viet-Nam Pictorial,* and they were reproduced on calendars and postage stamps. And as early as 1965, the North Vietnamese started issuing postage stamps to mark the number of aircraft shot down by air defense units. The Guerrilla Girl stamp, released in 1967, bore a caricatured re-creation of the Robinson–Nguyen Kim Lai photo, along with a flaming airplane tail section for added effect. It purported to recognize the 2,000th shootdown of an American aircraft; the North Vietnamese ultimately claimed to have shot down 4,181 aircraft. In actuality, the United States lost, by hostile action or accident, 2,257 aircraft during the Vietnam War (1965–1973), and fewer than half that number, 990, were lost over North Vietnam.[27] Nevertheless, the Guerrilla Girl stamp helped make the Robinson–Nguyen Kim Lai photo one of the most iconic images of the war.

The Scars of War

At the midpoint of the documentary, the filmmakers finally present Nguyen Kim Lai, covering her appearance at a twentieth-anniversary victory celebration in Ha Tinh Province. Sitting among military officials as an invited guest of honor, the forty-seven-year-old Nguyen Kim Lai wears civilian clothing adorned with several military medals. As a segue to her reunion with Bill Robinson, the narrator suggests that Nguyen Kim Lai "doesn't know when the picture was taken," but "she well remembers that she gave Mr. Robinson food and cigarettes." The two meet for the first time in thirty years in her home in Ha Tinh City, the province's capital. Once she sees Robinson, she has a fleeting moment of disbelief and asks, "Are you Mr. Robinson?" Once she is convinced that he is the American soldier from the photo, Nguyen Kim Lai invites Robinson and his wife Ora Mae into her house. The house consists of two rooms, a bedroom where the entire family sleeps and a living room. The kitchen area is detached from the dwelling. Nguyen Kim Lai remarks excitedly: "You are still young. You look the same as you looked then. It has been thirty years. I have gotten old. You are still young, Robinson." Reflecting on their fateful wartime encounter, Nguyen Kim Lai says, "I don't remember very well, but you looked sad. You might have remembered your family and your hometown." She recalls hoping that she had cheered up the American by reminding him of his sisters, and she wonders if he remembers her displays of sympathy. "That was a very difficult time," Robinson replies. "I do not remember everything, but I do remember the kindness of the people shown to me while I was in their hands." Speaking of the present, Nguyen Kim Lai tells Robinson, "We are so lucky in spite of what we encountered . . . [that] we could reunite with each other like this and have a family." She introduces her eldest child, a daughter, a first-year medical student, and her son, a freshman in high school. She also introduces her husband, whom she describes as a disabled soldier. This image of Nguyen Kim Lai, as a strong woman and mother, conformed with the communist narrative of Vietnamese history, albeit more authentically than the carefully scripted Guerrilla Girl myth of the war.

In postwar Vietnam the long-haired warriors who had helped achieve military victory often returned to a more traditional place in the family. Although their courage and sacrifices continue to be honored by Communist Party leaders, the women were called on to embrace the "gentler virtues" of motherhood. Reconstruction efforts, both economic and political, gave priority to the needs of men over those of women and promoted the mindset "that women's ultimate value in society rested in their domestic functions." These "maternal soldiers" were charged with rearing stable families in the newly independent Vietnam.[28] Working in a hospital as a lab technician, Nguyen Kim Lai epitomized those women who transitioned from the battlefield to the peacetime home front. She earned 270,000 dong per month, or the equivalent of $300 per year, and her husband received 230,000 dong per month as a disability pension. To make ends meet, the family relied on financial assistance from relatives in Thailand, a detail the documentary does not disclose. Similarly, the documentary offers only vague explanations about the husband's military service, revealing that he "was injured in America's bombing" of the area. He suffered brain damage, and a recurring nervous condition causes him to "stay mainly at his house because he cannot get a job." To Robinson it is obvious "that they had had a hard life," and while they chat he learns more about "the bad things in her life than the good." Robinson also discovered, through private conversations, that Nguyen Kim Lai's husband had a steel plate in his head. His disabilities and the consequences of war forced Nguyen Kim Lai to carry a heavy load on her shoulders. She allocates 60 percent of the family's income for her children's educational expenses. During their visit she tells Robinson that she does not reflect on the war; instead, she focuses on her family and their day-to-day needs. She sees education as the key to her children's futures and even her own, hoping that once her daughter becomes a doctor, she will have the connections and influence to help her mother obtain a better job. Nguyen Kim Lai speaks of the difficulty her friends have in finding meaningful employment. And the evidence is clear: recovery from the war had barely begun for many Vietnamese in 1995.[29]

Indeed, "the scars of bombing still remain" in Ha Tinh Province, the documentary notes. Aerial images show a physical landscape marred by bomb craters, which illustrate the lingering difficulties faced by those rebuilding their lives in the aftermath of war. Peasants rely on draft animals rather than tractors and modern equipment to farm the land, land too poor for rice cultivation, and so used for the production of corn and peanuts. As the group travels throughout the hamlets of Ha Tinh Province, the filmmakers emphasize the human costs of war. Robinson meets an elderly woman who remembers him from thirty years earlier, when he was held in her village while being transported to Hanoi. "It was me who made rice porridge with chicken when you were placed in this village," the animated woman informs Robinson. "I lost my arm three years after you left, and my house was destroyed. During the war I had a very hard time." This theme—the suffering of the Vietnamese people—now overshadows the reunion of Bill Robinson and Nguyen Kim Lai, as the filmmakers introduce Robinson to yet another individual and another story of sacrifice and personal loss. Standing before a photo of his deceased wife, a former militiaman recounts for Robinson and Ora Mae what happened in his village and to his wife and family. His military service sometimes tore him away from his family for extended periods. On those occasions his wife, Luong, was in charge of their household and dealt directly with American prisoners when they were brought to the village. She took care of American POWs in transit to Hanoi, allowing them to sleep in the family's bed. "The war left his bed but took her away," the narrator interjects. In a poignant and touching scene, Robinson and the widower burn incense to mourn Luong's death. "I lost my wife, my house, and all my property," the former militiaman reflects, "but it is not just me but everyone in this village." Robinson offers his condolences and concedes "that the Vietnamese people were deeply hurt by the war." But he quickly adds: "I also know that Americans are deeply hurt [by the war]. I hope all hurt will be healed some day, but we will never forget people who lost their lives for the greater good." After the ritual of remembrance, the viewer sees a determined survivor plowing the rocky Vietnamese soil in his bare feet, trying to eke out a subsistence on a small agricultural plot. Such was life in Ha Tinh Province twenty years after the war with the United States ended.

The documentary closes with a farewell conversation between Robinson and Nguyen Kim Lai. He offers words of encouragement to her, her family, and her nation. They both agree that peace has come to Vietnam for the first time in their lives. Her hope is simply to live happily with her husband and children without the pain of war. This dialogue is juxtaposed to a new image of Bill Robinson and Nguyen Kim Lai. This time, while walking along a dirt road much like the path they traveled thirty years earlier, they appear not as enemies but as friends, looking optimistically to the future, when their respective nations would be partners rather than foes. The narrator reinforces this message, interjecting the observation that the two countries had reached a point where each needed to "understand and forgive the other."

In terms of historical accuracy, the reunion documentary presents an objective account of Robinson's mission, shootdown, and capture, although it avoids any discussion concerning the torture of American POWs while asserting the claim of the humane treatment of prisoners of war. The documentary candidly reveals the fabricated nature of Nguyen Kim Lai's participation in Robinson's capture and explains how the staged photo was used for propaganda purposes. Interestingly, the Guerrilla Girl story as revealed in the documentary contrasts sharply with the Guerrilla Girl story delivered in Vietnamese museums. Whether at the Air Defense–Air Force Museum (formerly the Air Defense Museum) or the Women's Museum in Hanoi, images of long-haired warriors still repeat the war-era messages of "the unfairness of the conflict, the determination of the Communists to win, and the power of women." At the Women's Museum, the caption for the Guerrilla Girl photo incorrectly states that "Captain William Robinson, age twenty-two," was "shot down during the Christmas Bombing of Hanoi in 1972" and that Nguyen Kim Lai "led him out of the jungle to Hoa Lo prison." Countless inaccuracies continue to surround the Guerrilla Girl myth, none more egregious than the one repeated by the historian Sandra Taylor following her visit to Vietnam in the late 1990s. Taylor wrote that the Guerrilla Girl "story had a dramatic ending. Robinson, like many American service-men, returned to Vietnam, and in May 1985, he met with Kim Lai in Hanoi. He asked her forgiveness for his attempt to destroy her village, and she willingly gave it."[30] More recent studies of national remembrance in Vietnam indicate that the war-era propaganda version of the Guerrilla Girl story remains intact.[31]

On one level Robinson enjoyed his trip to Vietnam and was grateful for Ora Mae's support and companionship throughout the endeavor. It may seem strange, but Robinson "really felt welcomed there," by adults as well as children. He sensed a need for help among the Vietnamese people, and they did not shy away from asking for assistance. Reflecting on their experiences, Bill and Ora Mae were struck by the widespread poverty of Vietnam. "They still hadn't received what they needed," lamented Ora Mae, with considerable compassion for the Vietnamese people. Her husband shared those sentiments and blamed a corrupt communist government for limiting the scope of economic recovery. It was clear to them that all Vietnamese people "had not benefited from peace."[32]

Although he understood the intent of the documentary and its broader geopolitical purpose, he regretted that his family's saga had not been included in the finished product. Both sisters had been interviewed extensively for the project before his return to Vietnam, but neither Ginger nor Jackie appears in the documentary. Robinson had originally agreed to participate in large part because he wanted to honor his family for the heartache and pain they had endured in his behalf. The emphasis on postwar reconciliation between Vietnam and the global community left no room to contemplate the misfortunes of Robinson's relatives half a world away in North Carolina.

Beyond this disappointment, he was truly angered by the film team during his visit when, without any advance warning, they approached him about meeting "an old friend." A suspicious Robinson pressed his hosts for additional details, and despite their evasiveness, Robinson deduced that the person in question was none other than the One-Armed Bandit. Robinson despised the One-Armed Bandit and considered him a murderer. He refused to place American "blood" on his "hands by associating" with this war criminal, and he flatly rejected the proposal. Even so, several team members persisted, but Robinson remained adamant, and the meeting did not take place. Robinson's reaction perplexed the documentarians. In their words, they failed to comprehend how he "was able to forgive everyone" involved in the war except this one individual, a sentiment that forced the former POW to set the record straight. Robinson explained that in coming to Vietnam he was neither "offering forgiveness" nor "seeking" forgiveness. He accepted much of what had happened to him as well as to the Vietnamese people as the unfortunate consequences of war, but he reiterated his belief that the One-Armed Bandit had committed acts in violation of the established conventions of warfare.[33]

Rising Dragon

In July 1995, shortly after Robinson returned to the states, President Bill Clinton announced the normalization of diplomatic relations with Vietnam, and two years later Congress approved the nomination of the former POW Pete Peterson as the first postwar U.S. ambassador to Vietnam. The opening of diplomatic channels, however, did not eliminate existing trade barriers. The Jackson-Vanik Amendment to the Trade Act of 1974 prohibited U.S. trade relations with "nonmarket" or communist countries that restricted the immigration rights of their citizens. Because of Vietnam's troubled past regarding its refugee crisis, President Clinton had to request a waiver in order for American businesses to operate in Vietnam. Congress granted the waiver in 1998, by a vote of 260–193, in 1999, by a vote of 297–130, and in 2000 by a vote of 332–91. Between 1998 and 2000 U.S. imports from Vietnam rose from $553 million to $827 million, and U.S. exports to Vietnam increased marginally from $274 million to $330 million. The major imports from Vietnam were shrimp, coffee, cashews, footwear, and petroleum products, and the major exports to Vietnam were footwear parts, industrial and office machinery, telecommunications equipment, fertilizers, and cotton. On 13 July 2000 the two countries signed a bilateral trade agreement (BTA), which the U.S. Senate passed, by a vote of 88–12, in October 2001. In short, the BTA provided "reciprocal most-favored-nation" status between the two countries.[34] An Asian affairs analyst, Mark E. Manyin, believes that the BTA "was made possible by Vietnam's strategic desire to improve relations with the United States, continued improvements in POW/MIA cooperation, Vietnam's ongoing reform efforts, and by Vietnam's cooperation on refugee issues."[35]

The level of trade volume between the United States and Vietnam soared in the wake of the BTA. Total trade topped $1.4 billion in 2001, and the following year it grew a phenomenal 107 percent to $2.9 billion; additional growth occurred in the second half of the decade. The increases fell overwhelmingly—more than 80 percent—in the category of U.S. imports from Vietnam, and by 2008 and 2009 the U.S. had a nearly $10 billion trade deficit with Vietnam.[36] Industrialization and manufacturing headed Vietnam's new economy. Agriculture represented 20 percent of the gross domestic product (GDP) in the middle of the decade, down from 40 percent in the mid-1980s. Many Vietnamese, such as those working for the British footwear magnate Clarks, moved from the rice paddies to the factories. Depending on their skill level, these workers earned between sixty and eighty dollars per month in 2006. The country had met most of "the development targets set by the United Nations," and the Rising Dragon took its place alongside the Tigers of East Asia. The "broadly positive" results of Vietnam's economic modernization are indisputable. The reduction of poverty, in particular, has been impressive. Whereas 60 percent of the Vietnamese population lived below the poverty line in 1993, the number had been reduced to 20 percent by 2004.[37]

Vietnam's political liberalization has not kept pace with economic reform, however, and personal freedoms and civil liberties "are rigorously policed" by the Communist Party. There is no pretense of democratic reform in Vietnam; the goal is simply "to make one-party rule more efficient." On the surface, Vietnam manages "its social problems reasonably well," according to Bill Hayton, a reporter and producer with British Broadcasting Corporation News who covered Vietnam's application and admission to the World Trade Organization in 2006–7. Hayton, whose visa was revoked in January 2007, writes positively on the economic reforms in Vietnam, but he identifies several areas of concern, principally environmental issues and the lack of freedom of the press. Vietnam's Press Law obligates the media "to provide honest information about domestic and international situations" and "to carry out propaganda . . . and contribute to the building and protection of . . . [the] policies of the Party." With this mandate, "there is no press freedom" and the country "regularly placed in the bottom 10 (out of 170 or so) in . . . the annual Press Freedom Index—slightly above North Korea and Burma." The power of the state over the press includes the ability to fine, suspend, or ban editors or their publications. Censorship of the Internet is also pervasive in Vietnam. The government routinely blocks or filters political and religious sites, but it grants open access to online games and other sites. In Hayton's words, Vietnam "allows youngsters to consume plenty of porn but not Amnesty International reports."[38]

Diplomatically, the U.S. government deems Vietnam as an important player in such matters as the South China Sea dispute and nuclear energy development, and as a potential redoubt against Chinese militarism. Most Americans view Vietnam—aside from its cheap clothing and footwear—through the lens of the MIA issue. When the war ended, 2,585 Americans were unaccounted for in Southeast Asia. As of June 2003, "four hundred sets of remains had been repatriated by the Vietnamese, and another three hundred found" by American recovery teams. Army Lieutenant Colonel Thomas T. Smith arrived in Hanoi during the summer of 2003 to oversee the Joint POW/MIA Accounting Command field teams. Of his time in country he wrote: "I had a deep respect for the Vietnamese. We could learn much from them, and they have much to learn from us. Such is our future together." As the future unfolds for Vietnam, one can merely speculate on the place the Guerrilla Girl photo will occupy in the communist narrative of the nation's history. In his own country, Robinson's legacy is more certain.[39]

7

Legacies

In the mid-1990s Robinson started to receive invitations to speak publicly about his experiences as a prisoner of war, including one from an old friend in central Georgia. One day while driving north along Interstate 75 from his home in DeFuniak Springs, Florida, to Hampton, Georgia, a quaint community some thirty miles south of Atlanta, Robinson noticed a highway sign for the Andersonville National Historic Site (ANHS). In 1970 the U.S. Congress had transferred the historic grounds of the Civil War prison Camp Sumter, commonly known as Andersonville, and the Andersonville National Cemetery from the Department of the Army to the National Park Service (NPS). Part of the transfer agreement required that the ANHS interpret and commemorate not just the experiences of those held at Camp Sumter during the Civil War, but the experiences of all American prisoners of war throughout the nation's history. Located in a remote section of southwestern Georgia, straddling Sumter and Macon counties, the ANHS is nearly thirty miles from the nearest federal interstate. The state highway leading to Andersonville, as Robinson put it, "looked like a one-rut road" to nowhere. After several failed attempts, Robinson and his wife finally located the national historic site, and they received a rather dubious welcome on their first visit. At the time the ANHS had set aside two small buildings to display artifacts relating to American POWs. In one of the buildings Robinson spotted a copy of the famous Guerrilla Girl photo, and he informed a park ranger that he was the man in the picture. Robinson's revelation fell on deaf ears. He was given a "so-what response" from the park ranger. He felt it was like talking to a "brick wall." On that occasion a park visitor, Dr. Bill Arck, Alcohol and Other Drug Education Service Director at Kansas State University, was the only one with a desire to know more about Robinson's story. The two men exchanged addresses and intended to keep in touch. Although miffed by the outcome of his first visit, Robinson accepted it in stride, and when he returned to Andersonville a few years later, he received a more appropriate reception.[1]

National Prisoner of War Museum

Following the Civil War, the Department of the Army administered the Andersonville National Cemetery for more than one hundred years as an active national cemetery and the Camp Sumter prison site for sixty years before relinquishing them to the National Park Service. In an interview, Fred Boyles, who served as the ANHS superintendent from 1990 to 2009, succinctly described the Army's role at Andersonville: they "dug graves and cut grass." The extent of the Army's interaction with the general public was a card file that aided visitors in locating grave sites. By comparison, the first five Civil War military parks, Gettysburg, Antietam, Shiloh, Vicksburg, and Chickamauga, were transferred from the Department of the Army to the National Park Service in 1933; Andersonville did not become part of the NPS until nearly forty years later. Several factors contributed to the decision to make Andersonville a component of the NPS. According to Superintendent Boyles, the Department of the Army, facing the burdens of the Vietnam War, wanted to rid itself of Andersonville. Also, President Lyndon Johnson looked to Senator Richard Russell of Georgia for help in doing "something" that might one day benefit American POWs of the Vietnam War. Furthermore, local and state politicians as well as business leaders in Georgia recognized the potential economic effects that historical tourism would have on the surrounding communities and lobbied for the transfer.[2]

Once the transfer had been enacted, the first priority for the National Park Service was to conduct archeological and environmental studies to determine the historical accuracy of the location of the prison grounds and various buildings. The NPS also published several historical reports and booklets on the Andersonville Prison and worked to develop a broader interpretive vision.[3] The ANHS converted the former carriage house, the previous residence of the site's caretaker, into a museum to cover the history of POWs from modern wars. This building was the one that Robinson visited in the mid-1990s when he met the uninterested staff member. Another small building, the former cemetery chapel, served as a temporary museum for Civil War prisoner history. In the early 1980s Chief Park Ranger Alfredo Sanchez played a key role in focusing attention on the unfulfilled mission of interpreting and commemorating the stories of all American prisoners of war. As a result, the NPS, ANHS, and American Ex-Prisoners of War (AXPOW) formed a partnership in 1984 for the purpose of building the National Prisoner of War Museum at Andersonville. The U.S. Congress and the state of Georgia appropriated funds, and local governments and private organizations contributed in numerous ways to the initial efforts. For their part, AXPOW agreed to raise $2.5 million. Still, the project required additional funding, and not surprisingly, the former prisoners stepped forward to lead the campaign.[4]

On 21 January 1993 Pete Peterson introduced a bill in the U.S. House of Representatives that ultimately authorized the secretary of the Treasury to mint the Prisoner-of-War Commemorative Coin. The coins sold for thirty dollars each, and ten dollars of that went to fund the construction of the POW museum. The Treasury Department sold nearly 300,000 coins. In February 1994 AXPOW obtained permission to have the Veterans Administration insert a donation request card inside the 1.9 million checks mailed monthly by the agency to veterans receiving compensation or pensions. The level of response completely overwhelmed the staff at ANHS. Consequently, the former World War II POW Leon Swindell drove his motor home to Andersonville to set up a processing center for the incoming donations. For three weeks Swindell and other members of AXPOW "processed more than $77,000 in donations" from approximately 10,000 respondents. AXPOW chapters throughout the country participated in a vast array of fund-raising activities; for example, the Seattle (Washington) Chapter spearheaded an effort that raised eight thousand dollars. To many former prisoners, the National Prisoner of War Museum is *their* museum rather than one built *for* them.[5] Moreover, many prisoners attached great historical significance to the museum. "This is going to be as significant and memorable as the Arizona Memorial at Pearl Harbor, the Iwo Jima statue and Arlington Cemetery," proclaimed Carl Runge, a former World War II POW and a principal figure behind the creation of the museum. Runge also believed Andersonville's remote location was the ideal place for the museum: "Washington has enough monuments. When people come here and see this, they won't confuse it with anything. They will always remember. And that's all we have wanted all along."[6]

To their credit, the NPS and ANHS worked closely with AXPOW in developing the National Prisoner of War Museum. In fact, former POWs from both theaters of WWII, the Korean War, and the Vietnam War served on the Andersonville Task Force Committee that interacted with the NPS to produce interpretive plans and was involved in all design matters, especially that of the Commemorative Courtyard. The courtyard, an area adjacent to the museum and set aside for visitors to reflect on the nature of the prisoner-of-war experience, encountered some bureaucratic obstacles because of the difficulty in procuring art "via government contracts." AXPOW assumed full responsibility for the design of the Commemorative Courtyard and selected a sculpture. Construction on the museum finally began in the summer of 1996. Architecturally, the impressive 10,000-square-foot museum resembles a prison and "uses the thematic elements common to all POW stories: towers, gates, confinement, water and light."[7] There are nine themed exhibit areas in the museum that cover POW history from the American Revolution to Operation Iraqi Freedom. The exhibit areas focus on various aspects of the captivity experience, beginning with the definition of a POW, and continuing with the themes of capture, journey, living conditions, news and communication, those who wait (POW/MIA families), privation, morale, and freedom.[8]

"Under a cloudless sky," the National Prisoner of War Museum was formally dedicated on 9 April 1998 before more than two thousand former prisoners of war, many of whom were accompanied by family and friends. The day before, ex-prisoners, in groups of one hundred, received personal tours of the museum. The culmination of years of work stirred the emotions of all those involved. For the Civil War enthusiast, the dedication date of 9 April commemorated Robert E. Lee's surrender to U.S. Grant at Appomattox Court House. The official dedication literature, however, highlighted the museum's dedication date as the anniversary of the beginning of the Bataan Death March. Newspaper coverage focused on the heroism of the men and women who became prisoners of the Japanese after the surrender of Bataan and Corregidor early in World War II. James Downey, an eighty-three-year-old survivor of the Death March, was at the dedication with his forty-eight-year-old son, Gary. At one point during their museum tour, the two reached the original Camp O'Donnell cross, a large cement cross built and erected by some Bataan Death March survivors to honor their fallen comrades at Camp O'Donnell in the Philippines. Gary then remarked, "Dad, you made this monument. Let me take your picture on it." His father was somewhat reticent but agreed, and with a quavering voice he said, "I was in the march with my younger brother, Rob. Rob didn't make it." James Downey's story underscored the dominant theme of the day: the price of freedom.[9]

Indeed, in his introductory remarks printed in the accompanying program, President Bill Clinton wrote that "the legacy of America's POWs" was that they were "held as prisoners of war for the sake of our freedom," and their sacrifice reminds all Americans "that freedom does not come without a price."[10] When the former Vietnam POW John McCain stepped to the podium to deliver the keynote address for the grand opening of the museum, he, too, reflected on the incredible sacrifice of those individuals being commemorated by the museum, starting with the 13,000 Americans who had died in the Andersonville Prison. As McCain explained, they "gave their lives so that they might save a nation." McCain traced the lineage of prison survivors from Andersonville to Camp O'Donnell in the Philippines to the desolate camps in North Korea. These men "had been deprived of their liberty" by "enemies who attempted to commit them to the animal caste." They endured "terrible suffering, may have lost their faith for a time," lived on "meager rations," resisted the "daily regimen of brainwashing," and silently memorized "the ever-lengthening roll call of the dead, so that families may one day know the fate of their loved ones." To McCain, the legacy of the American prisoner of war was that, throughout their collective ordeals, they not only survived the horrors of captivity but remained loyal to "a cause greater than their self-interest" and maintained their dignity and honor in the face of extraordinary odds.[11]

McCain commented on his own time in captivity, referring to it as time spent "in the company of heroes," and he devoted nearly one-third of his speech to the story of Lance Sijan. Air Force Captain Lance Sijan, a backseater in an F-4 Phantom, was shot down over Laos on 9 November 1967. He sustained a compound leg fracture during the incident but evaded capture for forty-six days before the North Vietnamese recovered him on Christmas Day. Sijan, a former football player at the United States Air Force Academy, adhered to a literal and absolute interpretation of the Code of Conduct. He refused to answer questions during interrogation sessions, which caused his captors to kick, beat, and club him savagely and repeatedly. In his severely weakened state, Sijan contracted pneumonia and died on 22 January 1968. McCain had never met Sijan, but the naval aviator became part of the POW network that spread the word of Sijan's exploits. And as he concluded his address, McCain asked the audience: "When you leave here today, think of Lance Sijan, and carry his dignity with you. Keep his memory alive, confident in your faith that almighty God blessed him, and gave him the strength to prevail over his enemies. Though they took his life, they could not take his dignity."[12]

The dedication of the National Prisoner of War Museum represented a critical step in elevating public awareness about the history of America's prisoners of war. The completion of the museum also coincided with a turning point of sorts in the life of Bill Robinson, as he became more involved with the ANHS and began sharing his own captivity experience more frequently. Robinson had not participated in any of the museum's fund-raising activities. He did not really know very much about the project until it neared completion. He attended the dedication ceremonies, but the only Vietnam POWs he remembers meeting were Wayne Waddle, William Talley, John McCain, and David Terrell. Nevertheless, while attending the dedication, Robinson learned of the ANHS Guest Host Program.[13] As the relationship between AXPOW and the ANHS expanded in the mid-1980s, former prisoners offered to stay at the park for extended periods to give tours of the museum or just to talk casually with visitors about their time in captivity. Shortly after the museum dedication in 1998, the ANHS converted the carriage house—which had been the temporary museum of the modern-war POWs—into a studio apartment for these volunteers. The Magnolia (Mississippi) Chapter of AXPOW provided funding for the project. Since its inception, hundreds of POWs have contributed thousands of hours to the Guest Host Program.[14]

The Robinsons began participating in the Guest Host Program in 1998, and they soon discovered that they preferred serving during May because of the large number of students who pass through the park during that month. Most school districts in Georgia have completed their Criterion-Referenced Competency Tests (CRCTs) by April, giving teachers greater flexibility in scheduling field trips. It is not uncommon during these peak seasons for more than five hundred students to visit the ANHS on a particular day, and sometimes the number reaches one thousand. The Robinsons also prefer May because of Memorial Day commemorations.[15] One of the first observances of Memorial Day, originally known as Decoration Day, can be traced to May 1865 in Charleston, South Carolina, when African Americans placed flowers, wreaths, and crosses on the graves of Union soldiers who died in captivity at the Confederacy's Race Course prison. The ritual celebration soon spread, and on 5 May 1868 General John Logan, the national commander of the Grand Army of the Republic, issued a proclamation establishing a national Memorial Day "for the purpose of strewing with flowers, or otherwise decorating the graves of comrades who died in defense of this country."[16] Memorial Day at Andersonville has always held special significance, and since the 1970s the National Park Service has placed its imprint on the martial holiday. Memorial Day activities at the ANHS typically include a flag placement ceremony, at which hundreds of volunteers place an American flag at each of the nearly 20,000 graves in the Andersonville National Cemetery, and a laying of the wreaths ceremony at the cemetery's rostrum, to which various military, civic, and patriotic organizations are invited to honor those who died while serving their country. Additional features include instrumental music, generally performed by a military band,

and a keynote speaker. On numerous occasions Bill Robinson has represented the NAM-POWs organization during the laying of the wreaths or has invited a fellow POW to participate in the services. For the Robinsons May is indeed a special month at Andersonville, and each year that they serve in the Guest Host Program they encounter several thousand visitors and add to the rich legacy of the historic site and the National Prisoner of War Museum.[17]

A Family's Legacy

Bill Robinson never had a son to inherit his legacy, but, much to his delight, his nephew Tim Hux has filled this void in various ways. The only son and younger child of Bill's sister Ginger, Tim was only one year old when his uncle was shot down and captured in Vietnam. At the time Tim and his older sister, Pam, had not really formed a close bond with their uncle; however, their mother worked hard to keep Bill's memory alive. She often showed the children pictures of her brother and told them stories from their childhood so that they developed a sense of their mother's loss. The children were also part of the family gatherings that occurred when Bill's letters arrived from Vietnam, and Tim remembers accompanying his mother and aunt to the annual state fair, where they raised awareness for the POW/MIA issue. Bill's return in 1973 finally allowed uncle and nephew to forge a strong bond, but Bill's estrangement from his family limited contact between the two during Tim's adolescence. After graduating from high school in 1983, Tim decided to attend Wesleyan College in Rocky Mount, North Carolina, with the hopes of starring as a pitcher on the school's baseball team.[18] During the recruiting process, one of the Wesleyan coaches made a number of promises—especially regarding playing time—that raised Tim's expectations, but just a few weeks before the semester began, Tim learned that the coach had accepted a position at another school. Nevertheless, he enrolled, but he was unhappy at the college. He simply "didn't like it." Once the baseball season began, his playing time was less than promised and off-the-field issues, such as an incompatible roommate, intensified the disappointment, and he contemplated dropping out of college. Despite some efforts to address the off-the-field concerns, Tim decided to quit college and informed his parents that he intended to join the military. Ginger was devastated.[19]

She reminded Tim "of all that she had been through" with her brother and feared that she simply "couldn't handle" the constant burden of worry again. As a dutiful son, Tim reached back to his childhood to justify his decision. He presented his mother with a letter he received from the local Marine Corps recruiting office, one she remembered distinctly his receiving when he was eleven or twelve years old. Young Tim had stopped by the recruiting office one day on the way home from school to express his desire to join the Marines. Pleased with his enthusiasm and ever mindful of a potential recruit, the recruiting officer sent Tim a typed letter encouraging him to return once he reached the appropriate age. Using the letter as leverage, Tim told Ginger, "Momma, you see it is not just a whim. I really have for a long time wanted to join the Marines." Over time Ginger relented, telling her son, "It is not what I want for you, but I want you to do what you feel like you need to do."[20] Although Tim held his uncle in high regard and admired him for his years of military service and how he had handled himself while in captivity, his decision to join the Marine Corps was driven by his own deep and abiding respect for the military and his desire to serve his country and face the traditional challenges of manhood.[21]

Tim signed up as part of the delayed entry program and under the buddy system, which allowed, when certain conditions were met, for two friends to complete basic training and military occupational specialty training together, and to draw their first assignment together. Unexpectedly, Tim's friend changed his mind at the last minute, but Tim remained committed and formally enlisted in May 1983. After completing boot camp at Parris Island, South Carolina, he was assigned to Camp Geiger, a component of Camp Lejeune near Jacksonville, North Carolina. When he arrived, most of the 1st Battalion, 8th Marine Regiment had deployed to Beirut, Lebanon, and he learned that he would soon be joining them as part of a "rear party" attachment. Then, just three or four days before he was set to deploy, Tim received a transfer to the 3rd Battalion, 4th Marine Regiment. The timing of the transfer and the subsequent events of 23

October 1983 tested Ginger's resolve. On that October day suicide bombers detonated two truckloads of explosives outside the Marine barracks at the Beirut International Airport. Among the more than two hundred Marines killed that day were members of the 1st Battalion, 8th Marines. Throughout Tim's four-year enlistment, his mother relived, on some level and on a daily basis, what she had gone through with her brother.[22]

Fate spared Tim from the Beirut tragedy, but he found that for a serviceman in an uncertain world, danger or misfortune always seemed to be lurking nearby. In March 1984 Tim participated in "Team Spirit 84," a joint U.S.–South Korea field training exercise. On 24 March eighteen U.S. Marines and eleven Republic of Korea Marines were killed when a CH-53 Sea Stallion helicopter crashed near Pohang, Korea, as a result of poor weather conditions. Tim was not on board any of the six aircraft involved in the incident, but Ginger, upon hearing news of the accident, went straight to the local recruiting office seeking information. As a matter of courtesy, one of the recruiters promised to bring any information that he received regarding Tim directly to Ginger's house. Overwhelmed and reminded of the past, Ginger advised the recruiter that if he came bearing bad news he should prepare to deal with her death, too. The recruiter then reconsidered his offer and agreed not to come to her house. Even somewhat routine assignments alarmed Ginger. During the spring of 1986 Tim was in the midst of a seven-month stint in the Mediterranean aboard a U.S. Navy ship when President Ronald Reagan authorized Operation El Dorado Canyon, a retaliatory bombing strike against Libyan military targets for that government's role in the terrorist bombing of a Berlin discotheque. Tim, of course, was not part of the operation, although when his ship docked at a French port he was not allowed to leave for liberty. Each time an incident such as this occurred, Ginger relived a lot of the worry and heartache that she had experienced while her brother was a prisoner of war in North Vietnam. "It was just hard for all of us," she reflected, but she admits that her son "wouldn't take anything for the experiences that he had and it made him a better person." Ginger even believes that Tim would have made a career with the Marine Corps if he had received a military occupational specialty assignment with the Military Police.[23] Since completing his enlistment in May 1987, Tim has worked in law enforcement in North Carolina.

During his four years in the Marine Corps, Tim learned more about the history of America's Vietnam War captives and developed a deeper appreciation and respect for what his uncle had gone through as a prisoner of war. The fact that Tim had served in the military seemed to facilitate the lines of communication between the two men on those infrequent occasions when Robinson returned to North Carolina. Their relationship grew stronger after Bill's marriage to Ora Mae. Meanwhile, Tim sought ways to support the cause of POW/MIA awareness. Because of its dedication to the POW/MIA issue, Rolling Thunder, Inc., caught Tim's attention. Probably better known for its loud motorcycles, leather vests, and invasion of Washington, D.C., each Memorial Day weekend, Rolling Thunder is a nonprofit organization dedicated to a full accounting of American MIAs. The national organization and its numerous local chapters conduct charitable activities for veterans and their families and have lobbied Congress regarding veterans' benefits and concerns. Though the group's tactics and tenor (especially those of its national executive director, Artie Muller) have rankled some, many POWs are grateful for their efforts. Tim thinks Rolling Thunder does a good job "of keeping the memories of the POWs and MIAs alive," reminding those who will listen of the adversity POWs overcame and of the tens of thousands of American servicemen still unaccounted for, not only from the war in Vietnam but from all the nation's modern-day wars, and of the families still waiting for closure. In May 2006 Tim, his wife, Judi, and a few others left northeastern North Carolina and rode their motorcycles for three hours to take part in Rolling Thunder's Memorial Day rally in Washington, D.C. The monuments on the Mall, Arlington National Cemetery, and the nearly four-hour-long parade of motorcycles presented an impressive scene and atmosphere for the cause. Tim sees the annual event as a demonstration of respect, and it inspired him to be more active in similar efforts, especially those involving his uncle.[24]

In September 2006 Andersonville National Historic Site and Georgia Southwestern State University (GSW), located in nearby

Americus, cosponsored a POW/MIA Recognition Day program. Established in 1979 to recognize the sacrifices of POWs and to remember those still missing in action, POW/MIA Recognition Day has been observed nationally, by presidential proclamation, on the third Friday of September, beginning in 1986. Since its inception, the number of groups celebrating POW/MIA Recognition Day has grown to include military bases, veterans associations, governors' offices, schools, and civic organizations. When ANHS recruited participants for its inaugural event, it naturally turned to Bill Robinson, who eagerly agreed to join the two-day program. On 14 September a moderated POW symposium featured Robinson, Querin Herlik, an Army pilot held briefly as a POW in Cambodia during the Vietnam War, and Anne and Joy Purcell, the wife and daughter of the POW Ben Purcell. On 15 September, Colonel Ben Purcell, the highest-ranking Army officer held in captivity during the Vietnam War, gave a presentation on the campus of Georgia Southwestern. Several Rolling Thunder local chapters, primarily from Florida, provided a motorcycle escort as a prelude to Purcell's presentation, and the following day a memorial service was held at the Andersonville National Historic Site to close out the weekend's events. Over the years, the ANHS, GSW, and Rolling Thunder chapters have continued to sponsor POW/MIA Recognition Day in September in southwestern Georgia, and each entity maintains its own individual role in the observances. In 2009, as part of the "Ride Home" event, Rolling Thunder chapters held a recognition ceremony to honor those former prisoners attending the weekend's festivities. Once he decided to attend the event, Robinson invited family members to join him, and he specifically asked his nephew Tim to participate in the recognition service. As part of the ceremony, each POW in attendance has an escort who presents the POW with a welcome-home medal. Robinson asked Tim to serve in this capacity.[25]

Tim considered his uncle's request an incredible honor. He told his wife, "I am going to do whatever I have to to be there." Tim realized that Robinson attached great significance to these occasions, and he did not want to disappoint his uncle. So he and Judi accepted the invitation and traveled nearly six hundred miles from North Carolina to southwest Georgia. On Saturday morning, 18 September, several hundred POWs gathered at the ANHS to be recognized by Rolling Thunder. The protocol for the event called for each POW to be honored individually. When Robinson's turn came, the master of ceremonies announced his name and Robinson leaned forward in his chair. Tim, who stood directly in front of Robinson, placed the medal around his neck, stepped back, and rendered a salute, and his uncle, one of the first enlisted recipients of the Air Force Cross, returned the salute. It was truly an emotional moment for each man; Tim admits that neither he nor his uncle could look "each other in the eye. I would look at him and he would turn away, and he would look back at me and I would turn away. Neither one of us wanted to start crying." Needless to say, Tim has "a lot of respect" for his uncle and is "proud of his sacrifices."[26]

The day after the recognition ceremony, Robinson took Tim and his wife on a tour of the National Prisoner of War Museum at the ANHS. Tim marveled at how easily Robinson related exhibit items to his own prisoner-of-war experience in Vietnam, and he was especially moved by the discussion of the bonds of brotherhood that existed between the POWs. Tim regarded the guided tour as his "own personal history lesson," one that really opened his eyes to both his uncle's plight and life in captivity more generally. Robinson and Tim have also spoken privately about the incidents of torture that Robinson endured. Since the September 2009 event, the two men have stayed in touch and try to speak by phone every other weekend or so. Tim feels his uncle "deserves to be recognized" for the sacrifices that he made for this country and is committed to preserving his legacy. When given the chance, Tim shares the story of his uncle's ordeal, proudly referring to him as one of the longest held enlisted POWs in American military history. And Tim stresses his uncle's indomitable spirit. Practically everyone who knows Robinson well can testify to his proclivity to use catchphrases to illustrate a critical point, and Tim often quotes one particular saying to convey his uncle's valor: "Every day is a good day as long as I don't see leg irons and handcuffs coming." Robinson's optimistic and determined attitude helps Tim keep his own life in perspective and makes him realize that he has a role model who has overcome more obstacles than most people will ever face.[27] Similarly, Robinson holds Tim in high regard, appreciates his military service, and applauds his character and commitment to "doing things the right way."[28]

Duty, Country, Honor

On 23 May 2010, after experiencing leg pain, Bill Robinson relented to the concerns of his wife and daughter Cyndi and went to the emergency room at Perry Memorial Hospital in Houston County, Georgia. He spent five hours at the hospital receiving intravenous antibiotics to treat a case of cellulitis. After a few days of rest, he drove the thirty-odd miles to the Andersonville National Historic Site. Two weeks earlier at ANHS, he had spoken to a warrant officer candidate (WOC) class from Fort Rucker, Alabama, and made a promise to return on 26 May to speak to another WOC class from Fort Rucker. Despite having been ordered to keep his leg elevated as part of his recovery, he fully intended to keep his promise to the future noncommissioned officers. Just after two o'clock on the afternoon of 26 May, standing in the lobby of the National Prisoner of War Museum despite doctor's orders, Robinson addressed the class. The sixty-three candidates, wearing their digital camouflage battle dress uniforms and camel packs, had just completed a nearly two-hour tour of the Andersonville prison grounds, thereby completing their introduction to the American prisoner-of-war story. As he often does, Robinson started his talk with a bit of humor, joking that politicians, used-car salesmen, and military recruiters shared the same DNA. Several WOCs nodded in agreement, and an aura of respect quickly filled the room; this highly decorated POW was actually one of them.

Robinson began his life story with his entry into the Air Force in 1961 and his time in basic training, an experience shared by all servicemen and servicewomen. He described the early years of air rescue operations in Southeast Asia, in which members of the Air Rescue Service dealt with the problems of substandard equipment. He recalled the days of flying without protective armor and kicking fuel barrels out of the backs of helicopters. Robinson then explained how his "life changed forever" by recounting the Forby rescue mission, his shootdown and capture, the pep rally, his ar-

rival at the Hanoi Hilton, and Colonel Robinson Risner's dire warning, "Be prepared to give your life for your country." His captivity
spanned eight Thanksgivings, eight Christmases, and eight New
Year's Days. During this time he lacked adequate food and clothing,
but he praised his fellow Americans who were held in South Vietnam by the Viet Cong by calling his surroundings "deluxe accommodations" in comparison to theirs. He also stated that quite often
the only form of survival for his southern brothers was escape. He
summed up his mental approach to the seven and a half years of imprisonment with the "three-day motto: yesterday was the day I was
captured, today is today, and tomorrow is the day that I go home."
He had performed this exercise for more than 2,700 days. He spoke
of the importance of the Son Tay Raid and the formation of Camp
Unity. It was the first time that he had seen forty Americans in the
same place at the same time in five years. With great pride he held
up the senior officers among the POWs who had placed themselves
at the forefront of resisting the North Vietnamese interrogators,
frequently incurring brutal retaliation for their defiance. Robinson
judged their efforts as "leadership at its best." Part of his captivity
narrative outlined the struggles of families as they coped with their
loss and confronted the unknown. He pointed out that the families'
ordeals occurred against the backdrop of a deeply divided America.

Robinson posed a rhetorical question to the group: "How do
you measure eight years of captivity?" Given the eventual outcome
of the war in Vietnam, Robinson in essence was asking if they believed his sacrifice and that of the other POWs was worthwhile. In
short, his answer was yes. He recounted an incident involving one
POW who had patched together an American flag out of miscellaneous strings and bits of cloth. Each day all the prisoners in the
cell used the makeshift flag to reaffirm their faith in America. One
day the guards burst into the cell, demanding to know who was
responsible for the flag. The prisoner, naval officer, Michael Christian, stepped forward to accept his punishment. He returned to the
cell having received a severe beating, and his eyes were swollen
shut. His cellmates nursed him back to health with nothing more
than a cold rag. Within a week, Christian was busily collecting materials to craft another flag. Robinson felt these actions represented

the patriotic spirit of American servicemen in Southeast Asia. He described the Christmas Bombing run of Linebacker II as an all-volunteer mission designed to secure the release of all the prisoners of war. During that eleven-day aerial campaign, forty Americans were killed in action. He noted his happy homecoming of 14 February 1973, but he reminded the group of warrant officer candidates that America had forgiven those "who ran before thanking those who served," a veiled reference to President Jimmy Carter's decision, on the first full day of his presidency, to grant unconditional amnesty to Vietnam-era draft evaders. According to Robinson, the American soldier served on the "front line of the four corners of the earth" during the Vietnam War, supporting the nation's defense and promoting freedom and liberty. He considered it an honor to have served with them. Despite the ordeal of captivity, he "found something bigger than self," and he proudly trod down a path well-worn by a gallant band of men "who had returned with honor." He concluded his remarks by reciting Article VI of the Code of Conduct: "I will never forget that I am an American, fighting for freedom, responsible for my actions, and dedicated to the principles which made my country free. I will trust in my God and in the United States of America."

For forty-five minutes, the sixty-three candidates stood respectfully listening to Robinson's story. When he concluded, they applauded appreciatively, and Robinson offered them a chance to ask questions. One soldier stepped forward and asked the secret to surviving solitary confinement. Robinson explained the connective force of the tap code as well as the tricks and games some POWs employed to keep their sanity. A second officer candidate wondered how Robinson and the other POWs adjusted to postrelease life, given all the social changes that had transpired in America during the 1960s. He responded with an oft-quoted POW adage, "It's always a good day when the knob is on the inside of the door." When he returned to the states, Robinson, like many POWs, simply wanted to enjoy his freedom. Having survived a lengthy imprisonment under horrible conditions, he was confident that no matter what the future held, he would overcome any obstacle. The formal question-and-answer period ended after these two questions. Then, in a spontaneous gesture of respect and admiration, a little more than one-third of the sixty-three candidates formed a line to shake hands with Robinson. Some briefly exchanged information about hometowns. One candidate was the son of an Air Force mechanic whose father had served in Vietnam and serviced some of the aircraft used in the Son Tay Raid. Humbled by the revelation and ever grateful to the Son Tay Raiders, Robinson asked the young man to pass along his thanks to his father. Another candidate informed Robinson that he reminded him of his grandfather, who had just passed away. Robinson took a few moments to console the young man. And yet another candidate, a self-described immigrant, said it was an "honor to be accepted as an American soldier." The final warrant officer candidate, a female soldier, just wanted to express her gratitude. All the candidates then went into the National Prisoner of War Museum and concluded their visit with a brief tour of the Andersonville National Cemetery. The long green line between Fort Rucker and Andersonville continued on Sunday, as yet another group returned to the historical site to participate in the laying of the wreaths during the Memorial Day services.[29]

More Than Casualties of War

Since daytime temperatures are frequently in the upper eighties or low nineties, September sunsets in southwestern Georgia rarely announce the onset of autumn. Such was the case on 25 September 2010, when Robinson stepped to the podium to deliver the keynote address at the closing ceremonies of the Vietnam Traveling Memorial Wall exhibition at the Andersonville National Historic Site.[30] The Traveling Wall, a three-fifths-size replica of the more well-known Vietnam Veterans Memorial in Washington, D.C., served as a central component of the 2010 POW/MIA Recognition Day programs at ANHS. The original Vietnam Veterans Memorial, commonly referred to as the Wall, was born amid controversy. Maya Lin, the twenty-one-year-old Chinese American undergraduate at Yale University, won the national design competition, beating out more than 1,400 entries. Her design consisted of two polished black granite walls sunk into the ground, meeting "at an oblique angle and tapered to their extremities, forming a chevron shape." The tapered walls reached ten feet high at their tallest point and stretched some 250 feet in length. Inscribed on the walls would be the names of the Vietnam War's dead and missing. Lin's intent was to slice into the earth and create "an initial violence that in time would heal."[31]

Critics of Lin and the design, and there were many, described her concept variously as a "scar," a "trench," and most salaciously as a "black gash of shame and sorrow." H. Ross Perot, who helped fund the design competition, disapproved of the selection and labeled it a "tombstone" and a "slap in the face" to the war's veterans. His dissatisfaction was so great that he called on the former Vietnam POWs to join his effort to force changes to the original design. Specifically, Perot funded a poll of Vietnam POWs to document their formal opposition. The poll indicated that 67 percent disliked the original design, 70 percent believed "the color of the memorial should be white instead of black, 96 percent felt a flag should be a prominent part of the memorial and 82 percent felt the monument should be above ground."[32] The public outcry against Lin's design led to significant changes, most notably the inclusion of a bronze statue near the Wall, known as the Three Soldiers Monument. Robinson was not one of the 265 former prisoners who responded to the Perot poll; in fact, his opinion was not solicited. Yet he had concerns about the memorial, although they had less to do with the ethnicity of the architect or the architectural design than the simple fact that the monument recognized only those killed in the conflict and not all those who served during the Vietnam War. In this respect, he agreed with Perot's concerns. Robinson has "always been hesitant about [lists of] names because there is no way you will ever get it right—you reward some and you hurt some." Over time, Robinson's views on the Wall have softened, in large measure because of his attendance at Traveling Wall exhibitions, and he has come to realize "what the Wall really means."[33] On that sultry September day in 2010 at the ANHS, almost forty-five years to the day of his shootdown and capture in Vietnam, Robinson offered his reflections on the Vietnam Wall.

Robinson spoke first of a different wall, a wall he had visited with his grandfather while still a youngster in Roanoke Rapids,

North Carolina. This wall was not famous or controversial, but the younger Robinson did notice that it contained a list of names, of friends and family, including the name of William Jackson Robinson, Bill's father, as well as several uncles. Some of the names were accompanied by a star. When Robinson asked his grandfather about the meaning of the stars, a lump appeared in the elder's throat and tears formed in his eyes as he reminded his grandson that those stars represented "the ones that paid the ultimate sacrifice for the country that we enjoy today." As Bill grew older, he learned of "walls like this all over our country to honor the men and women who have given their all." Standing in front of the Vietnam Traveling Memorial Wall, Robinson announced, "Now I stand in front of the Wall of stars of my generation, over 58,000 strong, but over 1,400 of them still missing in action, part of 7.2 million men and women who wore the uniform during the Vietnam War"; more than three million of that number served "in country." He then identified five brothers whose names all appeared on the Vietnam Wall, each of whom played an important part in the man Robinson became while he spent eight Thanksgivings, eight Christmases, and eight New Year's Days in North Vietnamese prisons.[34]

Lieutenant Duane Martin's name, the first brother mentioned by Robinson, appears on Panel 2E, Line 91. Robinson explained that in the confusion of the shootdown, the two crewmates became separated as they both struggled to maintain their freedom. They experienced very different forms of captivity: Robinson spent "the duration of the war in camps outside the city of Hanoi," while Martin, a captive of the Pathet Lao, was held in a bamboo cage in the jungles of Laos. After what Robinson termed "many years, Duane and another gentleman escaped." In Robinson's opinion, "the only good thing about [the effort] was that Duane got to taste freedom for about four days before he was killed while trying to steal food and water in order to survive." Lieutenant Martin's final days were far more dramatic than Robinson implied.[35]

On 29 July 1966 Martin; a Navy pilot, Dieter Dengler; an Air America employee, Gene DeBruin; three Thai nationals; and To Yick Chiu of Hong Kong made their escape attempt. Their well-conceived plan was to catch the guards unaware during their afternoon meal break, confiscate the stacked weapons, hold the camp, and signal for a rescue plane. The guards detected the prisoners shortly after they left their cells, but the armed prisoners fired on the guards, killing five, while one managed to flee the shooting rampage, and another did not report as expected for the meal. Following a predetermined backup plan, the captives split up, and Dengler and Martin headed west toward Thailand. The barefoot fliers struggled from the beginning. The monsoon rains, the lack of food and supplies, and their weakened physical condition exacted a heavy toll. For four days the two men labored through the unforgiving jungle. On the fifth day they "awoke sore, sick, and dispirited." Then the situation worsened as Martin displayed symptoms of malaria: "fever, chills, and nausea." They traveled several days by river, and, despite hearing planes overhead, they were unable to start a signal fire and in many ways were closer to death than to freedom. Martin confessed to Dengler that he feared he would die in the jungle and made the naval aviator promise to make sure that his wife, Dorcas, was all right. When a Laotian fisherman spotted the two escapees, they reversed direction, abandoning the notion of reaching Thailand in favor of a shorter, more dangerous trek to North Vietnam, where larger rivers could carry them the twenty or so miles to the coast. After several more days of travel, their hope dimmed when they discovered that they had walked in a circle, but clear skies, a rousing fire, and a circling plane restored their spirits. The next day, when the expected rescue helicopters did not arrive, they resumed their sojourn. After three weeks of evasion, when all seemed hopeless, fortune changed for one of the two men. Flying in an A-1 Skyraider on the morning of 20 July, Lieutenant Colonel Eugene Deatrick, commanding officer of the 1st Air Commando Squadron based at Pleiku, South Vietnam, spotted Dengler on a riverbank, and the rescue operation was quickly under way. The discovery was an improbable happenstance in a known hostile area, but the experience and professionalism of the air rescue teams made the actual pickup practically a routine operation.[36]

Safely aboard an Air Force HH-3E Jolly Green Giant rescue helicopter, a delirious Dengler, stricken by "two types of malaria, intestinal worms, fungus, jaundice, and hepatitis," had avoided death by no more than forty-eight hours. Once he arrived at the hospital in Da Nang, naval intelligence officers questioned him about his time in captivity. He recounted his six-month ordeal, identified his fellow prisoners, and tried to pinpoint his escape route. He was surprised to learn that when he was extracted by the rescue team he was only thirteen miles from his prison camp and "at one point . . . had circled back to within two miles of the camp." Dengler also reported on the fate of Duane Martin. Just a few days before Dengler's rescue he and Martin had encountered a young boy carrying water along a trail. Shortly thereafter, villagers appeared out of nowhere and surrounded the two Americans, and suddenly "a wild-eyed young man in loincloth jumped in front of Duane, swinging a long machete about his head with both hands." The first blow struck Martin "deep in his thigh," causing the airman to scream in agony. The villager delivered a second blow "chopping" through the back of Martin's neck. With Dengler watching, the executioner completed his gruesome task with a final stroke that severed Martin's head. During the debriefing with the naval intelligence officers, Dengler broke down as he described Martin's death and had to be given time to recover. Lieutenant Duane Martin's wife, Dorcas, broke down as well. She never fully recovered from the heart-wrenching news of her husband's final days. For a while, she managed to cope and raised her two young daughters, Cheryl and Christine, through their formative years. Dorcas, however, in the face of her irreparable loss, deteriorated and "fell deeper into psychotic states." Eventually, the "vibrant, active, fun person" was institutionalized and family members view her "as much a casualty of the Vietnam War" as her husband.[37]

Perhaps Robinson felt restrained by the time limitations of the occasion, or possibly he decided that delving more deeply into Martin's escape might detract from the other four brothers whom he intended to honor. They were brothers whom Robinson wanted viewed in equal terms and as more than casualties of war. After Duane Martin, Robinson honored Ed Atterberry and John Frederick. Like Martin, Atterberry had been involved in a daring escape attempt, one that had cost him his life, but Robinson insisted that Atterberry was murdered by the North Vietnamese during a vicious

interrogation following his recapture. Robinson maintained that Atterberry sacrificed his own life rather than reveal the names of the
prisoners who had assisted his escape. "He knew their fate" would
have been similar to his, Robinson told the audience, "if he gave up
their names." Instead, "he carried those names to his death." Robinson admired Atterberry for his courage and fortitude in the face of
grave danger, and he harbored a deep resentment toward the Vietnamese for the Air Force captain's execution. He viewed John Frederick with similar esteem. Frederick was a battle-tested veteran who
"saw combat as a young man in World War II," and again in Korea
and Vietnam. Robinson watched helplessly from his own cell as the
Marine aviator suffered needlessly from injuries sustained during
his shootdown. Frederick spent 2,417 days in captivity, during which
he became known as a "Marine among Marines," a man's man, a
dedicated soldier and role model. Sadly, toward the end of the war,
Frederick, although having survived countless rounds of torture and
extended periods of deprivation, contracted typhoid and died in a
Hanoi hospital. Robinson heard rumors that Frederick died alone,
but he refused to believe them. As he explained, "I prefer to say
that he was cradled by angels as he ascended into heaven, where he
looked down upon the men he so proudly served with. He has gone
from us but long remembered." Edwin Lee Atterberry and John William Frederick were not simply casualties of war. Their names appear, respectively, on Panel 24E, Line 102, and Panel 3E, Line 136.[38]

Walter Ferguson, the fourth brother recognized by Robinson,
was a twenty-one-year veteran of the Air Force and a tail gunner
in a B-52 Stratofortress bomber. Robinson firmly believes that Ferguson, and everyone else associated with Linebacker II, was part
of a mission to bring him home. In late 1972 the United States and
North Vietnam established the parameters for "an honorable end to
the Vietnam conflict," but disagreements regarding U.S. backing of
South Vietnamese President Nguyen Van Thieu stalled negotiations
and by extension postponed the release of American POWs. This
was when President Nixon authorized Linebacker II. On 27 January
1973 the North Vietnamese signed the Paris Peace Accords, and the
United States ended its involvement in the Vietnam War. Following
his release and "over and over again in retirement," Robinson has

encountered Vietnam veterans who have said, "We wanted to come get you out, but no one would allow us." "Finally," said Robinson, President Nixon "decided it was time." The Linebacker II mission was a volunteer mission, and the first flight crews were ordered to take no evasive actions during their bombing runs. As Robinson reflected, he singled out Senior Master Sergeant Walter Ferguson, who "on the first night of the bombing, 18 December 1972, gave his life for the freedoms that I enjoy today." Ferguson's name appears on Panel 1W, Line 94.[39]

Robinson's longest tribute was for U.S. Army Private First Class Darrell Johnson. The two North Carolinians never met, but in 1968 their two families "lived less than thirty miles apart." Johnson was declared missing in January 1968 after an ambush on his unit near the shared borders of Laos, Cambodia, and South Vietnam. Because of the work of the National League of Families, the Robinson and Johnson families became well acquainted. They "prayed together, cried together, and laughed together." They convinced one another that their two sons, "whom they were very proud of, were sitting side by side in a cell, just waiting for the end of the war, waiting to come home." Not more than six months before that September 2010 day at Andersonville, while attending an American Legion meeting, Robinson had struck up a conversation with a veteran who had served as a casualty officer at Fort Bragg, North Carolina, during the Vietnam War. Robinson shared that conversation with the audience. Awakened in the middle of the night by a junior officer, the casualty officer learned that the official list of American POWs was soon to be released and that he drew the responsibility of informing the family of Darrell Johnson that his name did not appear on the list. "With a tear in his eye and a heavy heart," the casualty officer recounted to Robinson a thirty-seven-year-old story. "That was the longest sixty miles I ever drove," he said. "What was I going to say to that family . . . who believed for so long that their son would be coming home, that the war would be over for him." When the casualty officer finally arrived at the parents' home, he knocked on the door; when they answered, he "didn't have to say a word because they knew that their son was not coming home alive." Helpless, the casualty officer and the family "embraced and cried together for quite some time." As he repeated the story to the Andersonville audience, Robinson could not avoid a direct comparison to his own family: "That's the way it was: the Robinson family was blessed with the return of their son, who added to the family tree a loving wife, two wonderful daughters, and four beautiful grandchildren, and the tree will continue to grow. But the Johnson family, their family tree died in the jungles of Vietnam."[40]

In concluding his remarks, Robinson praised "Darrell, Duane, Ed, John, and Walter" for teaching him the meaning of "duty, honor, and country." They were not merely casualties of war. He linked the five men with their fellow "Vietnam brothers and sisters" and thanked them for a job well done. Robinson then issued a call to move beyond a narrow focus on the losses of the Vietnam War and its divisiveness. He championed healing as a more appropriate response and urged the audience to face the realization "that freedom is not free." He offered the Vietnam Wall as a transcendent symbol of the cost of freedom paid not only by those who served in Vietnam but by those "who came before" and by those "who will follow." Robinson closed his speech by affirming the importance of the Code of Conduct for today's men and women in uniform, "who stand ready today to defend freedom all over the world." And just as he had done with the warrant officer candidates from Fort Rucker four months earlier, he recited the words of Article VI of the Code of Conduct: "I will never forget that I am an American, fighting for freedom, responsible for my actions, and dedicated to the principles which made my country free. I will trust in my God and in the United States of America."

Greater Than Self

When the Andersonville National Historic Site announced plans for a 12,000-square-foot traveling exhibition, Victory from Within: The American POW Experience, Bill Robinson quickly volunteered to accompany the exhibit as it toured the country. Given his hundreds of hours of volunteer work with the Andersonville Guest Host Program, Robinson's remarkable gesture came as no surprise. After fifteen years of passionate devotion to the National Prisoner of War Museum, both Bill and Ora Mae have very clear views on its role and purpose, views that also apply by extension to the Victory from Within exhibit. First and foremost, Robinson expects any educational programs, historical displays, or special events to properly recognize the former captives for their accomplishments as prisoners of war and not simply to produce sympathy for those who survived the hardships of captivity. Moreover, he hopes the increased knowledge and awareness of the prisoner-of-war stories will provide a long overdue appreciation for World War II and Korean War POWs, who suffered unfairly under a cloud of alleged failure. Robinson has met World War II POWs who walked into their veterans' organizations, the American Legion or Veterans of Foreign Wars, and the membership "turned their backs" on the former captives. Robinson also feels that because successful escapes were so rare, especially after the Korean War, part of the National Prisoner of War Museum's mission is to illustrate the ability of individuals "to endure when there are no other options" and to frame "the wars within the war" that are often overlooked or neglected. In addition, he firmly contends that any serious effort to tell the American prisoner-of-war story must recognize "those who waited," the families—the mothers, fathers, wives, husbands, sisters, brothers, sons, and daughters—who lived through an unfortunate ordeal of their own. Even today, Robinson sometimes becomes furious at his stepmother for having said that it was his fault that his father "had a nervous breakdown." Nevertheless, he understands the difficult set of circumstances that his entire family faced during his captivity.[41]

Thinking somewhat like a historian, Ora Mae realizes that the prisoner-of-war story "needs to be told, and it needs to be recorded because when they are all gone there will be no one left to tell future generations. Their stories will be lost." She sees the National Prisoner of War Museum and its oral history collections as a guardian of the prisoner-of-war legacy. Over the years, the ANHS has conducted more than nine hundred interviews with former POWs and their families, and its holdings include interviews with former prisoners from World War I to the Persian Gulf War. On a personal level, Ora Mae intends to do whatever she can to assist and "move forward" in celebrating the legacy of American POWs. Membership in many AXPOW chapters has declined in recent years, a 10 percent decline each year for the first decade of the twenty-first century, but as Ora Mae vows, "as long as one can show up," she will continue to serve the POW organization. Her dedication to the legacy of the POWs extends to her holding the position of secretary-treasurer of the Smoky Mountain (Tennessee) Chapter of AXPOW, and the same position in the statewide Tennessee AXPOW. Ora Mae is now part of Robinson's legacy, though she is much more than the guardian of his story or the protector of POW memory more generally. She is his partner and his true love, and she helped restore his relationship with his family.

Robinson answers to many names; to his family he is Billy, to those he served with in the Air Force he is Robbie, and to everyone else he is Bill. No matter his name, his values and character have remained constant: an indomitable spirit, devotion to duty, and love of country. His is a legacy not only to be admired, but also to be emulated.[42]

Acknowledgments

I first met Bill Robinson at the Andersonville National Historic Site in March 2007. I was there to help with the Luminary Event, the placing of 13,000 candles on the old Civil War prison grounds to commemorate the death of U.S. soldiers who died in captivity while held at Andersonville Prison. Robinson was there as part of the POW Guest Host Program, whereby former prisoners of war volunteer their time to meet and interact with visitors to the historic site. The meeting had been arranged by Park Ranger Kim Humber, a former student of mine and a friend of Bill Robinson. I had recently completed a book manuscript on a Civil War prisoner of war, and Bill was looking for someone to tell his story. After we spent some time together, Bill asked if I was interested in writing his book. I consented. I don't think either of us understood completely what we had agreed to. Since that day, Bill and I have been together frequently. We have traveled together, and I have spent time with his family. Through the writing of the book we have become close friends. When Kim and I decided to marry, I asked my dad and my soon-to-be stepson Blake to stand as my best men. I also asked Bill Robinson, and of course he said yes. He views Kim as a daughter. Along with a friend and mentor, Joan Stibitz, Kim also had a former POW, Al Agnew, stand with her as part of the bride's party. The Vietnam POWs have been and will remain an important part of our lives.

As a professional historian, I am committed to writing history and constructing analysis based on the evidence. Bill, in effect, gave me his story and allowed me to determine how to present it. I have been careful and precise in allowing Bill's voice to come to the forefront of this biography. In many ways, this book is not simply the story of Robinson's captivity; it is as much a study of the perception and memory of Vietnam POWs as it is the history of a Vietnam POW. In this vein, and as the fortieth anniversary of the release of the Vietnam POWs has passed, Bill's own perspective is a crucial part of the historic record.

I have accrued many debts in completing this project. First and foremost, Bill Robinson gave me unlimited access to his personal papers as well as his thoughts and his time. At Georgia Southwestern State University, I have received financial assistance for research and travel. My colleagues John Stovall, Gary Kline, Richard Hall, Gary Fisk, Ellen Cotter, and Brian Parkinson have lent an ear or a helping hand on numerous occasions. DeDe Reyes has been a constant friend and has graciously assisted me over the years. I am grateful to the entire staff at the James Earl Carter Library at Georgia Southwestern, especially Valerie Anthony and John Wilson. Steve Wrinn, Allison Webster, and the staff of the University Press of Kentucky have been a pleasure to work with. I thank Steve for his enthusiastic confidence in this book. The three anonymous reviewers retained by the press provided professional and highly detailed commentary on the original manuscript.

I can never repay my debts to my family. My parents, Marvin and Phyllis Robins, have always loved me unconditionally. My in-laws, Buddy and Virginia Douglas, are more like a second set of parents, and I can always count on them. Blake, I am proud of you and excited to see what the future holds for you. And Kim, our first date was on Halloween, we were married on Veterans Day weekend, and each day you fill my life with love and a touch of craziness. I love you all.

Notes

Introduction

1. William Robinson interview, #906, Andersonville National Historic Site, Andersonville, Ga. (hereinafter cited as ANHS).

2. Edwin G. Burrows, *Forgotten Patriots: The Untold Story of American Prisoners during the Revolutionary War* (New York: Basic Books, 2008), x, xii.

3. William Marvel, "Johnny Ransom's Imagination," *Civil War History* 41 (September 1995): 181–89; James M. Gillispie, *Andersonvilles of the North: The Myths and Realities of Northern Treatment of Civil War Confederate Prisoners* (Denton: University of North Texas Press, 2008), 6–22.

4. Typically, sympathetic congressmen offered private pension legislation on Friday afternoons in the absence of quorums, when they were passed by unanimous consent. For more on the issue of pensions, see William Henry Glasson, *Federal Military Pensions in the United States* (New York: Oxford University Press, 1918).

5. For an examination of the postwar lives and legacies of Civil War soldiers, including prisoners of war, see James Marten, *Sing Not War: The Lives of Union and Confederate Veterans in Gilded Age America* (Chapel Hill: University of North Carolina Press, 2011).

6. For more on this issue see Glenn Robins, "Race, Repatriation, and Galvanized Rebels: Union POWs and the Exchange Question in the Deep South Prison Camps," *Civil War History* 53 (June 2007): 117–40.

7. Robert C. Doyle, *Voices from Captivity: Interpreting the American POW Narrative* (Lawrence: University Press of Kansas, 1994), 5.

8. Thomas Saylor, *Long Hard Road: American POWs during World War II* (St. Paul: Minnesota Historical Society Press, 2007), 257. For similar reports of the stigma of capture and the desire to remain silent about being a POW, see the comments of two former POWs, Louis Grivetti and Louis Pfeifer, in Lewis H. Carlson, *We Were Each Other's Prisoners: An Oral History of World War II American and German Prisoners of War* (New York: Basic Books, 1997), 231–43.

9. Saylor, *Long Hard Road*, 256.

10. Elliott Gruner, *Prisoners of Culture: Representing the Vietnam POW* (New Brunswick, N.J.: Rutgers University Press, 1993), 8.

11. Lewis H. Carlson, *Remembered Prisoners of a Forgotten War: An Oral History of Korean War POWs* (New York: St. Martin's Press, 2002).

12. Lori Lyn Bogle, *The Pentagon's Battle for the American Mind: The*

Early Cold War (College Station: Texas A&M University Press, 2004), 119–24.

13. Carlson, *Remembered Prisoners of a Forgotten War,* 222.

14. Mark Bowden, *Blackhawk Down: A Story of Modern War* (New York: Atlantic Monthly Press, 1999); Michael J. Durant with Steven Hartov, *In the Company of Heroes* (New York: G. P. Putnam's Sons, 2003).

15. Joe Dunn, "The POW Chronicles: A Bibliographic Review," *Armed Forces and Society* 9 (Spring 1983): 495–514. Although Dunn's piece is a bit dated, the early trends have continued. For two recent examples of the officer-aviator memoir tradition, see George R. Hall and Pat Hall with Bob Pittman, *Commitment to Honor: A Prisoner of War Remembers Vietnam* (Jackson, Miss.: Franklin Printers, 2005), and Leo Thorsness, *Surviving Hell: A POW's Journey* (New York: Encounter Books, 2008).

16. Maureen Ryan, *The Other Side of Grief: The Home Front and the Aftermath in American Narratives of the Vietnam War* (Amherst: University of Massachusetts Press, 2008), 115. For more on the issues of Vietnam POW narratives and of a master narrative or official history, see Craig Howes, *Voices of the Vietnam POWs: Witnesses to Their Fight* (New York: Oxford University Press, 1993).

1. Unfortunate Sons

1. For the transcript of the entire Johnson speech, see *New York Times,* 5 August 1964, p. 1.

2. H. R. McMaster, *Dereliction of Duty: Lyndon Johnson, Robert McNamara, the Joint Chiefs, and the Lies That Led to Vietnam* (New York: HarperCollins, 1997), 126–32.

3. Everett Alvarez Jr. and Anthony S. Pitch, *Chained Eagle: The Heroic Story of the First American Shot Down over North Vietnam* (Washington, D.C.: Potomac Books, 2005), 8–20.

4. Ibid., 20–25, 215–17.

5. Neither Alvarez nor Thompson was the first American serviceman captured during the Vietnam War. That distinction goes to Army Private George Fryett, who was captured on 26 December 1961 and released six months later. For more on Thompson's story, see Tom Philpott, *Glory Denied: The Saga of Jim Thompson, America's Longest-Held Prisoner of War* (New York: W. W. Norton, 2001).

6. Bill Robinson, interview by the author, 21 October 2008. (Unless attributed otherwise, all interviews cited were conducted by the author.) See also Robert B. Robinson III, ed., *Roanoke Rapids: The First Hundred Years, 1897–1997* (Lawrenceville, Va.: Brunswick, 1997), 21, 29.

7. Paul M. Gaston, *The New South Creed: A Study in Southern Mythmaking* (New York: Alfred A. Knopf, 1970), 7. See also Edward L. Ayers,

The Promise of the New South (New York: Oxford University Press, 1992).

8. Mimi Conway, *Rise Gonna Rise: A Portrait of Southern Textile Workers* (Garden City, N.Y.: Anchor Press, 1979), 12–15.

9. Bill Robinson interview, 21 October 2008.

10. Conway, *Rise Gonna Rise*, 15–16. For more on Stevens's anti-unionism and corporate strategy, see Timothy J. Minchin *"Don't Sleep with Stevens!" The J. P. Stevens Campaign and the Struggle to Organize the South, 1963–1980* (Gainesville: University Press of Florida, 2005).

11. Bill Robinson interviews, 15 May 2009 and 21 October 2008.

12. Bill Robinson interview, 21 October 2008.

13. Ibid.; Ginger Hux interview, 31 July 2010.

14. Ibid.

15. Bill Robinson interview, 21 October 2008.

16. Ibid.; Ginger Hux interview, 31 July 2010.

17. Bill Robinson interview, 21 October 2008.

18. Ginger Hux interview, 31 July 2010.

19. Ibid.

20. Bill Robinson interview, 21 October 2008.

21. Ibid. For a concise, state-by-state overview of school desegregation, see Brian J. Daugherity and Charles C. Bolton, eds., *With All Deliberate Speed: Implementing* Brown v. Board of Education (Fayetteville: University of Arkansas Press, 2008).

22. Bill Robinson interviews, 21 October 2008, 15 May 2009.

23. Bill Robinson interview, 21 October 2008.

24. Ibid.

25. Ibid.

26. Ibid.

27. Stuart I. Rochester and Frederick Kiley, *Honor Bound: The History of American Prisoners of War in Southeast Asia, 1961–1973* (1998; repr., Annapolis: Naval Institute Press, 1999), 60–61.

28. Bill Robinson interview, 21 October 2008.

29. Ibid.

30. Ibid.

31. Ibid.

32. Forrest L. Marion, *That Others May Live: USAF Air Rescue in Korea* (Washington, D.C.: Air Force History and Museums Program, 2004), 1, 6.

33. Ibid., 4–5, 18.

34. Allan R. Millett and Peter Maslowski, *For the Common Defense: A Military History of the United States of America* (New York: Free Press, 1994), 534–39.

35. Conrad C. Crane, *American Airpower Strategy in Korea, 1950–1953* (Lawrence: University Press of Kansas, 2000), 173.

36. Marion, *That Others May Live*, 48.

37. Drew quoted in Crane, *American Airpower Strategy in Korea*, 175.

38. Millett and Maslowski, *For the Common Defense*, 572–78.

39. Tilford quoted in Marion, *That Others May Live*, 48.

40. Alvarez and Pitch, *Chained Eagle*, 17.

41. Earl H. Tilford Jr., *Search and Rescue in Southeast Asia, 1961–1975* (1980; repr., Washington, D.C.: Center for Air Force History, 1992), 61, 70.

42. Quoted material from Wayne Mutza, *Kaman H-43: An Illustrated History* (Atglen, Pa.: Schiffer Military / Aviation History, 1998), 58, 61–62, 22. See also Tilford, *Search and Rescue in Southeast Asia*, 75.

43. Tilford, *Search and Rescue in Southeast Asia*, 60, 70, 76.

44. Bill Robinson interview, 21 October 2008; Joe Ballinger document, in the author's collection; Tom Curtis interview, 18 September 2010.

45. Tom Curtis interview, 18 September 2010; POW biographies are easily accessible at the following websites: www.veterantributes.org/POW.php and www.pownetwork.org/bios.htm; accessed 15 May 2010.

46. Tom Curtis interview, 18 September 2010; Bill Robinson interview, 21 October 2008.

47. Bill Robinson interview, 21 October 2008.

48. Ibid.

49. Chris Hobson, *Vietnam Air Losses: United States Air Force, Navy and Marine Corps Fixed-Wing Aircraft Losses in Southeast Asia, 1961–1973* (Hinckley, U.K.: Midland Publishing, 2001), 32–33.

50. Ibid., 32.

51. Bill Robinson interview, 21 October 2008.

52. Ibid.; William Robinson interview, #906, ANHS.

53. Ibid.; Tom Curtis interview, 18 September 2010.

54. Bill Robinson interview, 21 October 2008; William Robinson interview, #906, ANHS.

55. Ibid.; Tom Curtis interview, 18 September 2010.

56. Bill Robinson interview, 21 October 2008; William Robinson interview, #906, ANHS.

57. Bill Robinson interviews, 21 October 2008, 27 May 2010.

2. Separate Paths to Hell

1. Bill Robinson interview, 21 October 2008; Bill Robinson interview, 27 May 2010.

2. Ibid.

3. Bill Robinson interview, 21 October 2008.

4. Ibid.; Bill Robinson interview, 27 May 2010.

5. Bill Robinson interview, 21 October 2008; William Robinson interview, #906, ANHS.

6. Bill Robinson interview, 27 May 2010.

7. Bill Robinson interview, 21 October 2008; William Robinson Interview, #906, ANHS.

8. The other three central prisons were located in Saigon, Phnom Penh, and Vientiane. Peter Zinoman, *The Colonial Bastille: A History of Imprisonment in Vietnam, 1862–1940* (Berkeley: University of California Press, 2001), 52–53, 97.

9. Rochester and Kiley, *Honor Bound*, 88–90.

10. William Robinson interview, #906, ANHS.

11. Carlyle Harris, television interview, 1981, transcript, McCain Library and Archives, University of Southern Mississippi, Hattiesburg, 8–9.

12. Ibid.

13. Rochester and Kiley, *Honor Bound*, 135–40.

14. Bill Robinson interview, 27 May 2010; George Hall interview, 1 May 1973, McCain Library and Archives, University of Southern Mississippi, Hattiesburg, vol. 35.

15. Ibid.

16. Rochester and Kiley, *Honor Bound*, 129, 128.

17. Bill Robinson interview, 27 May 2010.

18. Ibid.

19. Rochester and Kiley, *Honor Bound*, 117; Alvarez and Pitch, *Chained Eagle*, 164–65.

20. Bill Robinson interview, 27 May 2010. For Frederick's biography, see www.pownetwork.org/bios/f/f053.htm; accessed 3 September 2010. For information about Pitchford, see www.pownetwork.org/bios/p/p063.htm; accessed 3 September 2010. For information on Marine aviators, see Rochester and Kiley, *Honor Bound*, 141, 264. For information on Operation Iron Hand and Wild Weasel, see "Iron Hand," National Museum of the U.S. Air Force, www.nationalmuseum.af.mil/factsheets/factsheet.asp?id=1308, accessed 3 September 2010; and James Stuart Olson, *Dictionary of the Vietnam War* (1988; repr., New York: Peter Bedrick Books, 1990), 487.

21. Bill Robinson interview, 27 May 2010; William A. Robinson to Beverly Fish, 3 June 1966, copy in the author's collection.

22. Bill Robinson interview, 27 May 2010.

23. Rochester and Kiley, *Honor Bound*, 145–46.

24. Bruce Henderson, *Hero Found: The Greatest POW Escape of the Vietnam War* (New York: HarperCollins, 2010), 5–47.

25. Ibid., 62–73, 94–96, 106–7; J. Nathan Campbell, "Yankee Station," in Spencer C. Tucker, ed., *Encyclopedia of the Vietnam War: A Political, Social, and Military History*, 3 vols. (Santa Barbara, Calif.: ABC-CLIO, 1998) 2:829; Dieter Dengler, *Escape from Laos* (San Rafael, Calif.: Presidio Press, 1979), 7–25.

26. Henderson, *Hero Found*, 163–64; William M. Leary, "CIA Air Operations in Laos, 1955–1974," https://www.cia.gov/library/center-for-the-study-of-inteligence/kent-csi/vol43no3/pdf/v43i3a07p.pdf, accessed 15 March 2013; Pisidhi Indradat, "Story of Escape," www.rescuedawnthetruth.com/Story_of_Escape.pdf. accessed 3 September 2010.

27. I am grateful to Routledge Press for permission to quote from my previous work, Glenn Robins, "The American POW Experience," in *America and the Vietnam War: Re-examining the Culture and History of a Generation,* ed. Andrew Wiest, Mary Kathryn Barbier, and Glenn Robins (New York: Routledge, 2010), 166–69.

28. Rochester and Kiley, *Honor Bound*, 278–79, 57.

29. Henderson, *Hero Found*, 166; Dengler, *Escape from Laos*, 91–105.

30. Henderson, *Hero Found*, 171.

31. Ibid., 172–76.

32. Ibid., 176–80, 194–98.

33. One of the best descriptions of Briarpatch is part of a study conducted in 1974 by thirty-five former Vietnam POWs while assigned to the Air War College at Maxwell Air Force Base. Armand J. Myers et al., *Vietnam POW Camp Histories and Studies*, 2 vols. (Montgomery, Ala.: Air War College, Maxwell Air Force Base, 1974), 1:75–78, 87; Rochester and Kiley, *Honor Bound*, 126–28, 159–60; Bill Robinson interviews, 27 May 2010, 16 May 2009.

34. William Robinson interview #906, ANHS; Bill Robinson interview, 18 May 2009.

35. Myers et al., *Vietnam POW Camp Histories and Studies*, 82–86; Bill Robinson interview, 18 May 2009.

36. Bertrand Russell, *War Crimes in Vietnam* (New York: Monthly Review Press, 1967); John Duffett, ed., *Against the Crime of Silence: Proceedings of the Russell International War Crimes Tribunal* (New York: Bertrand Russell Peace Foundation, 1968).

37. American Enterprise Institute, "The Prisoner of War Problem," study prepared for the 91st Congress, 2nd session, December 28, 1970, 15–23. The Article 85 stipulation is the actual language in the Geneva Convention.

38. Rochester and Kiley, *Honor Bound*, 194.

39. An excellent account of the Hanoi March can be found in John G. Hubbell, *P.O.W.: A Definitive History of the American Prisoner-of-War Experience in Vietnam, 1964–1973* (New York: Reader's Digest Press, 1976), 183–99.

40. U.S. Congress, *Congressional Record*, Senate, 15 July 1966, 15853.

41. Bill Robinson interview, 16 May 2009.

42. Bill Robinson interviews, 18 May 2009, 21 October 2008.

43. Bill Robinson interview, 27 May 2010.

44. Larry Guarino, *A P.O.W.'s Story: 2801 Days in Hanoi* (New York: Ivy Books, 1990), 105–6.

45. Rochester and Kiley, *Honor Bound*, 159.

46. Myers et al., *Vietnam POW Camp Histories and Studies*, 78–79, 92–94.

47. Harold G. Moore and Joseph L. Galloway, *We Were Soldiers Once . . . and Young: Ia Drang, The Battle That Changed the War in Vietnam* (New York: Random House, 1992), 323.

48. Bill Robinson interview, 22 May 2009.

49. Ginger Hux interview, 31 July 2010.

50. Jackie Robertson interview, 31 July 2010.

51. Ginger Hux interview, 31 July 2010.

52. Ibid.

53. William A. Robinson to Mr. and Mrs. William J. Robinson, 20 December 1965. Unless otherwise noted, copies of these letters are in the author's collection.

54. William A. Robinson to Mr. and Mrs. William J. Robinson, 26 April 1966, 3 June 1966, 19 July 1966, 23 October 1966, 10 November 1966; William A. Robinson to Beverly Fish, 3 June 1966, 19 July 1966, 23 October 1966, 10 November 1966, 7 December 1966.

55. William A. Robinson to Mr. and Mrs. William J. Robinson, 23 October 1966.

56. *Life*, 7 April 1967, 33–44.

57. Ibid., 43.

58. The fullest accounts of Stratton's story are Scott Blakey, *Prisoner at War: The Survival of Commander Richard A. Stratton* (Garden City, N.Y.: Anchor Press/Doubleday, 1978); Geoffrey Norman, *Bouncing Back: How a Heroic Band of POWs Survived Vietnam* (Boston: Houghton Mifflin, 1990).

59. *Life*, 7 April 1967, 43.

60. Ginger Hux interview, 31 July 2010; *Life*, 7 April 1967, 43.

61. "POW Symposium," National POW/MIA Day Program, 14 September 2006, Americus, Ga. DVD copy of program in possession of the author.

62. Rochester and Kiley, *Honor Bound*, 129.

63. Bill Robinson interview, 18 May 2009.

64. Bill Robinson interview, 27 May 2010.

65. Bill Robinson interview, 18 May 2009.

66. Arthur Cormier interview, #549, ANHS.

67. Bill Robinson interview, 18 May 2009.

68. Rochester and Kiley, *Honor Bound*, 388–89.

69. Bill Robinson interview, 15 May 2009.

70. Arthur Cormier interview, #549, ANHS.

71. Bill Robinson interview, 27 May 2010.

72. Arthur Cormier interview, #549, ANHS.

73. Bill Robinson interview, 27 May 2010.

74. William Robinson interview #906, ANHS.

75. Ibid.

76. Ibid.; Bill Robinson interview, 18 May 2009.

77. Bill Robinson interview, 18 May 2009.

78. Rochester and Kiley, *Honor Bound*, 324–26.

79. Ibid., 479–83.

80. Ibid.; Bill Robinson interview, 18 May 2009.

81. Rochester and Kiley, *Honor Bound*, 479–83; Bill Robinson interview, 18 May 2009.

82. Bill Robinson interview, 18 May 2009; Robert Coram, *American Patriot: The Life and Wars of Colonel Bud Day* (New York: Little, Brown, 2007), 207–15.

83. Bill Robinson interview, 18 May 2009.

3. After Ho

1. William J. Duiker, *Ho Chi Minh: A Life* (New York: Hyperion, 2000), 301–2, 561–63.

2. Jeremiah Denton with Ed Brandt, *When Hell Was in Session* (1976; repr., Mobile, Ala.: Traditional Press, 1982),145.

3. Ibid., 146, 151.

4. Duiker, *Ho Chi Minh*, 553.

5. Howes, *Voices of the Vietnam POWs*, 204–5.

6. The entire appendectomy episode is covered in Bill Robinson interview, 18 May 2009.

7. Vernon E. Davis, *The Long Road Home: U.S. Prisoner of War Policy and Planning in Southeast Asia* (Washington D.C.: Historical Office of the Secretary of Defense, 2000), 532.

8. For Sybil Stockdale's experiences, see Jim Stockdale and Sybil Stockdale, *In Love and War: The Story of a Family's Ordeal and Sacrifice during the Vietnam Years* (1984; repr., Annapolis: Naval Institute Press, 1990), 295–325, 361–91. For Anne Purcell's experiences, see Ben Purcell and Anne Purcell, *Love and Duty*, rev. ed. (Clarksville, Ga.: Patriotism Foundation, 2006), 93–97, 114–21. Quote from Robins, "The American POW Experience," 181.

9. H. Bruce Franklin, *M.I.A., or, Mythmaking in America*, expanded ed. (New Brunswick, N.J.: Rutgers University Press, 1993), 54–57, 83.

10. Ginger Hux interview, 31 July 2010; Jackie Robertson interview, 31 July 2010.

11. "POWs' Wives, Parents Promote Letter Campaign," unidentified newspaper clipping, dated by hand 18 April 1970, Robinson personal papers.

12. "POW-MIA Families Gather Thursday," unidentified newspaper clipping, dated by hand 18 April 1970, Robinson personal papers.

13. "POWs' Wives, Parents Promote Letter Campaign," unidentified newspaper clipping, dated by hand 18 April 1970, Robinson personal papers.

14. Rochester and Kiley, *Honor Bound*, 495.

15. William Andrew Robinson to Mr. and Mrs. William J. Robinson, 18 July 1968.

16. William Andrew Robinson to Mr. and Mrs. William J. Robinson, 3 December 1969.

17. Ginger Hux interview, 31 July 2010.

18. "North Vietnamese Acknowledge POWs," unidentified newspaper clipping, dated by hand 8 March 1970, Robinson personal papers.

19. "Saw Their Son in POW Film; Looked Healthy," unidentified, undated newspaper clipping, Robinson personal papers.

20. Rochester and Kiley, *Honor Bound*, 498–99.

21. Leo Thorsness, "Commissioned in Hanoi," *Air Force Magazine. Com* 93 (April 2010), www.airforce-magazine.com/MagazineArchive/Pages/2010/April%202010/0410hanoi.aspx; accessed 17 July 2012.

22. Bill Robinson interview, 15 May 2009.

23. Rochester and Kiley, *Honor Bound*, 498.

24. Bill Robinson interview, 15 May 2009.

25. Ibid.; Gerald Coffee, *Beyond Survival: Building on the Hard Times— A POW's Inspiring Story* (New York: G. P. Putnam's Sons, 1990), 263.

26. Rochester and Kiley, *Honor Bound*, 380–81.

27. Earl H. Tilford Jr., "Son Tay Raid," in Tucker, *Encyclopedia of the Vietnam War*, 2:653–54. See also Benjamin F. Schemmer, *The Raid* (1976; repr., New York Ballantine Books, 2002).

28. For a comprehensive account of the Son Tay Raid by a participant, see John Gargus, *The Son Tay Raid: American POWs in Vietnam Were Not Forgotten* (College Station: Texas A&M University Press, 2007).

29. Rochester and Kiley, *Honor Bound*, 522–23.

30. Bill Robinson interview, 22 May 2009.

31. Stockdale quoted in Rochester and Kiley, *Honor Bound*, 539, 523.

32. Bill Robinson interview, 18 May 2009.

33. Ibid.

34. Rochester and Kiley, *Honor Bound*, 544–45.

35. Bill Robinson interview, 18 May 2009.

36. Rochester and Kiley, *Honor Bound*, 440.

37. Howes, *Voices of the Vietnam POWs*, 109.

38. Dave Carey, *The Ways We Choose: Lessons for Life from a POW's Experience* (Wilsonville, Ore.: BookPartners, 2000), 107.

39. Bill Robinson interview, 18 May 2009.

40. Ibid.

41. Ibid.

42. Carey, *The Ways We Choose,* 104–5.

43. William Andrew Robinson to E. W. Robinson, 4 December 1971.

44. William Andrew Robinson to Mr. and Mrs. William J. Robinson, 4 August 1970, 4 January 1972, 19 May 1972.

45. William Andrew Robinson to Beverly Fish, 3 June 1966, 19 July 1966, 23 October 1966, 10 November 1966, 7 December 1966.

46. To trace Jane's reappearance, see William Andrew Robinson to Mr. and Mrs. William J. Robinson, 18 July 1968, 5 September 1968, 22 November 1968, in which he responds to their mention of her.

47. William Andrew Robinson to Mr. and Mrs. William J. Robinson, 20 November 1970.

48. William Andrew Robinson to Mr. and Mrs. William J. Robinson, 4 February 1971, 10 April 1971, 3 June 1971, 14 July 1971.

49. William Andrew Robinson to Mr. and Mrs. William J. Robinson, 4 December 1971.

50. William Andrew Robinson to Mr. and Mrs. William J. Robinson, 19 May 1972, 20 July 1972.

51. Bill Robinson interview, 17 May 2009. For Alvarez's perspective on the breakup of his marriage, in a chapter he titled "Betrayal," see Alvarez and Pitch, *Chained Eagle,* 202–17.

52. For more on the importance of smoking and the prison schedule, see James S. Hirsch, *Two Souls Indivisible: The Friendship That Saved Two POWs in Vietnam* (Boston: Houghton Mifflin, 2004), 96–97; Rochester and Kiley, *Honor Bound,* 491, 417–18.

53. Bill Robinson interview, 18 May 2009.

54. Hirsch, *Two Souls Indivisible,* 29, 103–7, 112–19, 126–44.

55. Bill Robinson interview, 18 May 2009.

56. Ibid.

57. Ibid.

58. William Andrew Robinson to Mr. and Mrs. William J. Robinson, 20 November 1970.

59. William Andrew Robinson to Mr. and Mrs. William J. Robinson, 4 December 1971, 22 November 1972.

4. Coming Home

1. Davis, *The Long Road Home,* 283–84, 491.

2. Ibid., 492–93, 514.

3. Rochester and Kiley, *Honor Bound,* 577–87.

4. "First Prisoners," *New York Times,* 13 February 1973.

5. Bill Robinson interview, 17 May 2009.

6. "First Prisoners."

7. Bill Robinson interview, 17 May 2009.

8. Ibid.

9. "First Prisoners."

10. *In Brief for the P.O.W: A Catch-up on News from the Missing Years* (Copley Newspapers, 1972).

11. Bill Robinson interview, 17 May 2009.

12. "First Prisoners."

13. Bill Robinson interview, 17 May 2009.

14. Ibid. For more on the military's assessment of the media, see William M. Hammond, *Public Affairs: The Military and the Media, 1968–1973* (Washington, D.C.: Center of Military History, U.S. Army, 1996). For more on the press reports of sexual frolicking, see Davis, *The Long Road Home,* 496–97.

15. Charlie Plumb, *I'm No Hero: A POW Story as Told to Glen DeWarff* (Independence, Mo.: Independence Press, 1973), 263; Richard Keirn, *Old Glory Is the Most Beautiful of All* (Pittsburgh: Dorrance, 1996), 112.

16. Bill Robinson interview, 17 May 2009.

17. Robinson Risner, *The Passing of the Night: My Seven Years as a Prisoner of the North Vietnamese* (New York: Random House, 1973), 250; Bill Robinson interview, 17 May 2009.

18. Bill Robinson interview, 17 May 2009; Hirsch, *Two Souls Indivisible,* 234–36.

19. Bill Robinson interview, 17 May 2009.

20. "The High Point," unidentified, undated newspaper clipping, Robinson personal papers.

21. "Clark Gets Thanked," *New York Times,* 15 February 1973, 16.

22. Ginger Hux interview, 31 July 2010; Tim Hux interview, 1 August 2010.

23. "Happiest Families in Area after Long Vigil," unidentified, undated newspaper clipping, Robinson personal papers.

24. Bill Robinson interview, 17 May 2009.

25. *Roanoke Rapids Daily Herald,* 14 February 1973.

26. Bill Robinson interview, 17 May 2009.

27. "Clark Gets Thanked."

28. Bill Robinson interview, 17 May 2009.

29. Ginger Hux interview, 31 July 2010.

30. *Greenville (N.C.) Daily Reflector,* 18 February 1973.

31. "POW Reunion Both Somber, Joyful," *Washington Post,* 16 February 1973; Jackie Robertson interview, 31 July 2010.

32. Bill Robinson interview, 17 May 2009.

33. "Absent Seven and a Half Years, 'Billy' Has Changed, Says Mother," unidentified, undated newspaper clipping, Robinson personal papers.

34. "POW Reunion Both Somber, Joyful"; "Absent Seven and a Half Years, 'Billy' Has Changed, Says Mother"; Jackie Robertson interview, 31 July 2010.

35. Bill Robinson interview, 17 May 2009.

36. Rochester and Kiley, *Honor Bound*, 581.

37. *New York Times*, 24 February 1973. For a discussion of the tension between the DOD and the media, see Davis, *The Long Road Home*, 526–30.

38. Bill Robinson interview, 17 May 2009.

39. Ibid.

40. Hirsch, *Two Souls Indivisible*, 243–45.

41. Bill Robinson interview, 17 May 2009.

42. Tim Hux interview, 1 August 2010.

43. *Roanoke Rapids Sunday Herald*, 4 March 1973.

44. Ibid.

45. Ibid.

46. Bill Robinson interview, 17 May 2009.

47. Jackie Robertson interview, 31 July 2010.

48. Ginger Hux interview, 31 July 2010.

49. Bill Robinson interview, 17 May 2009.

50. "3 PWs Promoted While in Captivity to Face Review," 15 February 1973, unidentified newspaper clipping, Robinson personal papers; Thorsness, "Commissioned in Hanoi."

51. Bill Robinson interview, 17 May 2009.

52. "P.O.W.s: Nixon Throws a Party," *Time*, 4 June 1973, 32; Guarino, *A P.O.W.'s Story*, 166.

53. Bill Robinson interview, 17 May 2009.

54. "Excerpts from Remarks by President to Gathering of Former Prisoners of War," *New York Times*, 25 May 1973. The Richard M. Nixon Foundation has posted the entire speech on Youtube; see www.youtube.com/watch?v=DRF3JBN6rK8; accessed 15 December 2010. For an analysis on Nixon's détente policy, see John Lewis Gaddis, *The Cold War: A New History* (New York: Penguin Press, 2005), 149–52, 199–202.

55. "Excerpts from Remarks by President."

56. Bill Robinson interview, 17 May 2009.

57. "Excerpts from Remarks by President."

58. "Operation Linebacker I" and "Operation Linebacker II," in Tucker, *Encyclopedia of the Vietnam War*, 1:378–80 and 380–81, respectively.

59. Howes, *Voices of the Vietnam POWs*, 159.

60. Tom Wicker, "Red Carpets and Other Hypocrisies," *New York Times*, 15 February 1973.

61. Ibid.

62. *Washington Post*, 9 February 1973.

63. Howes, *Voices of the Vietnam POWs*, 160.

64. For a discussion of some high-profile cases of POWs as corporate spokesmen, see Gruner, *Prisoners of Culture*, 64–78.

5. Forget and Move On

1. Bill Robinson interview, 17 May 2009.

2. Ibid.

3. Joe Ballinger, "Silver Stars Awarded to Eight Rescuemen," Release No. 42-J18-671, www.rotorheadsrus.us/documents/406.html, accessed 9 February 2013.

4. For a list of the recipients, see the Air Force Enlisted Heritage Research Institute website, http://afehri.maxwell.af.mil/pages/AFCross/AFCross.htm, accessed 1 August 2012.

5. Bill Robinson interview, 17 May 2009.

6. Ibid.

7. Also, on 27 June Marine Sergeant Abel Kavanaugh, who was held for a time in South Vietnam and later joined the antiwar Peace Committee at the Plantation prison camp in North Vietnam, committed suicide. Court-martial charges had been formally filed against Kavanaugh before his suicide.

8. Bill Robinson interview, 17 May 2009.

9. Bill Robinson interview, 1 December 2012.

10. Bill Robinson interview, 22 May 2009.

11. Ibid.

12. Ibid.

13. Ibid.

14. Beverly Fish to Mr. and Mrs. William J. Robinson, 22 July 1966.

15. Bill Robinson interview, 22 May 2009.

16. Bill and Ora Mae Robinson interview, 27 May 2010.

17. Bill Robinson interview, 22 May 2009.

18. Bill and Ora Mae Robinson interview, 27 May 2010.

19. Ibid.

20. Bill Robinson interview, 22 May 2009.

21. Ibid.

22. Ibid.

23. Ginger Hux interview, 31 July 2010; Jackie Robertson interview, 31 July 2010.

24. Bill and Ora Mae Robinson interview, 27 May 2010.

25. Ibid.

26. Bill Robinson interview, 22 May 2009.

27. Bill and Ora Mae Robinson interview, 27 May 2010.

28. Bill Robinson interview, 22 May 2009.

29. Ibid.

30. Ibid.

31. Ibid.; Bill Robinson interview, 1 December 2012.

32. Bill and Ora Mae Robinson interview, 27 May 2010.

33. Bill Robinson interview, 1 December 2012.

34. Bill and Ora Mae Robinson interview, 27 May 2010.

35. Ginger Hux interview, 31 July 2010; Jackie Robertson interview, 31 July 2010.

36. The institute is now named the Robert E. Mitchell Center for Prisoner of War Studies; see www.med.navy.mil/sites/nmotc//rpow/Pages/default.aspx, accessed 10 February 2013.

37. For more on the P.O.W. Network's involvement with the Branson Veterans Day event, see www.pownetwork.org/branson/Branson_99.htm, accessed 10 February 2013.

38. Aaron K. Ketchell, *Holy Hills of the Ozarks: Religion and Tourism in Branson, Missouri* (Baltimore: Johns Hopkins University Press, 2007), 11.

39. Gerald E. Parsons, "How the Yellow Ribbon Became a National Folk Symbol," *Folklife Center News* 13 (Summer 1991): 9–11, www.loc.gov/folklife/ribbons/ribbons.html, accessed 10 February 2013.

40. Bill and Ora Mae Robinson interview, 27 May 2010.

41. For an overview of the NAM-POWs organization, see their web site, www.nampows.org.

42. Durant with Hartov, *In the Company of Heroes*, 343; Bill and Ora Mae Robinson interview, 27 May 2010.

6. An Iconic Image

1. Le Manh Thich to William A. Robinson, 10 October 1994, Robinson personal papers.

2. Ibid.

3. Rumiko Sakai to William A. Robinson, 24 October 1994, Robinson personal papers.

4. Bill Robinson interview, 1 December 2012.

5. Bill and Ora Mae Robinson interview, 27 May 2010.

6. Arnold R. Isaacs, *Vietnam Shadows: The War, Its Ghosts, and Its Legacy* (Baltimore: Johns Hopkins University Press, 1997); James H. Willbanks, "The Legacy of the Vietnam War for the US Army," in Wiest, Barbier, and Robins, *America and the Vietnam War*, 271–90; B. G. Burkett and Glenna Whitley, *Stolen Valor: How the Vietnam Generation Was*

Robbed of Its Heroes and Its History (Dallas: Verity Press, 1998); Millett and Maslowski, *For the Common Defense*, 570–71; Raymond M. Scurfield, "Post-Traumatic Stress Disorder and Healing from the War," in Wiest, Barbier, and Robins, *America and the Vietnam War*, 187–208.

7. Marilyn Blatt Young, *The Vietnam Wars, 1945–1990* (New York: HarperCollins, 1991), 301–2; Millett and Maslowski, *For the Common Defense*, 571.

8. Mark Atwood Lawrence, *The Vietnam War: A Concise International History* (New York: Oxford University Press, 2008), 168. For an example of someone who endured for more than a decade in the hard labor camps and reeducation centers, see the story of the former ARVN officer Tran Ngoc Hue in Andrew Wiest, *Vietnam's Forgotten Army: Heroism and Betrayal in the ARVN* (New York: New York University Press, 2008), 273–303.

9. Young, *The Vietnam Wars*, 307.

10. Wiest, *Vietnam's Forgotten Army*, 286–287.

11. George C. Herring, *America's Longest War: The United States and Vietnam, 1950–1975*, 2nd ed. (New York: Knopf, 1986), 271.

12. Hy V. Luong, "Postwar Vietnamese Society: An Overview of Transformative Dynamics," in *Postwar Vietnam: Dynamics of a Transforming Society*, ed. Hy V. Luong (Lanham, Md.: Rowman and Littlefield, 2003), 8–10.

13. Gaddis, *The Cold War*, 214–15.

14. Luong, "Postwar Vietnamese Society," 9–13.

15. Mark E. Manyin, *U.S.–Vietnam Relations in 2010: Current Issues and Implications for U.S. Policy* (Washington, D.C.: Congressional Research Service, 2011), 7–8.

16. Senate Select Committee on POW/MIA Affairs, *Report of the Select Committee on POW/MIA Affairs*, 103rd Cong., 1st sess., 13 January 1993 (Washington, D.C.: U.S. Government Printing Office, 1993).

17. Michael J. Allen, *Until the Last Man Comes Home: POWs, MIAs, and the Unending War in Vietnam* (Chapel Hill: University of North Carolina Press, 2009), 275–76.

18. All quotes from the documentary are taken from NHK, *Reunion* (1995). I am grateful to Kyoko Sekimoto for translating the documentary from Japanese to English.

19. Bill Robinson interview, 1 December 2012.

20. Ibid.

21. Bill Robinson interview, 19 August 2012.

22. Christina Schwenkel, *The American War in Contemporary Vietnam: Transnational Remembrance and Representation* (Bloomington: Indiana University Press, 2009), 57–58.

23. William J. Duiker, "Ho Chi Minh and the Strategy of People's War," in *The First Vietnam War: Colonial Conflict and Cold War Crisis*, ed. Mark Atwood Lawrence and Fredrik Logevall (Cambridge: Harvard University Press, 2007), 173.

24. William S. Turley, "Civil-Military Relations in North Vietnam," *Asian Survey* 9 (December 1969): 890–91.

25. Sandra C. Taylor, *Vietnamese Women at War: Fighting for Ho Chi Minh and the Revolution* (Lawrence: University Press of Kansas, 1999), 115.

26. Turley, "Civil-Military Relations in North Vietnam," 890–91.

27. For statistics on U.S. air losses, see Earl H. Tilford, "United States: Air Force," in Tucker, *Encyclopedia of the Vietnam War*, 2:715–18.

28. Karen Gottschang Turner with Phan Thanh Hao, *Even the Women Must Fight: Memories of War from North Vietnam* (New York: John Wiley and Sons, 1998), 68–69, 150.

29. Bill Robinson interview, 19 August 2012.

30. Taylor, *Vietnamese Women at War*, 110, 155.

31. For example, see Schwenkel, *The American War in Contemporary Vietnam*, 190–91.

32. Bill and Ora Mae Robinson interview, 27 May 2010.

33. Bill Robinson interview, 19 August 2012.

34. Mark E. Manyin, "The Vietnam–U.S. Bilateral Trade Agreement," in V. Largo, *Vietnam: Current Issues and Historical Background* (New York: Nova Science Publishers, 2002), 29–34.

35. Manyin, *U.S.–Vietnam Relations in 2010*, 4.

36. Ibid., 9.

37. Bill Hayton, *Vietnam: Rising Dragon* (New Haven: Yale University Press, 2010), xiv, 11, 27–29.

38. Ibid., xiv, 98–100, 112, 106, 141–44, 77.

39. Thomas T. Smith, *Until They Are Home: Bringing Back the MIAs from Vietnam, a Personal Memoir* (College Station: Texas A&M University Press, 2011), 3–4, 125.

7. Legacies

1. Bill and Ora Mae Robinson interview, 27 May 2010.

2. Fred Boyles, interview by the author, 13 May 2009. For more on the first five military parks, see Timothy B. Smith, *The Golden Age of Battlefield Preservation: The Decade of the 1890s and the Establishment of America's First Five Military Parks* (Knoxville: University of Tennessee Press, 2008).

3. Edwin C. Bearss, *Andersonville National Historic Site: Historic Resource Study and Historical Base Map* (Washington, D.C.: Office of His-

tory and Historic Architecture, 1970); Raymond Baker, *Andersonville: The Story of a Civil War Prison Camp* (Washington, D.C.: Office of Publications, National Park Service, 1972), 3–20.

4. From the official dedication day program, *National Prisoner of War Museum, Andersonville, Georgia, Dedication April 9, 1998* (n.p., 1998), 7–10, www.nps.gov/ande/parkmgmt/upload/POW_Museum-dedicationbook.pdf, accessed 12 February 2013.

5. Ibid., 15–17.

6. "Together, in Andersonville," *Atlanta Journal and Constitution*, 9 April 1998.

7. *National Prisoner of War Museum, Andersonville, Georgia, Dedication April 9, 1998*, 14.

8. Glenn Robins, "The National Prisoner of War Museum," *Journal of American History* 99 (Summer 2012): 275–79.

9. "Together, in Andersonville"; "Telling the Story," *Atlanta Journal and Constitution*, 10 April 1998.

10. *National Prisoner of War Museum, Andersonville, Georgia, Dedication April 9, 1998*, 1.

11. John S. McCain, "Remarks at the National POW Museum," www.mccain.senate.gov/public/.

12. Ibid. For more on Sijan see Malcolm McConnell, *Into the Mouth of the Cat: The Story of Lance Sijan, Hero of Vietnam* (New York: Norton, 1985).

13. Bill and Ora Mae Robinson interview, 27 May 2010.

14. ANHS e-mail to the author, 12 May 2011.

15. Bill and Ora Mae Robinson interview, 27 May 2010.

16. David W. Blight, *Race and Reunion: The Civil War in American Memory* (Cambridge: Harvard University Press, 2001), 68–70.

17. ANHS, news release, 20 May 2011, copy in author's possession. See also Bill and Ora Mae Robinson interview, 27 May 2010.

18. Tim Hux interview, 1 August 2010.

19. Ginger Hux interview, 31 July 2010.

20. Ibid.

21. Tim Hux interview, 1 August 2010.

22. Ibid.

23. Ginger Hux interview, 31 July 2010.

24. Tim Hux interview, 1 August 2010. For more on Rolling Thunder, see their website www.rollingthunder1.com/.

25. Tim Hux interview, 1 August 2010. For more on the history of National POW/MIA Recognition Day, see Allen, *Until the Last Man Comes Home*, 206, 239–40.

26. Tim Hux interview, 1 August 2010.

27. Ibid.

28. Bill and Ora Mae Robinson interview, 27 May 2010.

29. This section is based on the observations of the author, who attended Robinson's presentation to the Fort Rucker warrant officer class.

30. This section is based on the observations of the author, who attended the ceremony. Audio copy in the author's possession. Hereinafter cited as Robinson speech, 25 September 2010.

31. Patrick Hagopian, *The Vietnam War in American Memory: Veterans, Memorials, and the Politics of Healing* (Amherst: University of Massachusetts Press, 2009), 97–102.

32. "Most Ex-POWs Polled Dislike Vietnam War Memorial Design," *Washington Post*, 12 October 1982.

33. Bill and Ora Mae Robinson interview, 27 May 2010.

34. Robinson speech, 25 September 2010.

35. Ibid.

36. Henderson, *Hero Found*, 198–224.

37. Ibid., 225–35, 262.

38. Robinson speech, 25 September 2010.

39. Ibid. For President Nixon's perspective on the stalled negotiations and Linebacker II, see Richard Nixon, *RN: The Memoirs of Richard Nixon* (1978; repr., New York: Simon and Schuster, 1990).

40. Robinson speech, 25 September 2010.

41. Bill and Ora Mae Robinson interview, 27 May 2010.

42. Ibid.

Suggested Readings

The most authoritative account written on the American prisoner-of-war experience in Vietnam is Stuart I. Rochester and Frederick Kiley's *Honor Bound: The History of American Prisoners of War in Southeast Asia, 1961–1973* (1998). Most Vietnam-era POW memoirs were written by Americans held in North Vietnam, and one of the best introductory works is Jeremiah Denton's *When Hell Was in Session* (1979). For a provocative look at the captivity experience in South Vietnam, see Frank Anton's memoir, *Why Didn't You Get Me Out? Betrayal in the Viet Cong Death Camps* (1997), and Zalin Grant's collection of interviews, *Survivors: American POWs in Vietnam* (1975). There are several memoirs written from the combined perspective of the POW and his spouse, including Jim and Sybil Stockdale, *In Love and War: The Story of a Family's Ordeal and Sacrifice during the Vietnam Years* (1984), and Ben and Anne Purcell, *Love and Duty* (rev. ed., 2006). Several of Bill Robinson's cellmates and former SROs have written books about their experiences: Larry Guarino, *A P.O.W.'s Story: 2801 Days in Hanoi* (1990); Dave Carey, *The Ways We Choose: Lessons for Life from a POW's Experience* (2000), George R. Hall and Pat Hall with Bob Pittman, *Commitment to Honor: A Prisoner of War Remembers Vietnam* (2005), Richard Keirn, *Old Glory Is the Most Beautiful of All* (1996).

The number of first-person POW accounts has garnered significant attention from literary critics. Robert C. Doyle's *Voices from Captivity: Interpreting the American POW Narrative* (1994) is an impressive analysis of prisoner memoirs as a literary genre. Whereas Doyle studies prisoner-of-war memoirs from throughout American history, Craig Howes, *Voices of the Vietnam POWs: Witnesses to Their Fight* (1993) limits his focus to the Vietnam War and challenges the notion that there was one common experience among the Vietnam POWs. As for thematic studies of American POWs in Vietnam, James S. Hirsch, in *Two Souls Indivisible: The Friendship That Saved Two POWs in Vietnam* (2004), uses the experiences of Fred Vann Cherry and Porter Halyburton to explore a unique interracial friendship that transcended North Vietnamese efforts to promote racial tensions among the prisoners, and Geoffrey Norman's *Bouncing Back: How a Heroic Band of POWs Survived Vietnam* (1990) examines how prisoners such as Richard Stratton and Al Stafford responded, both mentally and physically, to repeated rounds of torture and the dehumanization of captivity. Vernon E. Davis, *The Long Road Home: U.S. Prisoner of War Policy and Planning in Southeast Asia* (2000), chronicles the efforts of the State Department, Department of Defense, and the executive branch of the federal government to negotiate the release of the POWs as well as all aspects of repatriation.

No individual Vietnam-era prisoner of war has received more attention than the naval aviator Dieter Dengler. His autobiography, *Escape from Laos* (1997), is supplemented by Bruce Henderson, *Hero Found: The Greatest POW Escape of the Vietnam War* (2010), and two films, *Little Dieter Needs to Fly* (1998) and *Rescue Dawn* (2007), both directed by Werner Herzog. The most popular documentary on the Vietnam POWs is *Return with Honor: The American Experience* (1999), although it covers only the story of aviators captured and held by the North Vietnamese. Interest in the MIA question has declined somewhat over the years but still remains both a sensitive and a divisive issue. H. Bruce Franklin's *M.I.A., or, Mythmaking in America* (1993) explains the origins of the MIA controversy, and Michael J. Allen's *Until the Last Man Comes Home: POWs, MIAs, and the Unending War in Vietnam* (2009) is a compelling account of the cultural and political dimensions of the MIA controversy.

Index

CPSIA information can be obtained at www.ICGtesting.com
Printed in the USA
BVOW11s2112270715

410637BV00002B/2/P

9 780813 166216